THE WHICH? BOOK OF
INSURANCE

THE WHICH? BOOK OF

Insurance

Published by
Consumers' Association and
Hodder & Stoughton

Published by
Consumers' Association
14 Buckingham Street
London WC2N 6DS
and
Hodder & Stoughton
47 Bedford Square
London WC1B 3DP

ISBN 0 85202 261 1
and   0 340 34271 4

Typesetting by Paston Press, Bramerton, Norwich
Printed in Great Britain at the University Press, Oxford
by David Stanford
Printer to the University

Editor
Edith Rudinger

Contributors
Joan Astell
Mark Daniel
Ronnie Reece
Greg Wilson

Illustrations
Jo Bampton
Peter Smith
Jo Witney

Acknowledgement

During the preparation of this book, comments, information and advice were provided by many individuals and professional organisations, including

AA Insurance Services, Association of British Travel Agents, Associated Scottish Life Offices, Banking Information Service, British Association of Removers, British Insurance Association, British Insurance Brokers' Association, Building Societies Association, Chartered Institute of Arbitrators, Chartered Institute of Loss Adjusters, Chartered Insurance Institute, Industrial Life Offices Association, Institute of Insurance Consultants, Institute of Public Loss Assessors, Insurance Adjusters Association, Insurance Brokers Registration Council, Insurance Ombudsman Bureau, Life Offices Association, Lloyd's Motor Underwriters' Association, Lloyd's Underwriters' Non-Marine Association, Motor Insurers' Bureau, Office of Fair Trading, RAC Insurance Services, Scottish Consumer Council.

We would like to thank everyone for their help.

Contents

*'. . . upon the loss or perishing of any
ship, there followeth not the loss or
undoing of any man, but the loss
lighteth rather easily upon many
than heavily upon few . . . whereby
all merchants, especially the younger
sort, are allured to adventure more
willingly and more freely . . .'*

Insurance

Insurance cannot stop anything happening, it can only give you money towards making good the damage. So, although you cannot insure 'against' some unwanted event happening, you can take out insurance to lessen the loss.

Insurance started mainly to cover disasters at sea: the loss of lives, cargoes and ships. From this time comes the word still used today to denote the one who takes the risk: 'underwriter' – the person who wrote his name under the promise to pay.

Life insurance developed alongside marine insurance in that merchants who insured their cargoes while at sea also began insuring their own lives.

After the great fire of London in 1666, the thought arose that property on dry land also could be insured. The first fire insurance company established was The Fire Office or Phenix (not to be confused with the present-day Phoenix) in 1680. This was followed in 1710 by one that survives to this day – the Sun Fire Office.

Marine insurance soon expanded to transact fire business as well. From then on, insurance companies were formed, some fell and others amalgamated to become the huge conglomerates we know today.

Who provides it

INSURANCE COMPANY

Insurance companies dealing in general insurances for individuals and in life insurance are either 'proprietary', with shareholders and investments in the same way as other commercial companies, or 'mutual' companies without shareholders.

Other groups who provide insurance include friendly societies and provident associations with subscribing members and other non-profit-making bodies. There are also the 'industrial' life insurance companies or special societies whose representatives come to your own home and conduct business there, in a less formal way.

An individual consumer wanting to take out insurance is generally not affected by the legal structure of the different insurers.

Legislation incorporated in the Insurance Companies Act 1982.

An insurance company doing business in the UK, with its registered office in this country, has to be authorised by and come under the surveillance of, the Department of Trade and Industry, which has the power to intervene if there seems a threat to a company's solvency. You can find out from the DoTI's insurance division, Sanctuary Buildings, 20 Great Smith Street, London SW1P 3DB (telephone 01-215 5963/5) whether a company is authorised and for what class of insurance.

Some 340 insurance companies authorised to transact insurance business in the UK are members of The British Insurance Association.

Lloyd's

The Corporation of Lloyd's was created by Act of Parliament in 1871. The Lloyd's Act 1982, resulting from an enquiry into its constitution and the effectiveness of its powers of self-regulation, recommended the formation of a new body, the Council of Lloyd's, to assume the rule-making and disciplinary functions hitherto vested in Lloyd's membership as a whole.

Even after the formation of insurance companies, individual underwriters continued to do business. Traditionally, they tended to meet in Edward Lloyd's coffee house in the City of London. Edward Lloyd died in 1713, but his name lived on and when the underwriters moved to more commodious premises, they called them 'New Lloyd's Coffee House'. From here the first committee of Lloyd's emerged, which evolved into the Corporation of Lloyd's which exists today.

Lloyd's is not a company. It has no shareholders and accepts no corporate liability for risks insured there. Lloyd's is a society of underwriters, all of whom accept insurance risks for their personal profit – or loss, since they are liable to the full extent of their private fortunes to meet their insurance commitments.

The 20,000 individual members of Lloyd's are grouped into some 400 syndicates (varying in size from a few to hundreds of names), each syndicate managed by an underwriting agent.

In 1971, Lloyd's underwriters established a separate company, Lloyd's Life Assurance Ltd, to offer life insurance schemes through professional insurance brokers.

Originally, Lloyd's was exclusively for marine insurance. Nowadays, risks of every description (except long-term life insurance) are accepted by Lloyd's underwriters, who are renowned for their willingness to insure unusual risks.

Throughout this book for 'he' read 'he or she'

You can buy insurance policies
* direct from the insurance companies
by going to one of their own branch offices, or
by responding to their advertisements or direct mail shots, or
through an 'intermediary' between you and the company, or
from a company representative who calls on you
* through an insurance broker
by going to see him in his office, or
by responding to an advertisement for a special insurance scheme
set up by the firm of brokers
* through a full-time insurance agent or 'consultant'
by going to his office, or
by being called on at home after responding to a direct mail
coupon or advertisement
* through a part-time agent
such as a solicitor, estate agent, building society manager,
shopkeeper, travel agent, garage owner, removal firm, mail order
agent, accountant, to whom you have gone for some other
business or professional advice, or a friend or relative.

Although the policy you end up with may be the same and cost
you the same through whichever agency you choose, the scope
and obligations of each type of intermediary vary quite
significantly; some do no more than introduce clients to
companies.

From an insurance company direct

You can walk into any insurance company's office and buy what
you want over their counter or ask for a prospectus, a proposal
form, or just information. If anything is not clear after studying
the papers, ask to speak to someone in the underwriting
department for the answers to your particular queries.

Getting insurance direct from an insurance company will not
cost you less although the company will save the commission they
would normally pay to the broker, agent or other intermediary.

From an intermediary

*Good intermediaries do not simply
sell insurance. They help you to
determine your risks, quantify them,
and then buy the best insurance they
can for you.*

A broker or agent is paid commission by the insurance company
for the policies he sells. As a general rule, you do not pay him for
arranging insurance for you.

Commission rates differ between companies and are higher on
some policies, and to some intermediaries. On household
policies, the commission rate can be anything from 12½% to 25%
of the premiums you pay – not only when you first take out the
insurance but each time you renew or add to the policy. So, there
is likely to be a tendency to give you a push towards the

high-commission-paying insurance companies, especially if all other factors are more or less equal.

A handful of insurance companies do not pay commission to outside agents. A few are specific to an occupation, such as the Royal National Pension Fund for Nurses. Other non-commission-paying companies, who deal with the general public, are The Equitable Life Assurance Society and The London Life Association, and for life policies also the Ecclesiastical Insurance Office.

Insurance brokers

Insurance Brokers (Registration) Act 1977

Any person or any firm called 'insurance broker' must be registered with the Insurance Brokers Registration Council. Registration, which is renewable annually, commits a broker, amongst other things, to

* hold policyholders' money in a separate banking account used only for that purpose
* have had at least 3 years' experience within the insurance industry
* hold a current professional liability policy (this is an insurance policy covering the broker for legal action by clients who have lost money as a result of the broker's advice or acts)
* comply with the IBRC's code of conduct.

The following are some specific examples from the code of conduct drawn up by the Insurance Brokers Registration Council:

(1) In the conduct of their business, insurance brokers shall provide advice objectively and independently.
(4) Insurance brokers shall on request from the client explain the differences in, and the relative costs of, the principal types of insurance which in the opinion of the insurance broker might suit a client's needs.
(6) Insurance brokers shall, upon request, disclose to any client who is an individual and who is, or is contemplating becoming, the holder of a United Kingdom policy of insurance the amount of commission paid by the insurer under any relevant policy of insurance.
(9) Insurance brokers shall inform a client of the name of all insurers with whom a contract of insurance is placed. This information shall be given at the inception of the contract and any changes thereafter shall be advised at the earliest opportunity to the client.
(10) Before any work involving a charge is undertaken or an agreement to carry out business is concluded, insurance brokers shall disclose and identify any amount they propose to charge to the client or policyholder which will be in addition to the premium payable to the insurer.
(14) In the completion of the proposal form, claim form, or any other material document, insurance brokers shall make it clear that all the answers or statements are the client's own responsibility. The client should always be asked to check the details and told that the inclusion of incorrect information may result in a claim being repudiated.
(19) Insurance brokers shall display in any office where they are carrying on business and to which the public have access a notice to the effect that a copy of the Code of Conduct is available upon request and that if a member of the public wishes to make a complaint or requires the assistance of the Council in resolving a dispute, he may write to the Insurance Brokers Registration Council at its offices 15 St Helen's Place London EC3A 6DS.

For addresses of insurance brokers in your area, or further information about insurance broking, you can contact:
The British Insurance Brokers' Association (BIBA)
BIBA House
14 Bevis Marks
London EC3A 7NT

A broker will be an agent for a number of insurance companies. (Some brokers are also agents for syndicates at Lloyd's.)

It is commonly believed that a broker has entrée to any insurance company. This is true to a point – but a broker is likely to act only for a company that will pay him commission. The broker has to reveal the rate of commission if the client asks. Where a broker places your insurance with a company from whom he will get no commission, he may ask for a fee from you instead.

The broker's service in giving you information and getting quotations is free, but he may make a charge for arranging the policy finally for you. These charges are called something like 'policy charge', 'initial charge', 'administration charge'. Usually they are levied on each transaction, not just the first premium, and on renewals. They are generally asked for quite openly, and should not be disguised as part of the premium.

Any advice or service from the broker beyond general guidance regarding the issue and subsequent life of the policy is really an extra. You can ask a broker to handle any claim on an insurance company policy he has arranged for you, but find out whether he will charge for the service. (For example, helping with claims against third parties is a service often charged for by brokers because it entails some extra expenses.) The broker's expertise and his standing with the insurance company may be more effective in getting a good settlement than you, an unknown individual, could do on your own.

A list of names and addresses of Lloyd's insurance brokers is available from the Lloyd's Insurance Brokers' Committee at BIBA; price 25p.

brokers and Lloyd's
A Lloyd's policy can only be obtained through a broker: no direct selling system exists.

You cannot transact business at Lloyd's through just any broker – he must be a 'Lloyd's broker' or a broker who has an arrangement with a Lloyd's broker. Many brokers have such an arrangement; they have to be guaranteed and sponsored by a Lloyd's broker. Conversely, a Lloyd's broker does not deal exclusively at Lloyd's but can arrange policies with insurance companies.

You may have to pay a broker an administration charge for arranging a policy at Lloyd's.

A claim on a Lloyd's policy has to be made through the broker who arranges the settlement, collects the money from the underwriters and pays it out to you. You do not pay him a fee for this service.

Because all your dealings to do with a Lloyd's policy are with the broker, he may assume the role of insurer in your eyes. But the policy will always state clearly that the insurers are the '. . . at Lloyd's' or that it is the '. . . motor policy at Lloyd's', and it is there that the ultimate responsibility for your insurance lies.

Full-time insurance agents

Insurance 'consultant', 'advisor', 'specialist' – basically, these are all agents under different names. What an insurance agent sells is exactly the same as an insurance broker, and for the same premium. They sell the policies of a number of companies for which they hold an agency.

An agent is not required to register with any body and there is no law which says what he must do with his clients' money. So, in theory, anyone could set up as an insurance agent, with no experience and no money.

The British Insurance Association has a code of practice for all intermediaries other than registered insurance brokers. It is a condition of BIA membership that companies undertake to enforce the code on their agents. It includes general sales principles such as that the intermediary shall

- where appropriate, make a prior appointment to call. Unsolicited or unarranged calls shall be made at an hour likely to be suitable to the prospective policyholder . . . .
- make it known that he is the agent of one or a number of insurance companies (as the case may be) . . . .
- ensure as far as possible that the policy proposed is suitable to the needs and resources of the prospective policyholder . . . .
- give advice only on those insurance matters in which he is knowledgeable, and seek or recommend other specialist advice when necessary . . . .
- ensure as far as possible that the prospective policyholder understands what he is buying . . . .
- draw attention to any restrictions and exclusions applying to the policy . . . .
- not impose any charge in addition to the premium required by the insurance company without disclosing the amount and purpose of such charge.

There are many non-registered insurance intermediaries who rank on a par with registered brokers. Some are members of the Institute of Insurance Consultants or of the Corporation of Insurance & Financial Advisors and are subject to their codes of conduct and disciplines.

IIC
121a Queensway
Bletchley
Milton Keynes, Bucks MK2 2DH

CIFA
6–7 Leapale Road
Guildford
Surrey GU1 4JX

tied agents

Agents working directly for insurance companies may be on a 'commission-only' basis (and may have contacts with more than one company) or they may work on a 'salary plus commission' basis (usually restricted to one company only) in which case the commission element is smaller than if they are on a commission-only basis.

Other agencies for insurance

A part-time agent for only one or two companies may be someone such as a solicitor, estate agent, accountant, who takes on insurance agencies as a natural sideline to his professional business.

There are various other ways to buy insurance but with most of them you are not offered the choice of a number of companies. You could, for instance, complete a coupon put through your door or inserted in a magazine, or buy insurance through your mail order catalogue. Any shopkeeper or individual can be an agent.

Travel agents sell insurance for travel and holidays. The removal firm may offer insurance when you are moving house; so will your building society when you take out a mortgage.

building societies

A number of building societies have moved into the general insurance market in a wider role, in addition to being agents for arranging buildings insurance for properties they are lending money on. Their special schemes, marketed generally under the building society's own or created 'brand' name (for example, Leedsafe or Leicestercover), are mostly for household contents and buildings insurance. They are underwritten by insurance companies, with the building society acting as the intermediary. Some have negotiated better terms for their special policies than an insurance company's own policy may give.

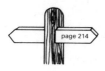

page 214

Nearly all building societies also arrange life insurance policies, including 'mortgage protection' policies.

banks

At one time, the bank manager used to act as an insurance agent in his personal capacity only. Nowadays, most major banks have set up their own insurance services division: Barclays, Lloyds, Midland, National Westminster, Trustee Savings Bank, Bank of Scotland, Royal Bank of Scotland. Most are registered brokers, and provide a full range of policies.

Anyone asking the manager at one of these banks about taking out insurance (perhaps initially in connection with getting a mortgage loan from the bank to buy a house) will have the enquiry dealt with by that bank's insurance division; there may be a regional office.

The bank may have arranged special policies or package schemes with a group of insurance companies or with a single company or with a Lloyd's syndicate, on terms that the bank has chosen as most attractive. These are often sold under the bank's name or exclusive description, such as 'Griffin' (Midland), 'Maxiguard' (Royal Bank of Scotland). The names of the underwriting insurers should be given in the printed literature. In other cases, the bank 'brokes' in the open market to find a suitable policy.

Although a bank's insurance schemes are basically directed towards the bank's own customers, anyone can make use of most of the banks' insurance services.

Life insurance offered by banks includes 'mortgage protection' policies and investment-type schemes. Two banks have subsidiary companies dealing exclusively in their own life insurance schemes: Lloyd's Black Horse Life Assurance Company and Barclays' Unicorn Group.

special offers

Members of groups such as professional associations (for civil servants, teachers, nurses, doctors, some trade unions) or of affinity groups (such as students, firms' employees, leisure organisations) may be offered 'special' insurance arranged by the particular body on terms exclusive to its membership. Premiums are generally on the low side, but there may be no flexibility in the cover because the schemes are negotiated as packages by the underwriting insurance company or syndicate. So, you would have to study carefully what is being offered to check that it provides what is suitable for you, and at terms that are better than you could easily get elsewhere.

It is not always clear who are the underwriters and who are the brokers, and many policyholders do not realise that the firm to which they pay their premiums are not, in fact, providing the cover but are acting as go-between. The name of the firm of brokers may easily be mistaken for that of an insurance company: many are called 'XYZ insurance services' or 'XYZ insurance facilities'.

Some organisations, such as the AA and the RAC, have their own insurance divisions with specialist brokers; others are merely intermediaries between the insurers and their members. Some schemes are handled, and in some cases virtually underwritten, by specialist brokers: for example, Endsleigh Insurance Services for students.

Some of the larger firms of brokers have set up their own schemes with insurers to cover certain risks or categories of insurance: for instance, for works of art, dental appliances, 'contingencies', electrical equipment, computers, boats, horses, house contents, travel.

Brokers' schemes available for individuals are advertised in the specialist and national press and through inserts in periodicals, often with an invitation to join before a certain date to take advantage of a discounted premium or guaranteed acceptance.

Some of these schemes may be good value because the brokers have been able to take advantage of their knowledge of the market and their standing with insurers to negotiate particularly good terms. But you should find out what the system is for settling claims and who will be responsible for handling a claim. Being tolerant about who is taken on ('easy underwriting') does not necessarily indicate equal tolerance when it comes to paying out on a claim.

There is no contingency against which one can not insure – but if one did, there would be no money left for the enjoyment of either the life or the property one had covered.
Which? reader

You yourself have to decide what you want to insure – your house, household possessions and personal valuables; your car; yourself, life and limbs; for your family after your death; specific possessions (caravan, boat, horse); your liabilities. You need to know what is on offer, where and how to buy it and what to be aware of.

What you want to find out is

- who provides the type of insurance you are looking for
- what can be covered
- what will be excluded
- what the basic premium rates are
- what premium you would have to pay for the cover you need
- what is likely to happen if you have to claim.

The proposal

You have to give the insurance company, agent or broker some facts about yourself and what it is you want to insure. From this, they will be able to tell you whether they will accept your proposal and on what terms, and give you some idea of the cost. This is in no way binding on them or you.

Proposal form

A proposal form is used in almost every type of insurance that a private individual is likely to want. It is designed to provide the insurers with full details of the 'risk' they are being asked to insure. The completed form is the basis of the contract between you (the proposer) and the insurers.

Proposal forms differ considerably between types of insurance and different insurers. Some of them incorporate brief details of the cover that will be provided by the policy. Some insurers' proposal forms are part of or come with a persuasive prospectus setting out details of the various types of cover and alternatives available for whatever it is that you wish to insure.

Before going as far as completing a proposal form, ask to be shown a copy of the actual policy document. Read it all (even if you find it difficult to understand), particularly the general and specific conditions and the exclusions – what is included will have been enthusiastically described in the prospectus.

If anything is not clear from the printed information you get, ask the insurers direct or get your broker or agent to find out for you.

In many cases, the prospectus or the proposal form includes the standard premium rates, so that you can work out for yourself what your premium will be, or at least check that the quotation you are given tallies with these rates; if it does not, find out why.

A spouse's occupation is asked because in the past, some people, realising that insurance would be difficult for them to obtain owing to their profession or occupation, got their partner who was not in the same occupation to take out the insurance in his or her name.

The seeker of insurance may have to disclose that he has had a proposal declined . . . I have come across instances of proposers who, having been turned down more than once, complain that they have been branded as 'difficult to insure' or, worse, as 'uninsurable' . . . While I cannot object to a decision taken on the basis of claims history or some equally cogent consideration, I do feel unhappy if the mere fact of a rejection by one underwriter is sufficient to cause other underwriters to follow suit.
INSURANCE OMBUDSMAN BUREAU
annual report for 1982

Some questions are common to all insurers' proposal forms:
* full names and address
* profession or occupation; with some types of insurance, also of your spouse.
(Some occupations are considered as making the insurance risk more hazardous.)

your insurance history
You may be asked whether you hold or have held any insurance with another insurer for whatever it is you now want to insure, and if so, to give the policy number(s).

These details are asked for in case your answers warrant further investigation by your prospective new insurers. They may contact your previous insurers for more information.
'Has any insurer declined a proposal?'
This does not refer to any times when you completed a proposal form, had a quotation given to you, but decided not to take that insurance. It means have you ever submitted a completed proposal form to insurers who then refused to accept you.

If so and you know the reasons for the refusal, state them: they may no longer apply (for example, different job) or bear no relevance to the insurance you are now asking for (for example, where you live).
'Have any insurers required an increased premium or imposed special conditions?'
To be relevant here, an increased premium or any special conditions must have been personal to you: for example, because you had a motoring or other conviction, not just that you had to pay a higher premium because you lived in a burglar-prone area. If you are not sure, say 'do not know'.
'Has any insurer cancelled or refused to renew a policy?'
It is a comparatively serious matter when an insurer cancels a policy. A reason for doing so may be that you claimed too much.
'Have you suffered any losses in respect of any of the risks proposed within the last x years?'
This question refers not only to claims you actually made but also any incidents, whether insured or not, for which you could have claimed. You may have to include your family's experiences, too.

 Previous claims may affect the premium you will be charged now or the terms of the policy. For example, the prospective insurers may make it a condition that you pay £xx of future claims – an 'excess'.

declaration
At the end of the proposal form comes the declaration that, to the best of your knowledge and belief, the answers to all the questions are true and you have not left out, misrepresented or withheld any information that may be relevant. You are bound by this declaration even when someone else filled in the proposal form for you.

Sometimes a broker or agent offers to fill in the proposal form for you – some just do it anyway. If you accept the offer, do not sign the proposal until you have been over it carefully and checked that all the questions have been fully and truthfully answered. It is your responsibility to answer the questions and, if a wrong answer is given, it is you who may be the loser – not the broker or agent.

So, if you do not fill in the form yourself, read it through and check all the answers very carefully before signing it.

Make and keep a copy of the completed proposal form: you may need to refer to it at renewals or if you make a claim.

duty to disclose

Somewhere on the proposal form there is a warning that you are required to disclose any 'material' facts for the insurer to take into account when deciding whether to accept your proposal. Failure to disclose relevant facts may invalidate your policy or parts of it.

Even where there are no specific questions to indicate what facts ought to be disclosed, nothing must be concealed by you or by the agent completing or helping you to complete the proposal form. The duty goes further than just not to conceal: everything which might affect a 'prudent underwriter' must be told. If the broker or agent knows something about the risk that you do not, he is under an obligation to make it known to the insurers.

It is hard for a layman to know what sort of facts an insurer would take account of in the assessment and acceptance of a proposal: as a rule of thumb, anything that makes your circumstances different from other people's might be 'material'.

Legislation is proposed to reduce the disclosure requirements for personal insurances.

Getting a quotation

After you have completed the proposal form, you will be told what premium you will have to pay, and any conditions specific to you. A broker or agent may, in many cases, make the quotation on the spot by merely referring to a chart. He will have guidelines on what he may quote for, and what he must refer to the insurers.

A broker's quotation may be altered when the underwriter has seen the completed proposal. Insurers can, if they wish, decline business – brokers or agents rarely do.

The quotation, written or by word of mouth, will tell you the premium required from you and details of any special conditions or terms that the insurers wish to impose on you. If you are given an oral quotation, take the name of the person giving it, make a note of the date on which it was given and ask if there is a quotation reference number.

Completing and signing a proposal form commits you to nothing. You may, if you wish, complete several proposal forms and take up none of them. Without specific acceptance, no insurance cover is operative and no claims will be paid.

Once you have said 'yes' to a firm quotation, there is a contract. In practice, you say 'yes' by paying the premium.

turned down

If your proposal is refused, ask why (although there is no obligation on them to tell you). If those insurers are adamant in their refusal, you will have to hawk your problem round the market, either direct or through a broker. A risk turned down by one insurer may be eagerly accepted by others.

If you have used a broker or agent in the first place, you may not know that you were initially turned down by the insurers he tried. The bad time comes when the broker says he cannot do anything for you. But then there are still specialist brokers. It is rare for someone, however poor a risk, not to be offered insurance somewhere – but at a price.

The premium

What you will be paying your premium for is to have prompt and proper settlement of valid claims.

Until you have paid or agreed to pay the first premium, you have no insurance and cannot claim on the policy. Where the insurer is unable to give an exact figure for the premium at the outset (for instance, because the sum insured has not yet been finally determined), insurance can come into effect with a deposit from you or a promise to pay.

For many insurance policies nowadays, there is a minimum premium which you have to pay even if the value of what you are insuring would merit a lower premium. When it is expressed as a minimum sum insured, you have to work out what premium this means you will have to pay. But when you claim, you will not get more than the value of your property even though the sum you had to insure it for is higher.

Paying

You may pay your insurance premium in cash to the broker or agent or over the counter at the insurance company office. Get a receipt. Or you may pay by credit card, or by cheque in person or through the post. Some premiums have to be paid by direct debit or banker's order.

by instalment

If you do not wish to pay the whole premium at once, with most insurance companies you can do so by instalments. In most cases, this has to be done by the direct debit system, and you have to have a current bank account. A minimum premium for payment by instalments is likely to be £50 or £30.

Companies' arrangements vary considerably, both in cost and in the number of payments over which your premium can be spread: five or ten, or even twelve. Some companies require an immediate cash payment for the first instalment; others give full cover after the completion of the form, even before a payment has been made.

Before opting to pay premiums through an insurance company's instalment scheme, check what it will cost you. There is a service charge: a percentage of the premium or a set amount per £100 (or part thereof) or a flat fee. If you have more than one policy with the same company, you may be able to save on the service charge by paying all premiums on the same instalment dates. Where the service charge is on a percentage basis, combining premium payments would not save anything.

If there are any additions or returns of premium due during the lifetime of the insurance, these are dealt with on a cash basis. For example, if you buy a more highly rated car halfway through the period of insurance, you will have to pay the additional premium in a lump sum.

Some brokers run their own instalment schemes: they pay the full annual premium to the insurers in one lump and charge you interest which you pay with the instalments.

With policies which allow you to pay a monthly premium, the 12 payments are likely to come to more than the annual premium paid in one go.

cash instalment collection

If you have an 'industrial' life insurance policy for which you pay regularly (usually once a month) and also a non-life insurance policy with the same company, you may be able to arrange to pay for this other insurance also when the company's collector calls.

Similarly, premiums for an insurance policy bought through a mail order catalogue can be paid in instalments to the mail order agent. But you will be paying more this way than by a lump sum direct.

If you are paying through an agent by an instalment system, make sure that you receive an insurance policy and not just a series of short-period cover notes.

Not going through with it

page 88

If you have paid a premium and then find when reading the policy that it is not covering what you expected, you should tell the insurers straightaway that you do not want it. (Some insurers let you have the policy 'on approval' for a specified time – perhaps 14 days.) Provided that you do this within a reasonable time, you should get your money back except for a charge for the time when the insurers actually were covering the risk.

What happens if you have paid the premium, the policy has been issued and then your circumstances alter in such a way as to make the insurance no longer necessary? For instance, you have to sell the car, house, horse, jewellery.

If it is your first year with those insurers, they will usually make what is known in the trade as a 'time on risk' charge and refund the rest to you. The charge will be on short-period rates, which are generally something like:

for 2 months' cover   25% of the annual premium
for 3 months' cover   33⅓% of the annual premium
for 4 months' cover   40% of the annual premium
for 5 months' cover   50% of the annual premium
and so on.

The broker or agent may make a small handling charge for expenses and time spent arranging all this for you.

If it is the second or subsequent year of a policy, the insurers may allow you a pro-rata refund because issuing renewals does not involve the same expense as the initial quotation and policy documents.

A motor insurance policy can be suspended rather than cancelled. Although you do not get your money back on the spot, this can prove more economical than cancellation if you are expecting to buy another car soon.

The policy

page 247

If the policy is not sent to you within about a month after the premium has been paid, ask whoever arranged the insurance for written confirmation that the policy is in force.

When you get it, read it carefully, particularly the schedule, to be certain that it sets out in detail what you have both agreed. Check against the copy of your completed proposal form. If any details are incorrect or not what was agreed, take or send it back to have it put right at once. If this is not done straightaway, there may be difficulties or complications when you have to claim.

Keep the documents in a safe place (and remember where you put them). Make a note of the policy number in your diary.

What is in it

Few policies are personalised to you. You get the standard policy, and with it or attached to it is a sheet of paper. This is known as 'the schedule'. It has on it your name, address, the policy number, the main details of what is insured and the sum insured.

THE SCHEDULE

Viewed without the schedule, the policy may appear to cover a number of things you do not want to have insured and may not even possess. For example, a household policy may have sections that cover a caravan, freezer, boat, computer, even motor car. The schedule contains a list of items that are not covered. Usually, these are referred to only by letters and numbers – A1(d), (c) or C2(d), (f) and so on. To understand these, you have to look up each item separately in the main pages of the policy.

To make things easier for yourself, go through the pages of the policy and, with reference to the list in the schedule, cross out in pencil all the items that are not insured. This will not invalidate the policy in any way and will make it a lot easier to refer to.

endorsement = to write on the back of

There may be endorsements – extra paragraphs for any warranties or additional risks or exclusions.

The schedule and endorsements override the printed sections of the policy if there is any contradiction between the two.

Any ambiguity in the policy wording would be construed against the insurer because he drew up the document and the law will therefore be biased towards you, the insured.

Policies, regardless of the type of insurance, have certain clauses in common:
* the geographical limits
* the sum insured or the limit of indemnity
* a list of general conditions
* a list of general exclusions.

CONDITIONS

The list of general conditions includes, for example
* time limits for making a claim
* what happens if there is another policy covering the same risk
* the insurers' rights of subrogation against third parties after a claim
* both parties' rights of cancellation (if there are any)
* that the insured has agreed to keep the insured property in a good state of repair and to take all reasonable steps to prevent loss or damage
* there may be an arbitration clause, setting out what must be done in a case of dispute.

EXCLUSIONS

The list of general exclusions differs according to the type of insurance. Nearly all policies exclude liability for damage, loss or destruction caused directly or indirectly by radioactivity or as a result of war or hostilities ('whether war be declared or not').

There are also usually special exclusions which apply in Northern Ireland.

Renewal

If you are paid the full sum insured on the claim, this may exhaust the policy and if you want to continue it you would have to renew or reinstate it by paying an interim premium.

Most insurance contracts (except some life and health insurance policies) run for one year and have to be renewed. With the insurers' acceptance of your renewal premium, a new contract begins.

At renewal time, you can decide whether or not to renew a particular insurance – car, household, personal accident – with the same insurers (or at all). It is not just a matter of the lowest premium. Also take into account
– has the insurer given a quick response to any claims made in the past?
– have increases in premium rates been above or below the market trend?
– have there been improvements in terms and conditions or new risks covered for no extra charge?

The insurers, on their part, may decide that they do not want you any more.

If you have decided not to renew the policy with those insurers, you need do nothing – the insurance will automatically lapse. As a

page
79

courtesy, however, you could inform the insurance company and/or the broker or agent.

Renewal notice

For insurance at Lloyd's, the renewal notice will come from the broker.

Many brokers issue their own form of renewal notice but should also send you the insurance company's renewal notice because it may contain extra information and instructions.

By issuing the renewal notice, insurers are saying two things to you:
'We will continue the insurance for a further year provided things have not changed with you
Our terms for the coming year are as follows . . .'.

With the renewal notice, the insurers should notify you of any changes. Study these in conjunction with your existing policy, and challenge any that are not to your liking. However, alterations to a policy's general terms are often an improvement on the previous contract, especially with household policies. Any condition, warranty or revision specific to your individual policy should be discussed with you in good time before renewal. If you do not understand or agree with what has been sent to you, ask for an explanation.

If you have no changes to notify and no queries, all you have to do is send the notice back with the premium payment requested. You should pay on or before the date shown on the renewal notice.

The wording of the renewal notice may say something like 'the premium must be paid within 15 days of the date shown above' – which is the expiry date of the policy.

When 'days of grace' are allowed, the insurers must meet a claim for a loss which occurs within 15 days of the expiry date, provided the premium is paid within this period. An insured person who does not intend to renew, however, cannot count on the 15 days of extra cover.

When you make a claim yourself direct with the insurance company, the first person you come across in the chain is the claims clerk at the company's office. If he says that you appear not to have a valid claim, ask why and check on the policy. His decision is not final; you can take the matter further.

If the loss is obviously covered, your claim will be allocated a number. Quote this number on all correspondence and calls. You may not always be dealt with by the same person, but by giving the claim number, you ensure that the right file is being looked at.

In the case of a small claim, where all the required receipts, bills, valuations, estimates, are attached to the claim form, the claims clerk gets the cheque sent to you.

When you have a claim that is not settled simply by exchange of pieces of paper, you may meet one or more of the people whose job it is to help in the sorting out of claims: the company's claims inspector, loss adjuster or engineer, depending on the type of claim.

The man from the company

A claims inspector is a person employed by the insurance company, whose job is to investigate the circumstances of a claim. He will want to come and to talk to you, to get further information about what happened, and may make suggestions on how to stop a similar loss happening again.

He will go through your claim form, perhaps make one or two visits, and finally write to you with a suggested payment. You do not have to accept this if you think it is unreasonable; when you ask for more, state your reasons why. He may make a revised offer in the light of what you have told him – or stand firm.

With a motor claim, it may be the insurers' engineer whom you meet, generally at the garage where he will go to see the car or its remains. He is most likely to be on the company's full-time staff, although some companies send an engineer from an outside firm.

page 110

The engineer is concerned only with the damage to the car, although he may be asked to comment on direction of impact and on any defects in your car that could have caused the accident.

Loss adjuster

Alternatively, the person who comes to see you after a claim may be a loss adjuster. He does a similar job to a claims inspector but is not an employee of the insurance company. Loss adjusters work as independent firms and are hired by insurance companies and Lloyd's underwriters to investigate and advise on claims for them.

The insurers will call in a loss adjuster if the claim is large or intricate. But for any claim it may be cheaper and more convenient for the insurers to use a loss adjuster than to send a man from their claims department perhaps a hundred miles away. It is the insurers who pay him, never you.

The loss adjuster will ask a number of questions to establish that the damaged or destroyed property is that described in the policy and that it was yours by right and that the claim falls within the policy wording, and may grill you about what happened.

The loss adjuster makes a report to the insurers, which usually includes the settlement figure he suggests. You do not get a copy of this report. He makes recommendations as to settlement but the final word is with the insurers. Although they are not bound to accept the adjuster's views and suggestions, the insurers rarely dispute them and the decision to pay (or not) is made on the basis of his report.

If the loss adjuster says you were not fully insured or reduces the amount you want to claim, do not accept his word without checking on your policy and, if necessary, arguing it out with him and the insurers.

Loss assessor

After a fairly substantial disaster, you may be approached by a loss assessor, offering to advise you on the preparation of your claim and help you negotiate a settlement.

What the loss assessor offers to do for you is to see to it
* that the claim is properly prepared
* that it is done quickly
* that all relevant aspects of the policy are brought to the insurers' or loss adjuster's notice.

A loss assessor can obtain values quickly for your damaged property, stolen jewellery and so on, because he knows how and where to get the information.

Although there is no way of knowing whether you will get more for your claim through a loss assessor than if you handle the whole thing yourself, he should ensure that you obtain the maximum to which you are entitled under the terms of your policy.

You pay the loss assessor a percentage of the settlement he obtains for you. This may be on a sliding scale according to the amount obtained – for example, starting at 10% for the first £1000. Before taking on an assessor, ask him to let you have an estimate of his charge in writing.

You are entirely responsible for his fee – whatever the outcome – and cannot make the fee part of your insurance claim.

Check his credentials: find out if he is a member of the Institute of Public Loss Assessors (IPLA).

IPLA
14 Red Lion Street
Chesham
Bucks
telephone: Chesham (0494) 782342

Glossary of some insurance terms

ALL·RISKS·COVER·LIABILITY·POLICY·PREMIUM·RENEWAL

abandonment
surrendering all proprietary rights in whatever was insured, the insurers having paid a claim for total loss (applies mainly to marine insurance)

accident
(1) a totally fortuitous event which nobody could foretell was going to happen which is either a specific peril listed in a policy or can be claimed for under the accidental damage or the all-risks section of a household policy
(2) name for a class of insurance business, which includes motor, liability, personal accident and, with some companies, household

accident report form
the form which you are required to complete when any accident or incident happens to your motor car, even when you have no intention of making a claim on your policy

actuary
a specialist in statistics who applies mathematical probabilities to life insurance risks

agent
a person who introduces business to insurers for which he receives commission; he may act for the insurer or for the insured

agreed value policy
a policy in which a specific sum for the item to be insured is agreed with the insurers at the time the

policy is taken out: the insurers undertake to pay this sum should a total loss occur; proof of value is normally required in the form of some kind of independent valuation at the time the policy is taken out

all-risks
insurance that covers all happenings that are not specifically excluded in the policy (as against a policy of specified perils which covers only the happenings that are listed)

annuity
in return for the payment of one lump sum to an insurance company, a set sum is paid out at agreed intervals for a defined period, which may be the lifetime of the annuitant

arbitration
the settlement of a dispute by an independent person whose decision has to be accepted by both parties; an alternative to litigation

assignment
transfer of ownership to another person of a right or a property (applies particularly to life insurance policies assigned to a building society to back a mortgage); a motor or household policy cannot be assigned: you cannot sell the insurance along with the car or house

assurance (life)
an undertaking to pay an agreed sum of money on the occurrence of an event that *will* happen (as against insurance for an event that *may* happen)

assured
in effect similar to 'insured'

averaging
the insurers reducing the amount paid in settlement of a claim by the proportion of any under-insurance (different in marine insurance)

benefit
payments made under a life insurance, personal accident or similar policy when the specified event occurs

betterment
any amount by which the insured person would be better off by virtue of the claim settlement; this is deducted from the amount paid out by, or must be repaid to, the insurers (for example, if after damage to a car, the whole exhaust system has to be replaced, you would have to pay an appropriate proportion of the cost)

broker
an intermediary registered with the Insurance Brokers Registration Council; he acts as an agent for the insurers and on behalf of the insured

certificate of motor insurance
a standard document issued by insurers to confirm that insurance has been taken out according to the requirements of the Road Traffic Act

commission
a fee paid by the insurers to the intermediary for the introduction of a client who buys insurance; it is a percentage of the premium, and varies according to the class of insurance and the insurers and who the intermediary is

conditions (of a policy)
stipulations written into every insurance policy, with which the insured must comply if he is to be paid under the policy

consideration
the premium

constructive total loss
when a damaged article is not totally destroyed, but is paid for by the insurers as if it were

contribution
where another policy (or policies) covers the same risk, each insurer pays only his rateable proportion of any loss

cover
the protection your insurance policy gives you: a risk is covered or held covered
– on cover
insurance term for saying that the contract is in force and claims will be paid out as agreed; this can happen before the policy has actually been issued
– cover note
document confirming cover temporarily, until the policy or certificate of insurance is issued

days of grace
number of days for which the insurance cover continues beyond the expiry of the term of a policy, which you intend to renew; if you do not pay the renewal premium

within these days, the policy lapses (motor policies have no days of grace)

deductible
another word for excess

declaration
statement at the foot of a proposal form or a claim form signed by the insured certifying the accuracy of the information that he has given

deferment period
in personal accident and permanent health insurance, the agreed number of days or weeks for which payment is not made on a claim; the lengths of deferment periods differ (the premium may be reduced if a longer period is taken)

duty of disclosure
the obligation of a person taking out insurance to tell the insurers everything that could influence an underwriter's judgment on whether the risk is acceptable and on what terms, even when no specific question about the matter is asked on the proposal form

endorsement
an amendment or addition to an insurance policy, to be fixed to or written on it, becoming an integral part of the policy
– endorsement charge
small fee sometimes demanded by a broker for altering a policy at a time other than renewal

endowment policy
life insurance which provides for payment of a certain sum at the end of a specified number of years or at death of the insured, whichever comes first

excess
specified amount of a claim, stated in the policy, which the insured has himself to bear; if a claim comes to less than this figure, no payment is made by the insurers

exception or exclusion
a happening which is specifically excluded from the terms of a policy

ex gratia
a payment made 'as a favour' by an insurer when he is not obliged to do so under the terms of the policy

extension
an addition to an existing policy to cover an extra item, another risk, a period of time, instead of taking out a separate policy for it (for example, a household policy can be extended to include a bicycle or possessions during a removal, a motor policy for driving abroad)

flat rate
a fixed premium rate, not a percentage related to the sum insured; often used for a package policy where a lot of small insurances are lumped together

franchise
an amount below which no claim is payable; if the loss exceeds this figure, the claim is paid in full (for example, a policy containing a £10 franchise would not pay anything on a loss of £6 but a loss of £11 would be paid in full)

green card
an internationally recognised document which can be issued to policyholders motoring abroad to show that their UK motor insurance has been extended in full to cover driving in the specified foreign countries; without a green card, only the minimum statutory insurance requirements within the EEC and certain other countries are met

hazard
aspects of a risk considered by insurers as likely to influence the occurrence or severity of a loss, including the attitudes and conduct of people
– hazardous activities
things in which an insured

indulges (or wishes to indulge) that either warrant an increased premium rate or, because of their dangerous nature, cannot be included in the insurance (for example, a holiday insurance policy may either exclude water skiing or charge an especially high premium to cover this activity)

home service
see industrial life insurance

indemnity
principle by which the policyholder shall be put in the same financial position after a loss as he was in immediately before it

index-linking
when the sum insured rises automatically in line with the durable household goods section of the general index of retail prices (for contents insurance) or in line with the house building costs index of the Royal Institution of Chartered Surveyors (for buildings insurance), the appropriate increase in premium having to be paid only at renewal; it can also be applied to life insurance and permanent health insurance

industrial life insurance
insurance (mainly life policies) for which premiums are collected by agents who call at the policyholder's home at intervals of less than two months; also known as 'home service'

insurable interest
a person has an insurable interest in property or a life to the extent to which the loss of it would involve him or her in financial loss; everybody has an unlimited insurable interest in their own life

the insured
the person who has entered into the contract with the insurers and is named on the policy

insurers
underwriter or company which accepts insurance risks

knock-for-knock
an agreement in motor insurance whereby each of the insurers pays for damage to their policyholder's car, regardless of who was to blame

liability
legal responsibility for injury to another person or damage to his property; also sometimes used in insurance as another word for the sum insured
– personal liability cover
insurance for what the policyholder and his family may be liable to pay in damages as a result of their negligence as private individuals

life office
insurance company or society which provides life insurance

limit of indemnity
the highest amount an insurer can be called upon to pay under any policy or section of a policy; separate sections of a policy may each have their separate limit of indemnity

loss
the insured-for event occurring; insurers refer to meeting a claim as a loss
– each and every loss
phrase used when some restriction, such as an excess, will be applied for every separate claim; that is, with more than one claim at the same time, the two will not be added together and one excess taken off: each will carry its own

loss adjuster
an independent professional who assesses losses and negotiates the settlement of claims on behalf of the insurers

loss assessor
a person who specialises in negotiating settlements of claims on behalf of the policyholder and who is paid by the policyholder

material fact
anything that could influence an underwriter in his acceptance or rating of the risk
see also duty of disclosure

maturity
an agreed date when a (life) policy will come to an end and a sum be paid

minimum premium
the premium which has to be paid even where the sum insured calculated at the rate per cent would result in a lower figure

moral hazard
an insured, or would-be insured, considered by insurers to present a higher risk because of his or her characteristics, occupation or connections (from careless person to criminal)

mutual company/office
an insurance company without shareholders: net profits go exclusively to policyholders (as against a proprietary company)

NCB **(no-claim bonus)**
another term for no-claim discount

new-for-old
insurance where a claim is met on a replacement-as-new basis

no-claim discount (NCD)
a deduction from a premium on renewal when there has been no claim in the previous year(s); mostly used in motor insurance

ombudsman
official to whom an unsatisfied complaint can be taken

onus of proof
the obligation of an insured person to prove that his loss was caused by one of the insured perils or of the insurers to prove that it was not or that an exclusion applies

paid-up policy
when premiums have stopped

being paid on a life insurance policy and the policy remains in existence but with a reduced sum insured payable

peril
any event which may be covered by or excluded from an insurance policy
– special peril
any risk added to a policy not originally designed to cover that risk (for example, adding to a fire-only policy the risk of bursting or overflowing of water tanks, apparatus or pipes)
'special perils' has become a term used by insurers and brokers for insurance consisting of the main risk (fire) but with many other risks covered by the same policy
– specified perils
the events listed in an insurance policy which, if their happening causes loss or damage to the property insured, will constitute a valid claim (as against 'all-risks' which covers everything that is not excluded)

permanent health insurance
a policy, designed to pay an income during long-term sickness, that cannot be cancelled by the insurers on account of the insured person's deteriorated health

policy
the document embodying the contract between the insurers and the policyholder

policyholder
the person in whose name the policy is; nearly always the same as the insured

premium
the amount paid to the insurers for the insurance cover set out in the policy

premium rate
the ratio of premium to sum insured, usually expressed as a percentage

proposal form
form to be completed by the person wishing to take out insurance, giving information required by the insurers in order to decide whether to accept the risk and how much to charge for it; when agreed by both parties, it forms the basis of the contract between them

proposer
not what it says matrimonially, but the person wishing to take out insurance who offers the proposal to the insurers; he becomes the policyholder or the insured as soon as his offer is accepted

proprietary company/office
insurance company whose net profits go to shareholders (as against a mutual company)

prospectus
a brief resumé, often lavishly illustrated, designed to give prospective policyholders an outline of the cover offered without having to read through the whole policy; does not contain all details of conditions and exclusions

proviso
exclusion, limitation or special exception

proximate cause
where there is a sequence of events, the one responsible for the loss or damage (for example, window broken by firemen to gain access – proximate cause: fire)

pro-rata premium
charge for the number of days a risk is covered, worked out as an exact fraction of the annual premium (as against short-period rates which work out higher than the appropriate fraction of the annual rate)

rate per cent
premium expressed as percentage per £100 of the sum insured (for example, building valued at £5,000 at 15p% = premium of £7.50)

rate per mille
premium expressed per £1,000 of sum insured (for example, building valued at £5,000 at £1.50‰ = premium of £7.50)

reinstatement
(1) when insurers replace or repair damaged property rather than pay out money for it
(2) restoration of the sum insured to the original figure, by paying a proportionate part of the premium after a claim has been met; where there is automatic reinstatement, no part-premium has to be paid before renewal

reinsurance
insurers securing themselves by transferring part of the risk to another insurer; does not affect the rights or obligations of the insured

renewal
the continuation of a policy for a further term on payment of a further premium

replacement-as-new
insurance where claims are met on the basis of the cost of a new equivalent to the lost or damaged item; for a building, repairs or restoration without deduction for betterment

risk
the risk is the property insured, not the perils it may fall prey to (for example, if an insurance person says to another 'what sort of risk is it?' the answer could be 'a small detached house')

salvage
property (damaged or undamaged) which is recoverable after an insured-for event; also the act of recovering it

schedule
section of an insurance policy which sets out details of the insured, the property to be insured, the period of cover, the application of any special terms,

and other details specific to the particular insurance, and the premium

subrogation
the insurers' right to take action in the policyholder's name against anyone who may be legally liable to the policyholder for all or part of the damage or loss

sum assured
in life insurance, the sum payable on death or at the end of the policy term

sum insured
in general insurance, the figure set against each item in an insurance policy or the total amount beyond which the insurer has no liability (limit of indemnity)

surrender value
the amount paid if premiums on a whole-life or endowment life insurance policy are discontinued and payment is required immediately

surveyor
in household insurance, a person employed by an insurance company who visits a property to be insured and advises the underwriter on the potential perils to which it is exposed and the policyholder on any ways in which they may be lessened – such as fitting extra locks, bolts, burglar alarm, fire extinguishers

syndicate
group of underwriting members of Lloyd's who undertake insurance placed with them through brokers

term insurance
a life insurance contract which pays out only on death within a specified period; also known as temporary insurance

third party
the person who is injured or whose property is damaged by the policyholder (the first party); the second party is the insurer

total loss
when something is totally destroyed or when it would cost more to repair a damaged item (usually a vehicle) than it was worth before the damage occurred (constructive total loss)

uberrimae fidei
of the utmost good faith

underwriter
(1) a person who decides whether to accept a particular risk and, if so, on what terms and the premium to be charged
(2) the person who carries the risk: a member of Lloyd's

uninsured losses
sums that are not met by the insurance: for example, with a motor policy, an excess or the cost of hiring a car while your own is being repaired (these sums may be recoverable from a third party if his liability can be established)

unit-linked policy
a policy providing some life cover but mainly intended as a savings contract: the bulk of the premium buys or is deemed to buy investment units such as units in equities or property

unoccupied
house standing empty; sometimes means insufficiently furnished for normal habitation

utmost good faith (uberrima fides)
the duty imposed on both parties to the contract: the insured to disclose all facts relevant to the risk and the insurers to deal fairly with the policyholder

void
a contract that is deemed never to have existed: for example, when it has been obtained by fraudulent means, or if an insured person had failed to disclose a material fact

voidable
an insurance contract that could be declared void by insurers because something is wrong, such as an omission or misstatement on the proposal form; usually overlooked by the insurers choosing not to repudiate it

waiver of premium
provision that premiums do not have to be paid on a life policy or permanent health policy during prolonged periods of illness

warranty
a condition which must be strictly complied with for a claim to be met under the policy (for example, that a burglar alarm will be maintained in full working order)

whole-life policy
a policy which provides for payment of a certain sum only when the person whose life is insured dies

with-profits policy
a life insurance policy where bonuses (varying according to the company's profits) are added regularly to the original sum assured paid when the policy matures

write-off
where an article is damaged beyond economical repair or is the subject of constructive total loss; the insurers pay you its total loss value

Household insurance

If you own or rent the roof over your head, you should have some kind of insurance for either the buildings or the contents, or both.

As an owner – and also as a tenant in cases where a rental agreement or lease imposes the responsibility on you – you should insure the actual structure. Where the landlord assumes responsibility for the structure, you need insurance for the fixtures and fittings you are responsible for, and may also want to insure your own furniture and belongings.

You can take out policies for
- fire
- fire and theft
- fire and theft and other 'specified' perils listed in the policy (anything not listed is not covered)

Some policies also cover
- accidental damage
- all-risks (everything is covered unless it is specifically excluded).

You can have a separate policy for the building and a policy for the contents, or a policy for both building and contents together. Many combined policies also offer insurance for other things or events as part of the package.

Some liability insurance is standard to a household policy:
* buildings insurance provides cover for your liability to the public as owner
* contents insurance covers your liability as occupier and may also include personal liability insurance for you and members of your family
* contents insurance includes employer's liability for domestic servants.

Beware with a fire-only policy: there is no liability cover.

The term 'buildings' in an insurance policy is defined as 'private dwelling which is brick, stone or concrete built, roofed with slate, tiles, concrete, asphalt, metal or sheets or slabs composed entirely of incombustible mineral ingredients'. It also includes
– all the domestic offices, stables, garages and outbuildings which are part of the property
– the walls, gates and fences around the property.
To this basic description is often added a list along the lines of
– swimming pool, tennis courts
– terraces, patios, drives, paths
– external service tanks, sewers, drains, soil pipes, drain inspection covers on the property
– fixtures and fittings (including landlord's)
– interior decorations, wallpaper.

Policies vary, especially regarding the outbuildings, walls, fences, hedges etcetera. Do not assume that a particular policy will automatically include everything listed here. Read the list for a policy very carefully in relation to your own premises and what they comprise. And if you are doubtful whether something which is part of your property is included, ask whether it is or can be included – for instance, a garage on a housing estate where garages are built in a group separate from the houses.

If your buildings do not conform to the standard description (for example, built of timber or with a thatched roof, or both), your policy will need an endorsement to the schedule stating that this is the case and you will need to pay a higher premium.

page 82

What you can insure for

Buildings are insured for damage or loss caused directly by

* Fire

There are no specific exclusions to this section (but if you deliberately set the place alight yourself, the claim would not be met).

Smoke damage where there have been no flames or burning is not usually covered. If you want cover for smoke damage, you must either ask to have the policy extended specifically to include smoke damage or insure with one of the few insurers that give all-risks cover for buildings.

* Explosion, lightning, earthquake, thunderbolt

Anyone who suspects that there has been an earth tremor can contact the Global Seismology Unit (Murchison House, West Mains Road, Edinburgh EH9 3LA) for confirmation.

These perils are usually listed along with fire. Earthquakes do occur in this country. The Global Seismology Unit of the Institute of Geological Sciences takes seismographic readings all the time and a tremor strong enough to cause damage to a building is likely to have been recorded.

* Storm, tempest
* Flood

The usual exclusions are: damage to gates, walls, fences, hedges; also subsidence, heave or landslip.

The 'first' £15 (or some other figure) of every claim is excluded in most policies.

Nowadays, although many insurers still automatically exclude subsidence from the storm and flood section, they include it as a separate specified peril.

* Theft, or any attempted theft

This means burglary, attempted break-ins, robbery – anything covered by the Theft Act.

This Act does not apply in Scotland.

Basically, there is only one exclusion common to all insurers: no cover while the house is unoccupied. This does not mean when you are just out for the evening, or at work. 'Unoccupied' is defined in the policy and it generally means either a period of 30 days or more when the house is insufficiently furnished for full habitation or normal residential purposes, or furnished but not lived in.

It is a general policy condition that the police must be told as soon as reasonably possible about any loss or damage for which a theft claim can be made.

* Riot, civil commotion, strikes, labour disturbances

Riot has an exact meaning in law. Because of some obligations of the Riot (Damages) Act under which insurers can get back from official sources the money they pay you, there is a time limit for making claims: a claim must be notified to the insurers within 7 days – some policies say 'immediately'. So, if the trouble was or appears to have been a riot, the next day will not be too soon, even if all the facts are not yet evident.

It takes only three people to constitute a riot. They must have a common purpose, and an intent to help one another, by force if necessary, displaying violence so as to alarm at least one person of reasonable firmness and courage.

Civil commotion is an intermediate state between riot and civil war. The policy conditions about the time limit for making a claim for this are the same as for a riot.

In Northern Ireland, cover for these risks is excluded.

* Malicious persons or vandals

Some policies restrict this to damage done during political disturbances or by malicious persons acting on behalf of some political organisation: avoid them.

Generally, it is a policy condition that the police must be told as soon as reasonably possible about any loss or damage for which a claim can be made under this section.

Excluded are loss or damage caused by the insured or his tenants, or when the house is left unoccupied. And generally malicious damage in Northern Ireland is excluded.

* Leakage of oil from any storage tank, pipe, fixed heating installation, or other apparatus
* Water overflowing or escaping from water tanks or apparatus or pipes

Old policies stop there; more recent policies have added, under 'apparatus', fixed domestic heating or water installations, plumbed-in washing machines or dishwashers, aquaria, water beds.

 The common exclusion is that there is no cover when the property is unoccupied/unfurnished. Most policies carry an excess of £10 or £15.

If the insurance requires you to meet £15 of any claim for damage due to a storm or flooding or burst pipes, you may be able to pay extra (in the region of £2 per annum per deletion) to have this excess removed.

There is one point to be aware of. The damage caused by water or oil escaping is always covered but the damage to the pipes themselves or other container is not covered with some policies, and in some this is left unclear. Traditionally, damage to pipes and apparatus never was covered, so it would be prudent to check. If you have an older policy, see whether this cover has been added by endorsement.

It can be argued that pipes are part of the building, so damage to them by any of the specified perils should be covered.

* Frost or the freezing of water (not in all policies)

Exclusions are damage to tennis courts, pools, dry stone walls, patios, drives, paths, gates, fences, hedges and garden water tanks, external paintwork and decorations, and while the buildings are unoccupied/unfurnished. There is usually an excess of £15.

Frost damage to the pipes or tanks is covered, but the wording may be obscure. In some policies, frost is not covered as a specified peril but the wording of the 'water overflowing' section may include 'freezing of water tanks, apparatus or pipes'.

* Subsidence and/or heave of the site on which the buildings stand or landslip (one company pessimistically adds avalanche)

There are many exclusions to this section – such as damage caused by coastal or river bank erosion; by the demolition of a building, or by structural alteration or structural repair; by the bedding-down of a new structure or the settlement of newly made-up ground; due to faulty workmanship or the use of defective materials.

Also excluded is damage to or resulting from movement of solid floor slabs unless the foundations between the external walls of the buildings are damaged by the same cause and at the same time.

Also excluded in most policies is damage to pools, hard courts, walls, patios, drives, paths, gates, fences, hedges, external service tanks (and in some policies, damage to sewers, drains, soil pipes, drain inspection covers) – unless the buildings are damaged by the same cause and at the same time.

There is a heavy excess of up to £500 or 3% or 5% of the current cost of completely rebuilding your home, whichever is the less.

Frost as such is not one of the insured perils listed under a normal household policy, whether or not frost damage is specifically excluded under the storm damage clause . . . The only frost damage normally covered by insurance is that to pipes.
INSURANCE OMBUDSMAN BUREAU
annual report for 1982

Under the Civil Aviation Act, compensation for damage attributable to sonic boom from Concorde can be claimed from Air France or British Airways. If caused by sonic boom from a military aircraft, compensation is payable from the government; claim through the Defence Secretariat, First Avenue House, High Holborn, London WC1V 6HE.

* Aircraft or other aerial devices and articles dropped from them
The exception is damage caused by pressure waves of aircraft travelling at supersonic speeds – sonic boom. Sonic boom is reputed to be able to shake tiles off the roof and to break windows. (This general exclusion was put into all policies when supersonic flights first happened and insurers thought the problem was going to be a lot greater than it is and wished to avoid the possibility of all sorts of claims for cracking and breakage being attributed to sonic bangs.)

* Breakage and collapse of television aerials, radio aerials, aerial fittings and masts

There are no exclusions, but only damage done 'by the collapse of . . .' is covered, so bear in mind that damage done to the aerials and masts themselves is not covered by a buildings policy.

Although damage to the house by falling trees is usually covered, the policy does not pay for the cost of felling any remaining parts or removing the tree.

* Impact
In some policies, this is limited to impact by any vehicle or animal; in others, the cover may be for impact by falling trees, telegraph poles, lamp posts and parts of them, aircraft, trains.
The main exclusion is the cost of repairing damage done to fences and gates by falling things.
With some policies, there is an excess (of £25) if the impact damage is done by a vehicle owned by, or belonging to, the policyholder or a member of his family. So, if you in your car hit the house or garage, or do not leave the brakes on properly and your car rolls on its own into the wall, you have to bear the excess.

* Accidental breakage of fixed glass and sanitary fittings
Some insurers go on to give a list of these such as washbasins, splashbacks, pedestals, baths, sinks, bidets, lavatory pans, shower trays, shower screens, fixed to and forming part of your home. If your policy does not give such a detailed list, it does not mean that these items are not covered: the term 'sanitary fixtures' applies generally to any of these, and fixed glass includes double glazing.
Always excluded is cover while the house is unoccupied for any length of time, or unfurnished. Other exclusions are breakage as a result of sonic boom, breakage of something that was already cracked and, in some policies, the cost of removing or replacing frames.

* Accidental damage to cables or underground service pipes supplying the property
Cover is limited to pipes and cables for which you are legally responsible. If, for instance, you put a garden digger through the main water pipe, you are legally responsible for the repair of the pipe.

* Loss of rent
The paying of a claim under this section depends on your having a valid claim under one of the other sections.

If you are the landlord, this covers the rent (including up to two years' ground rent) you would have received but can now not charge, up to a maximum of 10% of the sum insured.

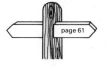
page 61

In many policies, this section covers alternative accommodation so, if you are an owner-occupier and your house is rendered uninhabitable by any of the happenings covered by the policy, you may claim for the cost of comparable accommodation up to a stated limit (usually 10% of the buildings sum insured).

There are no particular exclusions, but you can claim for staying in the alternative accommodation only for the period necessary to restore your property to a habitable condition.

* Additional expenses, fees
Somewhere in the policy, there will be a mention of the fact that the policy covers architects', surveyors', consultants' and legal fees necessarily incurred to rebuild or repair the building, the cost of removing debris and making safe; also any additional cost of rebuilding or repairing the damaged part of the buildings to comply with statutory regulations or local by-laws.

For accidental damage

Some insurers offer policies with accidental damage cover as standard.

Many policies have, in addition to the standard sections, an optional section headed 'Any accident or misfortune' or 'Accidental damage', for which you pay a higher premium (up to 20% extra) and carry an excess (£10 to £25).

Insurance companies give this optional additional cover names such as 'super' or 'maxi' or 'standard-plus', and the same terms used in different policies can mean different types of cover.

The main risks which this clause brings into the policy are accidental breakage or damage (such as splashing ink all over the wallpaper, smoke damage, putting your foot through the ceiling).

There are a number of exclusions: usually damage caused by tenants, by faulty workmanship, by defective design or the use of defective materials, by settlement, shrinkage or expansion, by wet or dry rot. Damage occurring while the dwelling is unoccupied/unfurnished, let, sublet or lent is not covered.

Also, some of the general policy exclusions are particularly pertinent such as wear and tear; gradual deterioration; electrical, electronic or mechanical breakdown; depreciation; damage directly caused by vermin, insects, fungus, condensation.

An exclusion may say '. . . damage for which claims are payable under paragraph xx' and the paragraphs it refers to are some of the specified perils. This is to your advantage because where any damage is covered under an ordinary perils section, the accidental damage excess would not apply.

The sum for which to insure the building

How much should you insure the building for? Do not just guess on the basis of how much the house next door was sold for.

When you sign the proposal form, you declare as a truthful statement that 'the sum insured represents the full cost . . . of rebuilding all the buildings in the same style, size and condition as when new'. In some older policies, this reads: 'the sums insured on the buildings are declared to represent not less than the full value of the buildings'. This may look as if it meant the market value. But in whatever way it is expressed, it means the full cost of rebuilding the lot – not just the house but also fences, gates, paths, sheds, garage, everything. This does not have any connection with what you could sell the property for – which may be much higher or much lower. The value of the land on which the building stands is irrelevant.

Alternatives which are being tried out include basing the premium on the square footage of the outside walls, or the age of the house and number of rooms.

It is unlikely that the house will ever have to be totally rebuilt, but premiums must be based on some figure that is realistic for the smaller claims that will arise for partial damage.

Even if a destroyed house is not to be rebuilt, the owner will be faced with substantial costs. The measure of the owner's loss is not the cost of rebuilding the house – it is the cost of doing what is necessary to meet his statutory requirements, obligations to adjoining owners and to the public at large, plus the market value of the property, less the value of the site.

Nearly all insurers supply a calculation table based on the chart in the British Insurance Association's pamphlet *The home owner's guide to buildings insurance*. If you have had your insurance for some time and would like to check that the sum insured is still on the right lines, you can either write to the BIA for a free copy of the pamphlet or ask for one at the counter of any insurance company's office or from your broker or agent.

In a street of identical terraced houses, where the houses at one end overlook the docks and the houses at the other end overlook the park, the cost of a new roof is the same at either end of the street but the market value of the houses will be rather different.

Approximate premiums
The likely rate is £0.15% (that is 15p per £100 of sum insured, or £1.50 per £1000); if including accidental damage, approximately £0.18%.

There may be a minimum sum insured of, say, £15,000, £17,500, £22,000.

British Insurance Association
Aldermary House
Queen Street
London EC4N 1TU

Regions

1 LONDON (GLC)

2 SOUTH EAST AND NORTH WEST ENGLAND
Oxfordshire, Buckinghamshire, Bedfordshire, Hertfordshire, Essex, Kent, East Sussex, West Sussex, Surrey, Berkshire, Hampshire, Lancashire, Merseyside, Greater Manchester and Cheshire.

3 WALES, SCOTLAND AND NORTHERN ENGLAND
The whole of Wales and Scotland together with Cumbria, Northumberland, Tyne and Wear, Cleveland and County Durham.

4 ALL OTHER COUNTIES AND NORTHERN IRELAND

Rebuilding costs for insurance purposes (September 1983)

		pre 1920 large £/ft²	medium £/ft²	small £/ft²	1920–1945 large £/ft²	medium £/ft²	small £/ft²	1946 and later large £/ft²	medium £/ft²	small £/ft²
detached house	region 1	45.50	49.00	48.00	43.50	45.00	45.50	37.00	39.50	39.50
	2	40.50	43.00	42.00	38.00	39.50	40.00	32.50	36.50	35.00
	3	38.00	41.00	40.00	36.00	37.50	38.00	31.00	33.00	33.00
	4	36.00	38.50	38.00	34.50	35.50	36.00	29.50	31.00	31.50
	typical area ft²	3450	1700	1300	2550	1350	1050	2550	1350	1050
semi-detached house	region 1	44.50	45.00	45.00	47.00	45.00	45.50	34.00	36.00	38.50
	2	39.00	39.50	39.50	41.00	39.50	39.50	30.00	31.50	33.50
	3	37.00	37.50	37.50	39.00	37.50	37.50	28.50	30.00	32.00
	4	35.00	35.50	35.50	37.00	35.50	35.50	27.00	28.50	30.50
	typical area ft²	2300	1650	1200	1350	1150	900	1650	1350	1050
detached bungalow	region 1				47.00	44.00	45.00	37.50	41.00	42.50
	2				41.50	38.50	39.50	33.00	36.00	37.50
	3				39.50	36.50	37.50	31.50	34.00	35.50
	4				37.50	34.50	35.50	29.50	32.50	33.50
	typical area ft²	The chart does not cover pre-1920 bungalows as few such properties were built			1650	1400	1000	2500	1350	1000
semi-detached bungalow	region 1				48.50	49.50	44.00	39.50	39.50	41.50
	2				42.50	43.00	38.50	34.50	35.00	36.50
	3				40.50	41.00	36.50	33.00	33.00	34.50
	4				38.50	39.00	34.50	31.00	31.50	32.50
	typical area ft²				1350	1200	800	1350	1200	800
terraced house	region 1	48.00	47.00	47.00	47.00	47.00	46.50	34.00	37.00	41.00
	2	42.00	41.50	41.50	41.00	41.00	40.50	30.00	32.50	36.00
	3	40.00	39.50	39.50	39.00	39.00	38.50	28.50	31.00	34.00
	4	38.00	37.50	37.00	37.00	37.00	36.50	27.00	29.00	32.50
	typical area ft²	1650	1350	1050	1350	1050	850	1650	1300	900

Typical garage rebuilding costs range from £5,600 for a detached double brick-built garage to £1,750 for a single prefabricated garage.

May 1984: the cost figures have gone up by 2.3%.

Notes
- The chart is unsuitable for certain types of property such as
  – properties which are not built mainly of brick
  – properties with more than three storeys or with a basement or cellar
  – flats
  – houses with special design features or of greater size than the largest shown on the chart.
- The figures are based on houses of average quality and finish, with central heating. If your home has, for example, double glazing, luxury kitchen and sanitary fittings, floor and wall coverings, you should increase the final figure by up to 25%.
- All the figures allow for demolition and professional fees.

You have to do the actual calculations yourself. This is how *Money Which?* December 1981 suggested you do it.

Step 1 To find out the size of your home, measure the area of the ground floor (outside if possible), including any integral garage. Add on the area of the first floor. If there is a third storey, you need to add only 3/4 of its area. Write the answer at A.

Step 2 In the chart, identify your type of home and the region it is in. Then look along the line until you reach the right age range and choose the column with the floor area nearest to yours (if your home has three storeys, use the area of only the first two for this). The figure in the chart is the rebuilding cost per square foot, and you write this in at B. But if your home has a lot of expensive features (*eg* solid oak floors or doors, a lot of expensive fitted furniture), you should increase the figure by up to 25%.

Step 3 Multiply A by B and write the answer at C.

Step 4 If you have a separate garage, find out the rebuilding cost and write it at D.

Step 5 Estimate the cost of rebuilding any outbuildings, walls, fences, swimming pool or other things fixed outside, and write the answer at E.

Step 6 Add up C, D and E: this is the amount to insure for.

How much to insure for

Total area of house	☐	A
Rebuilding cost per sq ft	☐	B
Multiply A × B	☐	C
Cost of rebuilding garage(s)	☐	D
Cost of rebuilding outbuildings, walls, fences, etc	☐	E
Add up D and E	☐	F
Amount to insure for C + F	☐	

The figure will need to be adapted for a house that is not of conventional construction or design: for instance, with a flat roof or thatched or incorporating large areas of plate glass or built on a steep slope. The figures assume central heating, so if your house is not centrally heated, deduct something like £2000 from the rebuilding figure.

You could ask your broker or agent for help and advice on getting the sum insured right for your home. But the final figure is your responsibility: if it turns out to be wrong, do not expect the broker or agent to pay the shortfall on your claim.

For an older property, or one of some architectural distinction, you may need to ask a building surveyor to give you a figure.

Flats

No guidelines are given by insurers about the sum for which to insure a flat. One of the problems is the common responsibility for shared parts of the building. How it should be insured depends largely on the lease.

One solution is for the owners of flats on a long lease to join together and insure all the flats as a block (for which a professional survey could determine the total rebuilding cost) and divide the premium amongst the flat owners. In some cases, the lease requires this.

Another arrangement normally found in modern leases is for the lessor to be responsible for the insurance of the building (including the common parts and the individual flats) under one central policy. The premium for the policy is then shared out between the individual flat owners, as part of the service charge. Individual flat owners remain responsible for their own contents insurance.

In older leases, the landlord may simply be responsible for insuring the common parts, leaving individual flat owners responsible for their own flats. This is not so satisfactory – you would find it difficult to rebuild your flat if the owner downstairs could not afford to rebuild his flat because it was under-insured. This is something you should look into carefully when you are buying a flat.

SCOTLAND

In Scotland, where you can own your flat freehold, the title deeds may specify that there must be a common insurance policy for the whole building, but often only for fire and storm. Arranging this is one of the jobs done by the factor.

Owner-occupiers who are buying a flat with a mortgage loan from a building society or bank are usually required by their lender to take out an individual insurance policy to cover their own flat and their share of the common areas.

The common insurance exists side by side with the flat owners' individual policies. Since each flat owner pays a substantial premium for his own policy, few wish to pay high premiums for the common insurance policy (payment would not be made twice over for the same claim). The present pattern is for common policies to be allowed to dwindle to a nominal amount, with low premiums. Nevertheless, there may be an element of double insurance.

Problems can arise with under-insurance where owners have finished paying off their loan and are not reminded to keep up their insurance cover.

Index-linking

When there is an upward movement in the average cost of rebuilding a house, a large claim at the end of a period of insurance could catch you with a sum insured that is nearly 12 months out of date. But there are index-linked policies to cope with inflation in building costs.

Index-linking works like this: the sum insured is automatically raised in line with the statistics provided by the Building Cost Information Service of the Royal Institution of Chartered Surveyors but no additional premium is charged on your policy until renewal. On renewal, your annual premium for the forthcoming year is charged on whatever the sum insured has risen to.

Index-linking is useless if your sum insured is not right in the first place, and it does not absolve you from having to re-consider it yourself at each renewal, particularly if you have improved the property.

Even with index-linking, you do not have to renew at the figure shown on the renewal notice. It is only a recommendation, not a stipulation. So, if at renewal the sum does not look right, have it altered. Explain your reasons for doing so when sending your insurers the renewal premium for the amended sum insured.

voluntary excess

A way of reducing the premium is by offering to pay a part of all claims yourself. For example, a £50 voluntary excess could bring the rate down by 2p%. This does not mean that you have to pay out the £50 to your insurers when you have a claim; the usual method of settlement is for the amount of the excess to be deducted from the payment for the claim. The premium is reduced not only because the insurers pay out less on a claim but because they save on administration costs: many losses will not be claimed for because the amount is under the £50.

On the other hand, you may be able to get deleted an excess that is normally part of the policy (for example, the £15 of a storm damage claim) if you are willing to pay a fee (for example £2), for this.

Building societies and insurance

Someone getting a mortgage from a building society must insure the building as part of his mortgage contract. The society usually offers to arrange this insurance, and will suggest three or more insurance companies whose policy you can choose. The building society will be paid commission by the insurance company.

Make sure you see the full details of the policy and check that the sum insured is adequate. The building society will suggest a figure, based on their valuation. If you are insured under the society's block policy, you can be reasonably confident that the insurers will not challenge this figure.

Building society block policies

A large building society, which may arrange insurance on hundreds of thousands of properties, has a streamlined procedure by means of what is called a block policy. This is one master insurance policy under which a large number of buildings are insured. The buildings which at any one time are insured under the block policy will be listed in a schedule. It is up to the building society to maintain this schedule, adding and deleting properties bought and sold by the society's members and collecting the correct premium on behalf of the insurance company.

The insurance company will not usually be aware exactly which properties it is covering, except in the event of a major claim or unless the society has had to consult it because the property concerned has some unusual characteristics from the insurance point of view.

Building societies insist on adequate buildings insurance but some do not cover the contents unless you ask; others offer a package policy including contents.

No individual policies are issued, but the building society should give its borrowers full details of the cover provided by the policy.

There is no proposal form as such. If you are taking out a mortgage with a building society, the details which you provide in the mortgage application form the basis on which your house is insured under the block policy. However, the duty of disclosure still applies and you should draw to the attention of the society (preferably in writing) any fact which you think might be relevant and ask that this should be passed on to the insurers.

The insurance is index-linked, and at renewal you are sent a letter showing the revised sum insured and premium. There is no renewal notice as such, and attention is not drawn to the revived duty of disclosure.

In the event of a claim, it is more likely that you know the office of the building society rather than the insurance company (you may even have forgotten which insurance company is involved), and building society offices are usually able to provide a claim form.

Insurance for the contents

Buildings and contents insurances are usually totally different covers. Do not assume that if you buy one you will automatically get the other.

The contents of your house or flat can be covered as part of a package with the building or insured on their own. They do not have to be insured with the same insurers as the building, but if they are, there are practical advantages when it comes to claiming.

Contents are usually household goods, furnishings and appliances, clothing and personal effects – all that it is normal to have in one's home, including a certain amount of money.

Each policy has its own specific exclusions and limitations on how much would be paid for some specific items.

Most policies exclude 'property more specifically insured', such as any part of the building, livestock, motor vehicles.

Contents are also defined by who owns them, which is generally put something like this: 'all belonging to or the legal responsibility of you or any other member of your family permanently residing with you'. People living together who are not married to each other can take out insurance in joint names, to avoid any quibbling when a claim arises.

In some policies, clothing and other personal effects (excluding money) of any resident domestic employee and any visitor are covered.

What you can insure for

The majority of contents policies are for 'specified perils'. The perils are almost the same as for a buildings policy, but some of the exclusions are different.

* Fire
No special exclusions. But if there have been no flames, damage from smoke and scorching is not covered unless the policy explicitly says so. If your oil heater goes wrong and, without bursting into flames, covers the place with dense, greasy smoke that gets into clothes and curtains, you cannot claim on your insurance. Similarly, if you scorch your clothes while ironing, the damage is not covered.

All-risks or accidental damage insurance does cover smoke and scorch damage.

page 32

* Riot, civil commotion, strikes, labour disturbances
* Malicious persons, vandals
Similar cover and exclusions as for buildings insurance.

* Theft, including attempted theft
There are exclusions here to be aware of. Theft by deception may not be covered: for example, what is sometimes practised by a 'knocker boy' in the antiques business who asks you to hand him something to take away to look it up in a book in his car, and then makes off with it.

If, however, deception is used to gain entry to the building, theft by the deceiver is covered. So, if a man knocks at your door and tells you he is from the water company and has come to check your bath taps, and you foolishly let him into the house and while inside he steals something, he has gained entry by deception so you can claim for that theft.

Theft of money may be excluded unless force is used to gain entry or exit from the building. So, if you accidentally shut the thief into your house, although he walked in or perhaps you even invited him in, and he has to break out (taking your money with him), you can claim.

Loss occurring while the house or flat is wholly or partly lent, let or sublet, or if it is not self-contained, is always excluded except when force is used to gain entry or exit. On the proposal form, you are asked to state whether premises are let or are not self-contained, but you may not be aware that, if so, this automatically excludes theft by anyone lawfully on the premises.

In some policies, theft is excluded while the house is unfurnished or unoccupied, as defined in the policy.

* Storm, tempest
* flood

There are no standard exclusions, but frost damage may not be covered, nor damage to anything outside the house.

* Bursting, overflowing or leaking from fixed fuel oil tank, apparatus or container
* Water leaking, overflowing or escaping from water tanks, apparatus or pipes

The exclusion here may be that there is no cover while the dwelling is left unoccupied/unfurnished.

Some policies still contain a warranty that whenever the dwelling is unfurnished or left unoccupied for more than, say, 30 days, the water is turned off at the mains and all pipes and systems are drained. This requirement has fallen into disuse in some parts of the country because keeping on the central heating system in an unoccupied house may prevent freezing. So, if your policy does contain this warranty and you have central heating which you want to leave on, suggest to your insurers that the warranty is removed.

Some policies do not automatically give cover for accidental damage to television and similar equipment but can be extended for this.

* Accidental damage to television, radio, recording and audio equipment

The kind of damage is not specified, but there is usually a limit on the amount that can be claimed (perhaps £500), together with the exclusion of recording tapes and discs, and any items designed to be portable (that is, with a handle).

The general policy exclusions particularly applicable to this section are: damage by wear and tear, condensation, cleaning, repairing; electrical, electronic or mechanical breakdown.

* Accidental breakage of fixed glass in furniture, mirrors
This may not be included in some cheaper policies.

* Aircraft or other aerial devices, and articles falling from them
There are no particular exclusions here, except for the general
exclusion of damage caused by sonic boom.

Vibration transmitted through the
ground from a passing train which
causes a plate to fall from a shelf is
not 'impact by a train'.
INSURANCE OMBUDSMAN BUREAU
annual report for 1982

* Impact – by animals, vehicles; falling trees, telegraph poles or
parts of them; aircraft, trains
The exclusions are similar to those for buildings insurance.
　　The cost of removing whatever fell or crashed into the house is
included, provided that there is a valid claim on the policy for the
damage done to your belongings inside the house.

* Subsidence and/or heave of the site on which the building
stands, or landslip
No excess here, unlike a buildings policy, but much the same
exclusions.

* Television and radio masts and aerials
Most contents policies include somewhere (under the defined
perils, or under a special television section which some policies
have), damage to the aerial itself – but not the damage it does on
the way down; that would be covered by buildings insurance.

* Rent

You can pay an additional
premium to increase the amount of
loss of rent/alternative
accommodation cover.

This may mean that you can claim up to 10% of the sum for which
the contents are insured if your home is rendered uninhabitable
by one of the insured happenings and you have to find alternative
accommodation. Or, if you are a tenant and have to go on paying
rent while you cannot live there, it may mean that the rent
payments can be included in your claim. In a good policy, the cost
of alternative accommodation and of rent are both included.
　　The limitation of 10% of the sum insured may not provide
enough to pay for hotel expenses and rent for the length of time
the place is uninhabitable. However, the happening is likely to
have damaged the building, too, and you may be able to claim
first on your buildings policy under the 'loss of rent' section up to
10% of that sum insured, and, together, the two lots of 10% will
provide your alternative accommodation expenses for much
longer.

page 61

* Liability as tenant
A contents policy includes some cover for a tenant's responsibility
for his landlord's property, fixtures and fittings. The lease or
tenancy agreement makes clear what this liability is. The cover is
for damage by specified perils, but only for up to 10% of the total
sum insured by your contents policy – so you would have to foot
the bill for the rest of the cost of repairs or restoration.

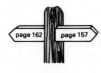

page 162　　page 157

Not in the house

Anything you take outside is included (by most policies), and so is anything that is kept habitually in the open. There are exclusions: theft, for example, or storm and flood, depending on the policy. Trees, plants and other garden produce are generally excluded.

There is a limit (usually in the region of £100 to £250) on what will be paid for belongings out of doors, and there may be an excess of £10 or £25.

property temporarily removed

Your belongings are insured for most of the specified perils while temporarily removed from the premises up to a limited sum, usually expressed as a percentage (perhaps 15% or 20%) of the total sum insured for contents. The geographical limits are usually the British Isles; a few companies include the continent of Europe. The possessions of your children while at school or college are generally covered – but check. (Students at college can buy a special policy for their personal belongings and liability.)

Theft is covered from any building where you or any other member of your family are employed or are carrying on business, and – with some policies – also from any occupied dwelling. Theft from any other building would not be covered unless force was used to gain entry to or exit from the building.

An exclusion under this section may be damage to property not in a building caused by storm or flood – which effectively stops claims for clothes damaged by excessive rain.

Also excluded are contents removed to any furniture depository or for sale or for exhibition. But your possessions are covered for theft or attempted theft while in a bank or safe deposit including, with some policies, while you are taking them there or back. If you take property to repairers, it may or may not be insured, depending on the types of cover both you and the repairer have. Do not rely on anyone else's insurance – check on your own.

Some policies cover the contents of your house while they are being moved permanently to another home or can be extended for this. This cover is usually for all-risks or accidental damage.

Money

The definition of 'personal money' usually includes not only current legal tender (coins and notes) but also cheques, postal orders, postage stamps (but not stamp collections); some policies also include in the list travel tickets and traveller's cheques, premium bonds, certificates and securities. Because definitions vary from policy to policy, check what yours covers and ask about any realisable pieces of paper you keep at home that you would like to have covered by insurance.

Borrowed goods:
Policyholders who have lost borrowed equipment or had it stolen . . . have then claimed under their own policy, only to be told that they had no insurable interest in the borrowed goods and could not expect indemnity. . . . The proper course of action is for the lender to make sure that the goods are insured under his own policy before lending them – and inform his company of the loan.
INSURANCE OMBUDSMAN BUREAU
annual report for 1983

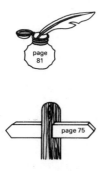

page 81

page 75

Money, however defined, is covered under a contents policy for loss due to any of the specified perils, but for loss elsewhere than in the home, cover may be limited to money lost when there was forcible entry to or exit from a building.

There is a limit on how much you will be paid back for lost money: either a set sum (from £25 to £300) or a percentage of the sum insured (perhaps 5% up to a maximum of £100 or £200). Always excluded is loss due to confiscation or to depreciation in value or to errors in payments you have made or received.

By paying an extra premium, you can extend your contents policy to cover loss of money, up to a higher set sum, wherever you are and however it happens – the stolen handbag or picked pocket in an unguarded moment.

CREDIT CARDS

Some policies include credit cards as 'money'; others offer optional extra cover for unauthorised use of a credit card before you can notify the credit company that the card has been lost or stolen. A loss not reported to the issuing company within 24 hours of discovery, or losses arising from your failure to comply with all the terms and conditions under which the credit card was issued, will not be covered. It may be a policy condition that you have to report the loss of the card to the police.

Food in a freezer

With some policies, you have to insure for a minimum amount (£250 or £500); premiums range from 1% to 4%.

Cover is usually offered as an extra, at an additional premium, for the contents of a freezer; in a few policies, this cover is thrown in for free.

Deterioration of food in the freezer as a result of deliberate acts of the electricity authority or of strikes or lock-outs is excluded in nearly all policies. There are, however, a few freezer policies issued through specialist brokers at Lloyd's which do cover these risks. Some policies include the cost of hiring a replacement freezer temporarily.

Most freezer extensions also cover deterioration due to breakdown, but usually put a limit on the age of the freezer. Check this: you may well be paying a premium for cover that is excluded because of the age of your freezer. Some make it a condition that you have a maintenance contract for the freezer if it is more than a certain age or impose an excess.

But you may not really need extra cover. The freezer and the food in it, being household contents, are anyway covered for all the specified perils. So, if a storm – or a burglar – cuts off the electricity supply, the damage to the frozen food can be part of your claim.

Bicycles

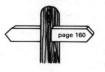
page 160

Bicycles can be insured as an extension to a household contents policy. The cover should be for all-risks. Cover for damage or injury you or members of your family cause by using a bike (third party liability), is usually part of your general contents policy.

Some policies restrict cover to the British Isles, others cover you if you take the bicycle abroad.

The main exclusions are loss or damage while the bike is being used for racing; some policies also exclude pace-making and speed testing. A bicycle that is hired out is not covered. With some policies, theft of or damage to tyres or accessories is not covered except when the cycle is stolen or damaged at the same time, or an excess applies.

With some policies, you are expected to pay a premium for each bike separately; with others, the extension covers all the bikes in the household (useful if there are a lot of cyclists in the family). There may be a set maximum sum insured for each bike.

One of the general conditions of a contents policy is that you must take all reasonable steps to prevent loss, damage and accidents, and to maintain all property insured in a sound condition. This is what is known as the 'duty of care', and it means that just because the bike is insured, you cannot leave it propped up against the railings unlocked: locking it, which is a reasonable precaution, becomes a condition of the insurance even if it is not referred to specifically in the part of the policy dealing with bicycles.

DUTY OF CARE

The only way to ensure that one's goods remain covered by insurance is to exercise towards them the same care as if they were not insured.
INSURANCE OMBUDSMAN BUREAU
annual report 1983

Other extensions

Other extensions that you may find offered on a contents policy include sports equipment, horses and ponies, keys (which provides for the cost of installing a replacement lock to the front door if the keys have been stolen or, with some policies, lost), home computers, personal accidents, legal expenses, caravan, small craft, and even for a motor car.

page 138

The cover given is fairly similar to that given by a separate policy but the rates may differ a little. With motor insurance, there may be some fringe benefits to be had by doing the lot together, such as a 'loyalty bonus'.

fatal injury
In some policies, there is a 'death benefit' section, once traditional in every household policy. This, with slight variations, will say 'If you and/or your spouse die as a result of, and within three months of, a fire or theft occurring at the buildings during the continuance of this policy, we shall pay a total of £1000' (with some policies, up to £5000).

Some insurers go further than this and pay out the £1000 also if you die as a result of any accident or assault in your home, and also after an assault in the street or an accident while travelling as a fare-paying passenger in a train, bus or taxi. With this wider cover, someone over 70 years of age is excluded, and so are accidents outside the United Kingdom.

Premiums for accidental damage are approximately £1.50 more per £1000 than standard cover.

Damage to a carpet and other soft furnishings by spilled paint is not covered under a standard (household) policy.
INSURANCE OMBUDSMAN BUREAU *annual report for 1982*

Accidental damage

Policies nowadays usually have an optional section headed 'valuables' or 'accidental damage to valuables' or 'all-risks'.

Accidental damage is generally restricted to a happening in the home. It includes cover for careless actions, such as paint dropped on the carpet, and smoke damage and scorching.

A policy may exclude damage done by pets, another may exclude damage to clothing. Other exclusions may be damage to brittle articles in the course of ordinary use, damage to clocks by overwinding; there are various other exclusions in different policies.

All-risks insurance

A few insurers offer a household contents policy on an overall all-risks basis. All-risks cover is for
- all the 'specified perils' (subject to the standard exclusions)
- accidental damage
- unexplained loss.

The premium is higher (at least 25% more) and there is an excess on most sections.

At one time, all-risks insurance for particular valuable items was provided by a separate policy. Then claims experience got very bad (the insurers' way of saying that expenditure on claims began to exceed premium income) and all-risks insurance was then offered only as an extension to contents policies. Now the pendulum is swinging back and it is possible (but not very popular with insurers nor widely advertised – and expensive) to have separate all-risks insurance policies again.

all-risks extension

All-risks cover offered as an optional section in a contents policy is usually divided into unspecified and specified items. Some policies divide it into three parts, with two categories of unspecifieds. (Some insurers split it up further – for instance, there may be a separate all-risks extension for money and credit cards.) You can choose which of them you want to have.

Never included in this category are contact lenses, money and documents, manuscripts, pets.

* unspecified personal effects

What constitutes 'personal effects' is not always defined, but what does not fall into this category is always set out in the policy. It varies considerably with insurers, so read your policy carefully and make sure that everything for which you want this insurance is covered by this unspecified section or the next.

Most insurers require that the sum insured for unspecified personal effects represents the maximum total value of those items which you and your family may have on or with you when outside the home, so beware of under-insurance.

You can include the possessions of all the family permanently living with you, not just your own. Cover is usually anywhere in the British Isles; world-wide for holidays up to 30 or 60 days away in the year. If you want more holiday cover, the policy can be extended temporarily.

single article limit

Each policy stipulates a limit on the maximum that will be paid for any one article; £200 is a likely sum. No article will be deemed to be worth more than that limit and you will not get more than the £200 for any one item, whatever its value. But you may have a whole lot of things worth up to £200 each in your unspecified effects, so the sum insured should be the total value. For example, a sheepskin coat at £200, leather jacket at £100, husband's dinner suit at £150, and various bits and pieces from £20 to £50 each, making a total of, say, £750. This should be the sum insured for this section, so that if you lost the lot, you would get £750.

With some policies, there is a minimum sum insured (perhaps £400) and you have to pay the premium for this sum even if the value of your assorted possessions is less.

Do an add-up job on these things, to arrive at the figure that should be the sum insured. And when you decide for how much to insure the rest of the contents, deduct this amount.

* unspecified valuables

This category generally includes cameras, binoculars and suchlike objects, furs, gold and silver articles, jewellery. 'Valuables' and 'personal effects' overlap and you may need both sections to be fully covered. The main difference is that the limit for any one article under unspecified valuables is higher, say £500; the sum insured should be the value of these items, added up. There may be a minimum sum insured, say £1000, and an excess (£5).

You are not generally expected to get the pieces valued individually or to provide proof of the values you have based the sum on. But if you make a claim, you may have to produce evidence of value.

The cover is the same as for unspecified personal effects.

* specified valuables

The premium rate depends on where you live because of the high risk of theft. Some insurers do not publish these rates so you have to ask.

You can insure any valuable objects under this all-risks section except furniture and similar household goods. This insurance is meant to apply mainly to jewellery, small curios, stamp or coin collections, pictures, expensive cameras and the like. Insurers also ask you to specify pieces of equipment such as an electric typewriter, domestic sewing machine, musical instruments, hi-fi equipment, portable televisions.

These items have to be listed individually, with a separate value for each of them. The individual values will be above the 'single item' limit for unspecified valuables. For any which are over a set figure (which may be £500 or £1000), a valuation or receipt must be produced to the insurers when first taking out the insurance, to prove the value.

The cost of any valuation done has to be paid by you. The charge may be 2% of the value of the articles, with a minimum

page 80

ISVA
3 Cadogan Gate
London SW1X 0AS

fee. The days of insurers having a jeweller who did valuations for nothing are gone, and insurers nowadays give no advice or help over valuations.

The Incorporated Society of Valuers and Auctioneers lists in its journal *The Valuer* (£1.50 per single copy) members of ISVA with fine art and chattel salerooms who undertake valuations for insurance.

index-linking and all-risks

One point to watch for is that although your contents' sum insured can be index-linked, in some policies the sums insured for specified items will not be. This means you should regularly adjust the sums insured to keep in line with market values. And even if the all-risks section is index-linked, it would also be advisable to re-consider the values every few years: some things appreciate more than others (silver, for instance) and some depreciate (furs, for instance).

when going on holiday

People tend not to think about their household contents insurance when they buy holiday insurance, and often therefore insure the same things twice without realising. So, when you go on holiday, do not forget that if you have an all-risks extension to your contents policy, you can increase this rather than take out holiday insurance for your baggage unless you are going outside the geographical limits of your household policy.

page 168 page 170

without all-risks insurance

If you do not have all-risks insurance for your personal effects and valuables, they are covered for only the 'specified perils' and certain limits apply. 5% or 10% of the total sum for which the contents are insured is usually the limit for any one item such as a piece of jewellery, fur, article of gold or silver or other precious metal, picture or other work of art, curio, stamp or coin collection. Also, the aggregate of all valuables is put at 25% or 33$\frac{1}{3}$% of the total sum insured.

Buildings, contents, all-risks and other optional extensions are all included on the same proposal form. The main purpose of a proposal form is for the insurers to find out as much as possible about the risk you are asking them to insure. Insurers each produce their own form, differing in style and format, but all ask much the same questions.

All proposal forms start with the usual request for your name and address, and the occupation of yourself and your spouse, and for the address of the property to be insured if it is not the same as your own.

There will be a number of questions about the construction of the property and what it is used for, and about yourself and your family which you have to answer by ticking boxes 'yes' or 'no'.

Is the property

■ *occupied by anyone other than you or your family?*

If the answer is 'yes' because you have got a lodger, cover for theft unless accompanied by forcible entry or exit will be deleted automatically.

If the domestic arrangement is one of sharing with someone who is not related by blood or marriage, ask whether the other person's property will be covered or whether he or she needs to take out separate insurance or whether you can/should have the policy in joint names.

■ *used in whole or in part for any business or professional purposes?*

If you are starting a small business from home – for example, a workshop in shed or garage, or an office in a spare bedroom – a household policy may not cover these activities and you may need separate business insurance.

If you are asking for insurance for a self-contained flat, there are no extra exclusions and you will pay normal premium rates. If it is not self-contained, the 'forcible entry and exit' stipulations will apply to a theft claim. If it is over a shop which might present a fire hazard (paintshop, ironmonger, for example), a higher premium will be charged.

■ *used as a holiday or weekend home?*

Depending on how isolated it is, the insurers will impose restrictions, such as excluding theft, water damage and accidental breakage of glass and malicious damage. The insurers may stipulate that water, gas, electricity are turned off at the mains when the place is unoccupied.

The premium will be high and the excess figures may be increased.

■ *regularly left unoccupied for more than one (or two, depending on the insurers) months at a time?*

The conditions imposed on a holiday home are likely to apply, perhaps less stringently if the home is regularly visited by a neighbour during your absences.

■ *built of brick, stone or concrete, and roofed with slates, tiles, concrete, asphalt or metal? (referred to by insurers as BSST, which stands for brick, stone, slate, tiles)*

Some underwriters at Lloyd's specialise in insuring thatched cottages.

All premium rates are based on 'BSST' buildings. When other materials are incorporated, the premium goes up, particularly if the materials are wood, thatch or a combination of the two. Some companies will not insure such a building at all; others get you to fill in an additional proposal form which asks a lot of questions, such as 'Where is the nearest water supply?' 'How long does the fire brigade take to get there?' (many thatched cottages are very isolated) 'What sort of thatch is it?' (Some burns more quickly than others). The question does not specifically refer to outbuildings, but you should tell the insurers if the garage roof or other small flat roof of an outbuilding is timber covered with felt.

■ *in a good state of repair? and will it be so maintained at all times?*	If your answer is 'no.' and you cannot give a good reason (such as 'we bought a wreck and are doing it up'), you will usually be offered limited cover, such as for fire only. 'Yes' to the second part of the question commits you to good maintenance – which is, anyway, a general condition of the policy.
■ *in an area that has been free from flooding in the last ten (or five, depending on the insurers) years?*	Depending on how bad the flooding history is, you may be accepted with no restrictions or an excess may be imposed, or a higher premium charged. Only in exceptional circumstances will flood cover be refused.
■ *free from any sign of damage by landslip, subsidence or heave? not in an area where there has been evidence of damage by these causes?*	Any signs may be hidden: the damage may have been repaired or if it is a house you are just buying, no one lets you see it. So, you may well inadvertently give a false answer to this question. Your agent or broker may know more about the district than you, particularly if you have just moved there, and he has to disclose what he knows even though it may cause restrictions of some kind to be put on your insurance.
■ *has there been any loss, damage or liability, whether insured or not, over the last five (with some insurers, three) years?*	If you reveal that you have had a string of small claims for minor damage, the insurers may want to send someone to have a look at the property. The same applies to your having been burgled more than once recently, depending on the incidence of burglaries in the area in which you live. One burglary in a small country town may be ignored but in a large city where the burglary risk is high, insurers may stipulate some additional burglary protection. The insurers want to be told of such happenings even if you made no claims on a previous policy.
■ *has any insurer refused insurance or imposed special conditions?*	If the special conditions were because of the locality of your last home, this revelation will be ignored. If the insurance was declined or terminated because you had arranged to pay monthly and were unreliable with your payments or your cheques bounced, you will have to pay cash for this insurance. If there were any other reasons, the insurers will want to discuss the matter with your previous insurers.
■ *have you or any member of your family permanently residing with you ever been convicted of any offence involving actual or threatened damage to or loss of property or dishonesty of any kind?*	(Some insurers ask more bluntly about arson, theft or fraud.) If it comes to light that you say 'no' when you should have said 'yes', the policy could be voided – and no claims met. If your answer has to be 'yes', there is usually a large space on the form wherein to tell all. If, under the Rehabilitation of Offenders Act, the conviction has become 'spent', a prospective policyholder may omit the information.

Spent convictions
An offence becomes spent
according to the sentence:

imprisonment over 30 months never spent	*conditional discharge or probation* after 1 year
imprisonment between 6 and 30 months after 10 years	
imprisonment less than 6 months after 7 years	In specified professions, certain offences never become spent: exceptions include doctors, dentists, lawyers, accountants, veterinary surgeons, nurses.
fine or community service order after 5 years	

general

Then follow some questions that merely help the insurance company's records, such as *'Have you got any existing policies with this company?'* and *'Is another of our policies being cancelled by this policy?'* (If so, you have to give the policy numbers.)

You are usually asked to give the name and address of any mortgagee or other interested party. This would include part-owners (perhaps you have been left the property with a brother or sister) or when you have borrowed money privately with the property as security. The reason why the insurers want to know this is that in the event of a claim, particularly for a total loss, they will pay the appropriate proportion of the settlement money to any other party who has a valid insurable interest in it.

'When do you want the insurance to commence?' This will be the date on which the policy will become renewable each year and an annual premium due.

You may be asked if you would like to pay by a monthly instalment plan, by credit card, or any way to make parting with your money a little less painful.

The sum insured

Where there is a minimum figure shown beside the box in which you have to state the sum insured, you cannot insure for less. This may be the first time you learn of such a stipulation. There is no point in over-insuring, so if the minimum sum insured is too high for you, try to find another insurer who either does not impose a minimum or has a lower one.

For the building

You are asked to state the sum for which the building is to be insured 'to represent the full rebuilding cost, including all fees and associated costs'. Some insurers stipulate a minimum sum even if your laborious calculations work out at less.

For contents

Look carefully at the prospectus or brochure for the description of what the alternatives (such as 'super', 'standard', 'standard-plus', 'economy', 'Maxplan', 'Golden Key' or 'Silver Key') include.

The way to assess your possessions is to arm yourself with a check list and go from room to room. Most insurance companies provide a list for doing this and there is a BIA pamphlet *'A guide to home contents insurance'*. These check lists should prod your memory about items you might forget or overlook.

There is usually a note that reminds you when calculating the sum insured for contents generally, not to include items insured under an all-risks extension.

Available free from the British Insurance Association, Aldermary House, Queen Street, London EC4N 1TU.

The official definition of the term indemnity is insurance 'designed to place the insured in the same financial position as he was immediately before the happening of the event insured'. That is, he must not be better off nor worse off than before.

If you lose a carpet that has been down for 4 years and could have been expected to wear for 12 years, it will be assumed that a third of its life has already gone, and if a comparable new carpet costs £150, you will receive £100 from the insurance.

Write down not the value of each piece but what it would cost to buy new today. What you do next depends on the basis on which any claims would be settled: replacement-as-new or indemnity.

indemnity

With indemnity cover, you should insure your possessions for what they would cost to buy new, less a deduction for wear and tear, depending on how old or used they are. This deduction will be different for each item. Even if you bought all your furniture and household items at the same time, some things will have worn or depreciated more than others. Some articles – for instance, an antique carriage clock – appreciate rather than depreciate with age. 'Indemnity' allows for that.

replacement-as-new

With replacement-as-new (also referred to as new-for-old), you are paid the full cost of an equivalent new article when you make a claim for one that has been lost or destroyed.

Some policies do not insure clothing and household linen or bicycles on this basis, some stipulate an age limit (items not older than, say, three or five years old). Such items are insured on an indemnity basis.

Since most of your possessions have to be insured for what you would have to pay for them if you went into a shop and bought them new today, your sum insured is likely to be a good deal higher than for insurance on an indemnity basis. And so, also, will be the premium you pay.

Where the indemnity premium rate is 30p per £100, replacement-as-new would be 35p.

If you are under-insured with replacement-as-new insurance, when you make a claim, the insurers will pay on an indemnity basis: that is, deduct for wear and tear from the sum you claim for the lost articles.

index-linking

Some insurers give you the choice of having the sum insured index-linked, so that it increases automatically in line with an official prices index but without your having to pay an increased premium until renewal. Most replacement-as-new policies are index-linked.

Check whether index-linking applies only to general contents or includes items covered under policy extensions, such as all-risks.

Index-linking is a safeguard – so long as you get the figure right in the first place. And if you do not agree with what the index has upped your sum insured to at renewal, you can then alter it up or down, provided you keep the sum insured to its correct value.

Some policies contain an under-insurance clause, which means that if not index-linked and you had not kept the sum insured up to its proper amount, averaging would apply in the case of a claim.

AVERAGING
value of property   £20,000
insured for only   £15,000
claim for   £ 1,000
paid only   £   750

high-risk items

You may be asked to state the total value of articles that might constitute a high risk. The proposal form will suggest what these might be: cameras, clocks, furs, audio equipment (but not any article you are insuring separately under an all-risks extension). If the value of these items comes to more than a set percentage (perhaps $33\frac{1}{3}\%$) of the sum insured or a set figure (perhaps £4000), you will have to pay a higher premium.

And if any one object among the contents you are insuring is worth more than a percentage (say, 5% or 10%) of the sum insured or a set figure (say, £1000), you have to give details and a figure for its value. This might apply to a piece of antique furniture, for instance.

optional extensions

page 48

If you want to have all-risks cover for any of your personal possessions and valuables (the actual words 'all-risks' may not appear), you have to give the sums for which you want to insure these valuables: an overall sum for personal effects, another sum for unspecified valuables, and separate sums for each specified valuable. There will be spaces in which to list and describe each specified item individually, with a sum insured for each.

There may be a note that valuations or receipts should be provided for any item over £xxx. When sending these valuations or receipts, it is customary to send the originals and the insurers should send them back. But if you do not trust the insurance company to remember to send them back, send a photocopy – nearly all insurers will accept photocopies (but may ask for the originals if you make a claim).

For personal money and credit cards, merely tick the box. With some policies, you can state how much you want covered (up to a maximum); with others, there is a set figure for the amount that will be covered.

For food in the freezer, you may be asked to state the year of manufacture of your freezer: some insurers do not insure freezers over a certain age, perhaps 5 or 8 years – but some, up to 10 or 15 years.

To insure bicycles, it may simply need a 'yes' or 'no' answer; with some policies, you will have to state how many bicycles, and the value of each. There may be a maximum sum set for each bike.

If any of the maximum sums insured for these optional insurances is inadequate for you, ask the insurers whether it can be increased and what the extra premium would be.

Duty of disclosure

You are expected to reveal everything (about the building, contents, yourself and your household) that may influence a prudent underwriter in his assessment of the risk. Most proposal forms carry a warning to this effect, and tell you that failure to disclose could make your insurance invalid.

What might influence a prudent underwriter against you? It

may be the sea coming close to the property at very high tides (not asked on the proposal form but very relevant); that a neighbour keeps stocks of combustible materials; that there are poplars in your garden or very tall trees nearby; that your house is particularly exposed to gales. Some forms ask specific questions about such aspects of a property, others do not. But you are meant to tell, regardless.

the declaration

You are the only person who knows all the facts about yourself and the family, the use of the home, the quality of its fixtures, fittings, decorations, the nature and value of its contents. The insurer can only quote a premium on the facts you give, so it is vital that these are detailed and true. If they are not, it could affect the position when a claim arises.

You have to sign the declaration that, to the best of your knowledge and belief, all the statements are true and that the proposal and the declaration shall form the basis of the contract between yourself and the insurers.

Remember that some of your answers to the questions commit you into the future: for instance, 'yes' against the question 'Is the building in good repair and will it be so maintained?' or 'Is the property in the sole occupation of yourself and members of your family?'

If you are insuring with a mutual company – that is, one that does not have shareholders – the wording of the declaration will be slightly different: something on the lines of 'I wish to effect an insurance with and apply to become a member of the association . . .' and then follows the ordinary declaration for you to sign.

the proposal completed

Keep a copy of your completed proposal form. Some companies' forms come with an attached duplicate that copies automatically. If yours does not, take a photocopy of the form before you send it off.

Take or send the completed form to the insurance company, and wait to hear whether you have been accepted. You will in due course be told how much premium to pay. If you take the form to your broker or agent, he may be able to tell you on the spot.

The cost

Insurers have standard premium rates for buildings, for contents (for indemnity and for replacement-as-new) and for all-risks. But the premium you will be asked to pay depends very much on the part of the country you live in, and also on how isolated your house is. For buildings insurance, the areas are in counties or large regions. For contents, there is a more precise delineation. Reason: although fire, burst pipes and similar risks are the same wherever you live, theft is a different matter. Some areas of London and the large cities have a huge number of break-ins and insurance premium rates there are correspondingly high and may not be standard but quoted individually.

In some areas, where burglaries are rife, insurers will require you to install especially good locks and, depending on the sum you are insuring for, may stipulate burglar alarms and other protection devices and may send their surveyor to check. The cost of such installations has to be borne by you.

---

from Phoenix Assurance home policy prospectus (1983)

The Cost (normal risks)

Buildings £1.50 per £1000 sum insured – plus £1.50
Minimum Premiums
Scotland and Wales and counties of
Cleveland Cumbria Durham Northumberland
Tyne and Wear £30
Elsewhere (not otherwise stated) £32
Northern Ireland £37
South Eastern Counties £40
London (G.L.C.) £45

Contents

District	Postcode and District Definition		Indemnity	New/ Old	Accidental Damage
		RATES PER £100 SUM INSURED Bracketed Figures = Minimum Premium			
A	The Counties of Cornwall, Cumbria Devon (not EX1 to 6,PL1 to 9) Lincolnshire, Norfolk (not NR1 to 8) Northumberland, Somerset and Suffolk (not IP1 to 6, IP8 to 10) The Counties of Dyfed, Gwynned and Powys The Regions of Borders, Central (not FK1 to 5) Dumfries and Galloway, Grampian (not AB1 to 2) Highland and Tayside (not DD1 to 5, PH1 to 2) Paisley post codes PA21 to PA40 and Scottish Islands.		£0.27 (£18)	£0.32 (£20)	£0.47 (£30)
B	Elsewhere (not otherwise stated)		£0.30 (£20)	£0.35 (£27)	£0.50 (£35)
C	Birmingham	B1 to 21,B72 to 76,B90 to 93	£0.35 (£22)	£0.45 (£30)	£0.60 (£40)
	Croydon	CR3			
	Enfield	EN7 to 11			
	Glasgow	G46,G61 to 62,G64,G66 to 67 G71,G74 to 77,G82 to 84			
	Guildford	GU6 to 10,GU18 to 26			
	Leeds	LS1 to 15			
	Liverpool	L23,L29,L31,L37 to 40, L46 to 66			
	Manchester	M9 to 15, M26 to 35			
	Motherwell	ML1 to 6			
	Paisley	PA5 to 15			
	Redhill	RH1 to 9			
	Slough	SL0,SL1 to 9			
	Sunderland	SR1 to 6			
	Sutton	SM7			
	Twickenham	TW15 to 20			
	Warrington	WA8 to 9			
	Watford	WD1 to 3,WD5 to 6			

District	Postcode and District Definition	Indemnity	New/ Old	Accidental Damage
D	Bromley — BR1 to 7 Dartford — DA1,DA5 to 8,DA14 to 18 Glasgow — G5,G11 to 12,G14, G40 to 41,G43,G51.G69, G72 to 73,G78 Guildford — GU1 to 5 Ilford — IG1 to 11 Kingston — KT7 to 24 Manchester — M1 to 8, M16 to 25 Newcastle — NE1 to 4 Paisley — PA1 to 4 Romford — RM1 to 14	£0.45 (£25)	£0.55 (£35)	£0.70 (£45)
E	Croydon — CR0,CR2.CR4 Enfield — EN1 to 6 Glasgow — G1 to 4,G13,G15,G20 to 23, G31 to 34,G42,G44 to 45, G52 to 53,G81 Harrow — HA0,HA1 to 2,HA4 to 5, Kingston — KT1 to 6 Liverpool — L1 to 22,L24 to 28,L30, L32 to 36,L41 to 45 Southall — UB1 to 10 Sutton — SM1 to 6 Twickenham — TW1 to 14	£0.50 (£30)	£0.60 (£40)	£0.75 (£50)
F	Harrow — HA7.HA9 London — E1 to 18 EC1 to 4 N1 to 22 NW1,NW5,NW7,NW9, NW11 SE1 to 28 SW1 to 20 W1 to 5,W7 to 8,W10 to 14 WC1 to 2	£0.85 (£50)	£0.95 (£60)	£1.10 (£70)
G	Harrow — HA3,HA6,HA8 London — NW2 to 4,NW6,NW8, NW10,W6,W9	£1.00 (£55)	£1.10 (£70)	£1.25 (£80)

'All Risks'

The rates relate to the Districts above

Rates per £100 sum insured – up to £10,000 (special rates will be quoted for higher amounts)

	Specified items	Unspecified items			Specified items	Unspecified items
District A	£0.80	£1.00		District E	£2.00	£2.50
District B	£1.00	£1.25		District F	£2.50	£3.00
District C	£1.25	£1.50		District G	£3.00	£4.00
District D	£1.50	£1.75				

Phoenix Assurance 1984 rates:

	RATES PER £100 SUM INSURED			
	CONTENTS			ALL RISKS
DISTRICT	INDEMNITY	NEW for OLD	ACC. DAMAGE	up to £10,000
A	£0.27 (£18)	£0.32 (£27)	£0.47 (£40)	£0.80 (£12)
B	£0.30 (£20)	£0.35 (£30)	£0.50 (£45)	£1.00 (£15)
C	£0.35 (£23)	£0.45 (£38)	£0.60 (£50)	£1.25 (£20)
D	£0.45 (£30)	£0.55 (£45)	£0.70 (£60)	£1.50 (£25)
E	£0.55 (£35)	£0.70 (£60)	£0.85 (£75)	£2.00 (£30)
F	£0.90 (£60)	£1.10 (£95)	£1.25 (£110)	£3.00 (£45)
G	£1.05 (£70)	£1.25 (£105)	£1.40 (£120)	£4.00 (£60)

NOTE: Figures in brackets indicate the minimum premiums charged in the various districts.

The policy

When you receive your policy, check that all the details on the
schedule specific to you and the property are correct. Read the
whole policy carefully to make sure that you understand what is
covered and what the conditions and exclusions are, and that any
optional sections you wanted have been included on the schedule.

Keep the policy in a safe place; you will not get another one at
renewal, and any endorsements that come later, either sent out
generally by the insurers or specific to a change in your insurance,
should be attached to the policy.

Make a note of the policy number (and the name, address and
telephone number of the insurers) in your diary or at work, so that
if the policy gets destroyed or stolen, you can still quote the
number and make a claim without delay.

Renewal

Although you do not fill in the proposal form again, you implicitly
confirm the answers you gave on it. So, look at your answers to
every question on the original proposal form and particularly at
■ your occupation and part-time occupation, and the occupation
of your spouse and others insured by the policy.

If not all the same as before, it is important to tell the insurers –
for instance, that you have become a market trader or member of
parliament.
■ the property insured – is it still the same and is it still worth the
same?

Recall whether you have acquired or disposed of possessions of
any value during the past year; built an extension to the house,
put up a garage. If so, tell the insurers what the sum insured
should be adjusted to. You can, and should, do this at any time
during a period of insurance, whenever what you are insuring or
its value changes significantly. Still operative is the duty of
disclosure. So, if you are now taking student-lodgers, for instance,
or your neighbour's house has had to be propped up, tell the
insurers.

new premium
The renewal notice will tell you what premium you are required
to pay for the coming year. With a policy that is index-linked, the
sum insured will be a little higher than the previous year's (if
present inflationary trends continue). The percentage increase
will not be shown as such, so if you want to know, you would
have to ask.

Index-linking may not apply to items specified in an all-risks
extension, so make sure to look at their current values. A fur coat
will have gone down in value, a gold bracelet gone up.

Claiming

When a claimable event has happened, get in touch with your insurers direct or via the broker or agent, at the earliest possible opportunity, by telephone, by letter or in person. Try to give some indication of the extent of the loss or damage. Notification by word of mouth is a valid way to establish a claim, but you will nearly always also be expected to fill in a claim form.

Immediate action

If structural damage, no matter how caused, is extensive, ask your insurers what they want you to do. In any case,
- try to minimise further loss through looting, water or weather (if this costs money, it can be included in your claim)
- if there are remains, keep them (the insurers may want to see what is left)
- if anything is salvageable, try to keep it safe.

When your property has been damaged by, say, a storm, and emergency repairs could save further damage, insurers normally authorise such repairs straightaway.

If any damage was caused by a burglar, you have to notify the police immediately, even if he did not manage to get into the building or take anything.

The policy may say that any temporary repairs necessary to make the property weatherproof (if, for example, the roof has been damaged) can be put in hand immediately. However, the insurers should be given an opportunity to inspect the damage before permanent repairs are done.

Where there has been a fire, the firemen will cover over a partly burnt roof and advise you about the demolition of any dangerous structure remaining. Where there is flooding, try to get the fire brigade to come as soon as possible to start pumping the water away. If you can, move anything away from the possibility of its being looted and get it locked up in the garage or a store if you can find one. It is a condition of the policy to minimise loss by taking such action.

The steps you take, and what you will be reimbursed for, must only be to prevent already damaged property getting further damaged or prevent undamaged being put at risk. If this includes paying out money, do so, but keep receipts so that you can get it all back. If you act on the advice of the police or fire service, no insurer would query the need.

You can contact your broker or agent and he may be able to help: he may be experienced in practical matters arising from disasters and property damage.

He will be able to get in touch with the right people in the insurance company's office, and see that a loss adjuster is immediately appointed if the damage is serious.

It depends on the individual insurers whether they will send someone to see you. They each have limits below which they do not bother, but these differ and there are no hard and fast rules.

The insurers will send someone to see you as soon as possible. Whoever comes – claims inspector or loss adjuster instructed by the insurers – will ask you what happened. He may bring a claim form with him and offer to fill it in with you. (You may want to have your broker or agent with you at this time, provided he is willing.)

Dealing with the loss adjuster

Before the loss adjuster comes, sort out in your own mind what you need to tell him, and go through your policy again to check the relevant clauses, and any general conditions, so that you know all that you are entitled to claim.

You are likely to be upset and distraught, but he will have seen it all before. Do not worry too much if you lose your cool or forget half of what you wanted to say or ought to have told him. There will be other opportunities – this first visit is mainly to get things started and to tell you what to do next and how to do it and what you can expect the insurers to do.

When a loss adjuster arrives, you should ask for proof that he is the person appointed by your insurers (there are unscrupulous people who turn up at the scene of a disaster such as an accident or fire or after a burglary). If in doubt, telephone the insurance company or your broker and check before giving the loss adjuster any information.

The loss adjuster will want to see the damage probably before a builder gets to work. He may be able to recommend a builder who is known to the insurers as a firm that does not overcharge, will do a good job and start without too much delay. When an estimate is received, the adjuster will decide whether the price is right and, if necessary, negotiate with the builder.

You should arrange with the adjuster and the builder how payment will be made and how and when the insurers will settle the bill, so that you do not have to make the payments yourself.

Do not forget to include in your claim the cost of debris clearance, and the fee for applying for planning permission, if required. If you intend to use an architect or a surveyor, you may have to get the consent of the insurers so that his fees can be included in the sum you claim.

Any fees you incur in preparing or furthering a claim under your policy have to be met out of your own pocket.

alternative accommodation

If you cannot go on living in the house and your policy includes payment for alternative accommodation, it will pay up to, say, 10% of the sum for which you have insured the buildings; on your contents policy, you also get 10% of that sum insured. This lengthens the period for which you can get paid for living in a hotel, or somewhere else.

The policy wording says 'comparable' accommodation, so if your normal home is modest, a 2-star hotel would seem appropriate for the emergency. But there are no hard and fast rules, so if only the best is available, you will just have to take it for the time being. The insurers will not pay for your food, which you would have had to buy anyway nor, if you have to stay for some length of time, can you claim for outgoings you are saving, such as gas and electricity. But you will be paid for the reasonable difference between the cost of hotel food and what you would normally have bought. (If you have to find and make arrangements for your animals to be fed or put into kennels, some insurers pay for this, too; with others, it is strictly your own expense.)

Instead of going to a hotel, you may be able to rent furnished accommodation, and this will be paid for under the policy.

Or you may prefer to stay with relatives or friends, if that is possible. What you claim when staying with relatives or friends, whether you actually pay them anything or not, would have to be a case of negotiation between the insurers, yourself and your hosts.

Tell the adjuster about your temporary accommodation and get his confirmation that it will be considered suitable by the insurers and ask how and when you will be reimbursed. As soon as your house is fit for habitation, you will be expected to move back into it.

Subsidence

Some subsidence damage can only be satisfactorily dealt with by substantial reinforcement, and in some cases complete replacement of foundations (as happened with claims for subsidence after the droughts in 1975 and 1976).

Such a claim may include alternative accommodation costs while the necessary work is being done. If the whole house has to be cleared of its contents while work is done on the foundations, the storage costs can be included in the claim. There is a limit – a percentage of the sum insured – to what will be paid for alternative accommodation (for possessions and people).

The onus is on you to prove that the damage was caused by subsidence (not due to lack of maintenance, for example). You may have to produce a structural surveyor's or consulting engineer's report – at your own expense.

There may also be a question of deciding whether a third party, possibly a neighbour, a builder or a local authority, is legally liable for the damage caused.

A claim for subsidence damage is therefore likely to involve considerable delays (and there is a hefty excess).

For lesser damage

Even for a claim which is relatively small and does not warrant emergency action, report the matter to the insurance company, broker or agent as soon as possible and get a claim form. You can ask someone at the office to help you fill it in.

A straightforward claim for a relatively small amount may be settled on the basis of just an explanatory letter with the receipt for the repair or replacement attached.

Claim, even if you are not certain that the loss or damage falls within the terms of your policy. It does not go against your record with the insurers to have asked whether something was covered.

If it is not, you will simply get a letter from the insurers or broker, telling you so and usually explaining why – and probably offering you an extension to your policy that would have covered it. For example, you have a standard household contents policy and you knock over a tin of paint on your new carpet, totally ruining it: your insurance as it stands would not cover this but you could, by paying extra, have had accidental damage or all-risks insurance that would have covered it.

Excess

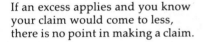

Where an excess applies to a claim (for example, £15 for storm damage to a building), claim for the full amount of the cost of the repair or restoration, but expect to receive payment less the £15. Leave it to the insurers to deduct this.

If you know that you will not get paid £xx of the cost of the repair or replacement because there is an excess, do not fall for the temptation of inflating your claim so that when the excess is deducted you get the right figure. If you are caught out, and the chances are that you will be because insurers have seen it all so many times before, no claim will be paid, your insurance will be cancelled (there is a cancellation clause in the policy) and when you come to try to get insurance elsewhere, you will have to answer 'yes' to the question 'Has any company ever refused . . .?'

If an excess applies and you know your claim would come to less, there is no point in making a claim.

The claim form

If the disaster has damaged both the structure of the building and the contents and you have the building and contents insured with the same insurers, you need complete only one claim form and the claims will be processed as one.

The form will ask a lot of self-explanatory questions, such as

■ *When and where did the damage occur?*	If you cannot answer the question, do not just cross it out: say why you do not know – for example, 'I was out at the time'.
■ *State the nature of the damage*	Here you have to say which 'peril' has happened to cause the damage or loss, such as fire, storm, theft.
■ *Give brief details of the occurrence*	It is sufficient to state at this stage how you discovered the outbreak or damage and how bad it was. The form may state that 'Claims in respect of damage to the building must be accompanied by a builder's estimate for the repair of the damage, obtained at the insured's own expense'. If you have not yet been able to get an estimate, put 'to follow'.
■ *For what purposes were the premises being used at the date of the occurrence?*	The form is used for commercial premises as well, so 'private dwelling' is all that needs to be inserted. The form may go on to ask whether the premises and their occupation were at the time of the occurrence exactly as described

in the policy schedule. The answer will most probably be 'yes', unless you had recently let off rooms in your house or taken in a party of foreign students and had not yet had time to advise your insurers. (It will not at this stage make a great deal of difference to the progress of your claim.)

■ *Are any other policies in force that could also cover the damage?*

If you say 'yes', you have to give the policy number and name of the other insurers. Who pays what proportion of the claim will be sorted out by the two insurers.

On the reverse of the claim form, there are usually columns with headings such as 'articles damaged or destroyed', 'date of purchase', 'current price', 'estimated value at time of occurrence', 'value of salvage', 'net amount claimed'.

* With a replacement-as-new policy, you can simply enter under the 'net amount claimed' today's price of a new equivalent of anything that has been destroyed, and ignore the other columns. (You may have to go round the shops to find out current prices of equivalent articles.)

* If your policy is on an indemnity basis, you have to deduct from the current price an amount for depreciation according to the life of the article. You will have to try to remember what everything was like; the loss adjuster should be able to give some guidance about estimated values.

The date of purchase need be only approximate unless on an indemnity policy you wish to prove the item is nearly new so that a deduction for wear and tear need not be made.

Remember that you have to make due allowance for wear and tear only if your policy is on an indemnity basis and (with most policies) for clothes or linen you have lost.

'Value of salvage' means the value of the remains of a damaged article. The figure you put in can be what you would be prepared to pay for it in that state (a scrap dealer might pay a lot less).

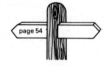

page 54

Good faith over building repairs: a claim affecting a roof was paid on the strength of a builder's estimate; the claimant then called in a different builder who botched up a repair for a lesser sum than the policyholder had received. . . . The company pays out on the understanding that the builders whose estimate is chosen will be instructed to do the work . . . the contract is one of indemnity so there is no room for profit. Strictly speaking, the money not spent on repairs should be returned to the insurers.
INSURANCE OMBUDSMAN BUREAU
annual report 1983

repairs

If any articles are repairable, get an estimate for the repair and send it with the claim form, asking whether you can go ahead with the repair or restoration.

Even with a replacement-as-new policy, you will get only the cost of the repair, not of a new article. And if indemnity insurance applies to the damaged article, it is no good going ahead with repairs that will eventually put you in a better position than before if you cannot afford to contribute your share of the bill. In that case, tell the loss adjuster or the insurers and ask them for the amount they will pay as their share of the estimated cost of the work if it were carried out. Provided you agree that the proposed payment is a proper settlement, you will be given the money and it is up to you to do what you like: have a lesser repair done or perhaps sell or keep the article in its damaged condition.

reinstatement of property

Many insurers make it a condition of the policy that they have the option to reinstate (replace) or repair a damaged article rather than give you the money to do so. The majority of claims are settled by means of cash payments but in a case where the claim appears perhaps exaggerated, the insurers may elect to replace the insured property or get it repaired themselves. They would arrange for the repair work to be carried out in the manner they think fit or arrange for a similar article to be supplied from any source of their choice.

There is nothing to stop you asking the insurance company if they will arrange for reinstatement or repair on your behalf, but you cannot require the insurers to reinstate an article, nor can you prevent them if they choose to do so. However, once they have stated that they are dealing with a claim by replacement, they cannot change their minds halfway through if they run into difficulties.

Extra claims

The claim form does not provide a space specifically for claiming for resultant damage – for example, caused not directly by flames but as the result of a fire, such as smoke affecting other areas of the house (clothes and curtains upstairs needing to be cleaned) or water from the firemen's hoses soaking the carpets. If there is so much mess that you have to get a firm of cleaners to clear it all up, the cost of this work can be claimed. If you do not yet know what all this will cost, state when sending in the claim form that you will be submitting a further claim with estimates or receipts for this extra work.

The insurers' stipulation *'We may take over and conduct in the name of the insured, with complete and exclusive control, the defence or settlement of any claim'* then comes into effect.

page 85

You may get a claim from your neighbour for damage done to his property as the result of a fire in your premises. This you should pass directly to your insurers, without comment.

There is a warning in the policy that you must not admit, negotiate or even reject any claim by another person without the insurers' written consent. In other words, if as a result of what has happened, someone else's property has been damaged, you should not say 'My insurance will pay you for that'. The other person has to write and claim against you personally, and you must pass the letter to your insurers.

On the other hand, the policy gives the insurers the right to start legal action, in your name as the insured but at their expense and for their own benefit, for compensation from anyone who is liable for any damage covered by the policy.

You must give the insurers all the help and information they may need to settle or defend any claim or start legal proceedings. This situation could arise, for instance, if your neighbour's bonfire gets out of control and the flames set light to your property.

Settlement of the claim

The amount you claim may be based in part on estimates from, say, builders or repairers. As soon as you get bills for the completed work, you should send them to the insurers, either for payment direct or for reimbursement. Insurers are usually prepared to settle a large claim in instalments as the work gets done. If at a later date you want to claim more – for hotel accommodation, for instance – or the final cost is less than the original estimate, inform the insurers as soon as the additional information is known.

If a claim takes a long time to settle, many insurers keep the index-linking going on that part of the sum insured that is subject to the claim, so that, in a time of quickly rising prices, your claim will be suitably adjusted as it goes along.

betterment

It used to be the normal procedure, after a reasonable figure for the new work and decorations had been arrived at, for the insurers to say 'But this puts you into a better position than you were before the loss – that is, you have got a partly rebuilt house, or newly decorated rooms'. They then knocked a certain amount off the payment of your claim for the improvements – betterment. Some insurers' policies still impose this.

Others have a clause in their policies that a deduction for betterment will only be made if the sum insured is not up to full rebuilding cost at the time of the claim, or if the buildings have not been kept in good repair.

If your policy is on an indemnity basis, you have to expect some deduction for any betterment. The amount is based on the estimated life of whatever it is that has been damaged or lost. If, for example, you had had your house totally redecorated 4 years ago and the decorations would be expected to last for 10 years, 60% of the cost of the new redecoration would be offered as payment. This principle would apply also to the building of a new wall or replacing part of the roof.

If it is a replacement-as-new policy, the question of betterment should not arise unless you choose to have a better quality replacement, in which case you would have to pay the difference.

under-insurance

The policy may say '*If at the time of any loss or damage the sum insured is less than the full rebuilding cost* (for buildings, or *less than the full value* for contents), *we will pay the cost of repair or replacement less a deduction for wear and tear*'. In other words, your insurance is on a replacement-as-new basis and you are under-insured, you get settlement on an indemnity basis only.

If your policy has what is known as an 'average' clause

If you engage a professional surveyor to give his opinion on what the insured value should have been, his fee cannot be included in your insurance claim.

Under-insurance clause:
'If the property insured is at the time of any loss destruction or damage collectively of greater value than the Sum Insured the insured will be considered as his own insurer for the difference and will bear a rateable share of the loss accordingly.'

If you paid to have an excess deleted, check that the excess has not been deducted.

If you signed a satisfaction note when you received the settlement cheque and further damage or loss comes to light, contact the broker or the insurers immediately and ask to reopen the claim.

(sometimes called an 'under-insurance' clause), this tells you what proportion of a claim will be paid if you are found to be under-insured at the time of a loss. It will be proportionate to the amount that you are under-insured. For example, if you are 20% under-insured when you claim £1500, you will be paid £1200.

Where there is no average clause in a policy, the insurers cannot insert one in the middle of the term (although they can refuse to renew the policy unless one is put in – but you would have to be a party to that). However, you had agreed to insure the property for its full rebuilding cost and you have invalidated the policy because you did not do so.

Although under-insurance technically invalidates the insurance, the insurers may offer you an 'ex gratia' payment (usually the same amount as if they had applied average), provided the sum insured is immediately increased to its proper level. (If the insurers offer a low or no ex gratia payment, you can argue – but, technically, you have no claim.)

what you get
You will in due course get either a cheque for the full amount you claimed (minus any excess) or an offer of a lesser amount. If the insurers have reduced your claim or rejected some items, check the reason. You may find out for the first time that your photographic equipment was not covered by the policy, or that your camera was over the single article limit so you cannot get the full amount for it. But ask the insurers to explain any reduction in what you claimed.

If your claim involved a number of items or was complicated, it is wise to go through the settlement offered to you very carefully. Insurers often quote an overall figure even though the claim will have been itemised separately on their own records, so you can ask to see the itemised figures. If you are not satisfied or would like more details of any item, do not hesitate to take it up directly, or through your broker, with whoever has been dealing with your claim. In many cases, an offer is improved after new facts have been pointed out to the insurers. Also, ordinary arithmetical errors have been known to occur.

If your claim is a small one and obviously comes within the terms of the policy, and there is no query or administrative delay, you may well receive a cheque within a fortnight. You should not let a lengthy delay or protracted correspondence go unchallenged. If a sternly – but politely – worded letter brings no response from the office with which you are dealing, a letter to the company's general manager at the head office should bring immediate action.

Some insurance companies still use what are known as discharge receipts, for you to sign and send back to the insurance company. It is merely a normal receipt form quoting your policy number, the date of the loss, and the amount you have been paid.

Some receipts have a phrase that the payment is 'in full and final settlement' of your claim. Signing such a discharge receipt

page
86

would mean that you could not reopen the claim if you should find afterwards that other things are missing or that something you had not previously noticed has also been damaged.

reinstatement of sum insured

Most policies contain what is known as an 'automatic reinstatement clause', so that the sum insured is not reduced or exhausted following settlement of a claim (provided that you carry out any recommendations that the insurers make in order to prevent further damage, and that the damage that has been done is made good without delay).

Check that your policy does contain this clause, because if it does not, you must remember to contact your broker or agent or the insurers and arrange for the sum insured to be reinstated to its original level. Technically, there would be a premium due on the reinstated amount (that is, the amount of the claim), charged pro rata from the date of reinstatement to renewal date. Whether or not you are asked to pay this additional premium depends on the insurers and whether they consider the amount worth collecting.

Claims when there is a mortgage

If your house is mortgaged to a building society, you should inform it of any claims – you will have to do so anyway if the society arranged the insurance, in order to obtain a claim form and details of the policy.

Usually the building society will leave it to you to negotiate the claim, although it will be able to help if there is any difficulty. Some building societies are willing to handle the claim on their borrowers' behalf, if requested; some do so as a matter of routine.

If the claim is for a very large amount, the building society may play a major part in negotiations with the insurance company. Part of the settlement money may go to the building society, and the building society may inspect the repair or reconstruction work before releasing the rest of the money to you.

In the event of the house being completely destroyed, the building society may get from the insurers the amount you owe on the mortgage.

After a burglary

As soon as you know or suspect that someone has tried to get in, whether or not he has succeeded, ring the police. (If you know who it was and do not wish to initiate police action that might identify him or her, you cannot make a claim on your insurance policy.)

There will be a question on the claim form asking 'When were the police notified and at what station?' So, when the police come

round to investigate, ask which police station they have come from. The police will want a list of the property that has been stolen; keep a copy of the lists you make for the police and the insurers.

If you have insurance for the building as well as the contents, you can claim on that for making good any damage the burglar did to the building and fixtures, such as breaking a window or a washbasin.

The question on the claim form 'Have you ever before sustained loss or damage of this nature?' applies to incidents, not necessarily to claims. So, if a potential thief had previously tried to get into your home but had been unsuccessful, you should mention this, too. The insurers may ask your local police if there have been any previous occurrences in your district or at your house.

What you say now may be compared with the answers given on your proposal form, or disclosures at subsequent renewal dates, so you may have some explaining to do.

The insurers should not avoid a claim just because you did something foolish like leaving a window open. But there is the general condition to take all reasonable precautions to prevent loss, so leaving a key under a door mat may allow insurers to avoid a claim.

Some policies contain a warranty for certain conditions to be complied with at certain times: for example, that whenever the property is left unoccupied for any period, all windows and doors must be locked or a burglar alarm set. The loss adjuster may ask you questions designed to find out if you have complied with any such warranty. If you have not, the claim may be repudiated.

If you build up a history of carelessness or recklessness, you become what insurers consider a bad risk or moral hazard, and they may not be willing to continue your insurance when the time comes for renewal.

The claim form

Some insurance companies have a claim form specifically for theft claims.

The main part on the claim form asks for a list and description of the missing property, its approximate date of purchase, the amount paid for it, the value before the loss and the amount you are claiming for each piece.

After a burglary, it may take some time for you to discover and list everything stolen. You can either fill in the details that you know already and send in the claim form straightaway saying that there is more to come, or keep the form until later but tell the insurers approximately how much the claim may come to. If you discover that more has gone than you had originally thought, you must tell the police (let the insurers know that you have done so when you add the extra losses to your claim).

page 85

If your insurance is for replacement-as-new, enter the current prices and ignore the other spaces. You should support your claim with some evidence of the quality of the stolen articles. Photographs showing an article can be helpful, even if they were not taken with insurance in mind.

With a policy of indemnity, you have to allow for depreciation (or appreciation) for the figure you put down as the 'value before the loss'. Rather than just guessing how much to claim for items whose present value you find it difficult to assess, put 'not known' with a note explaining why – for instance, 'home made' or 'heirloom' or 'gift from a friend'. Discuss with the loss adjuster any articles which are difficult to describe, let alone evaluate.

If you had brought in an article from abroad and cannot produce a customs declaration, the insurers may try to refuse to pay out for it.

Personal possessions and valuables that you had insured without specifying them separately should now be listed individually, with a current value or replacement cost claimed for each, even though this was not required when you took out the policy. Remember the 'single article limit' – you will not be paid more than a certain amount for any one article (a specified figure, or a percentage of the sum insured, according to the policy).

For articles insured for all-risks as 'specified items', you cannot claim more than the amount quoted against each in the schedule to your policy, even if you now realise (too late) that the value or replacement cost of an article has gone up – for example, if you have a valuable ring under-insured as a separate specified item, you cannot choose now to claim for its full value as part of the general contents.

You can claim for accidental or wilful damage done by the burglar, even if you do not have cover for accidental breakage as part of your policy. All necessary cleaning up and repairing can be claimed for; estimates for this should be sent to the insurers.

When you send in the claim form, point out that if you later discover other things had been taken, you will be adding these to the claim. There is no set time limit; if you can give a reason why you did not find out before, additional claims will be met later. The insurers will not scrutinise the latecomers more carefully, unless you give them cause by continuing to add items.

If you are asked to sign a 'satisfaction note' or 'discharge receipt' when accepting the insurers' payment and you think that yet other things may have been stolen, endorse the note as being settlement 'only so far'.

Afterwards

One way in which theft claims differ significantly from other claims is that there is a chance that you may get some of your things back. The police will tell you about the recovery first, probably because they will want you to identify your property.

If your claim has been paid, these articles do not belong to you any more. If you would like any back, you must negotiate with the insurers about repaying the amount you had been paid for it – or only part of the sum if the article has been damaged. If you do not want to repay the insurers to get your property back, they will take it over and probably sell it.

After the claim has been paid, the specified items that were stolen are automatically deleted from the policy (until you buy replacements and give the necessary details about them to the insurers).

burglary distress insurance
A scheme to insure for the cost (maximum £1000) of moving house following a break-in is available as a separate policy or extension to one insurer's special household policy.

Compensation is paid if you or a member of your family living with you need to have physical or psychiatric treatment as a result of the event and you therefore decide to move away from the home within 12 months of the break-in.

anti-theft installations
You may have to comply with any requirements that the insurers now make to prevent further loss, such as installing better locks or bolts or bars, or an alarm system.

The insurance company's own surveyor (an expert on protection and preventive measures of all kinds) may call on you, by appointment, to see what locks and bolts, bars and alarms you have. If he is not satisfied, the insurance company will then write either direct to you or via your broker or agent, setting out what they want done and will expect you to get it done (and you have to pay for it).

They usually say quite firmly what sort of locks they want – 7-lever mortice deadlock or whatever – or what burglar alarm system, where they must be put, and may recommend certain makes.

Sometimes they make only recommendations – that is, they expect you to carry them out as part of the policy condition that you must make every endeavour to protect the insured goods, but they do not endorse the policy to that effect. If you have another burglary and the new measures have not been fitted or are not being used, the insurers will meet the claim but make fitting of preventive devices a condition of the policy.

Where the situation is more serious, the insurers make the fitting and use of these devices a stipulation in the first place and issue an endorsement of the policy to this effect. This means that if you do not use the protective devices, you have no insurance cover for burglary. And at renewal date, the insurers may refuse to renew either theft cover or the whole policy until the precautions they have specified are carried out.

A word of warning: if a surveyor has called and made his recommendations but you have said 'no', you are in trouble if you want to go elsewhere for your insurance because now you must answer in the affirmative the question on the proposal form whether you have had any insurance or proposal cancelled, withdrawn, declined, or made the subject of special terms. Every new insurer you go to will want to know what these were, and almost certainly will want the same.

Theft today is such a serious problem in some parts of the country that insurers take a tough line in these cases, as well as charging higher premiums.

Some simple precautions against burglars

There is a British Standard (BS 3621) for thief resistant locks.

Doors
the main door is the most vulnerable because you cannot bolt it from the inside when you leave the home – fit two locks: top one an automatic deadlocking latch, lower one a 5-lever mortice deadlock
doors inside the home – fit mortice bolts at top and bottom
aluminium sliding doors – fit an extra security lock to prevent doors being lifted from the tracks

Windows
shut them all whenever you leave the house (even when just going round the corner to shop)
fit security locks on all accessible windows (ground floor and any near drain pipes or a flat roof)

Keys
never leave keys in a lock
never leave a key in 'secret' hiding place (thieves know them all)

When going away
do not make it obvious that you are away from home: cancel milk and newspapers (make arrangements in person or by letter – do not leave a note outside the door that any passer-by can see), ask trusted neighbour to keep an eye on your house, and to

remove leaflets or circulars that are stuck into the letterbox
take jewellery and other valuables to the bank for safe-keeping
do not leave valuable items, video equipment, hi-fi, silver ornaments in full view from a window

When you are out
always lock up when you are going out, for however short a time
shut all windows, even the smallest ones
keep garage and shed locked (may contain tools useful to burglar), ladder padlocked
when out for evening, leave light on in a room (not just the hall), radio on (not too loud, switched to a talking station)

Be prepared
Do not open the door to unknown callers. A security chain on the door allows you to check caller's credentials without opening the door fully. If caller claims to be some kind of official, do not be fooled by a uniform: ask for some identification.

Keep a detailed description of your property; photographs of jewellery and other valuable items will help you and your insurers after any loss, and the police after a theft.

Weddings and funerals are an open invitation to thieves, so remember to arrange for someone to remain in the home while the ceremonies and after-proceedings are taking place.

Advice on burglary protection can be obtained, free, from your local police station. A crime prevention officer will come to look at your house and advise you on locks, bolts and bars, and general precautions on how to keep a thief out.

The BIA's free pamphlet *Beat the burglar*, obtainable from insurance companies, brokers or direct from the British Insurance Association, describes some security devices and precautions generally, and so does the Home Office pamphlet *As safe as houses?* available free from citizens advice bureaux and police stations. The Consumer Publication *Securing your home* deals with the whole subject in detail.

When moving house

While negotiating to buy a house

If you are nervous that you may be left with fees and expenses if your proposed purchase of a house or flat falls through at the last moment due to the seller withdrawing, it is possible to take out 'last-minute hitch' insurance. This has to be arranged by a solicitor or an estate agent and cannot be taken out direct.

You can claim only if the decision not to go through with the agreed sale is made by the other side, the seller, and you must have made a genuine offer to buy, subject to survey and contract.

You can be reimbursed for fees to solicitors, surveyor and building society's valuer that you have had to pay, but only up to £250. The insurance will also pay a lump sum of up to £250 for removal costs that you have to meet if completion is delayed, plus a daily accommodation allowance (£25 for up to 14 days). The premium is a flat £36.

The premium also covers the possibility of a defect in the title to the property coming to light within two years of completion.

For the period between exchange and completion, insurance is available for costs and expenses arising from delay or failure to complete due to a cause beyond your control, whether buyer or seller (or you can be insured for both roles in a transaction). Expenses incurred because of a defect in the title which you could have been expected to know about are excluded. The premium is £15 for a house selling for up to £50,000, £25 for prices above that, for a maximum period of cover of 3 months. The limit on what will be paid is 5% of the contract price (which may not be sufficient to cover, for example, interest on an extended bridging loan).

after exchange of contracts
A clause in some buildings policies gives cover to the buyer of your house during the period between exchange of contracts and completion. This extends to the buyer your policy's cover for damage or loss if he has not otherwise insured the property. As seller, this provision is irrelevant to you; your buildings policy continues to cover your property until you move out, and the buyer would be well advised not to rely on someone else's insurance.

The Consumer Publication *The legal side of buying a house* explains:

'Once contracts are exchanged, the risk in the property passes to the buyer and the seller is under no duty to maintain any insurance on it. Thus if, for example, the property was flooded between exchange of contracts and completion, the buyer would still have to go through with the purchase and bear the cost of repairs. So the insurance of the property you are buying should start from the moment you exchange contracts.'

Structural defects insurance

A scheme is available through some building societies that covers major structural defects emerging in a mortgaged house or bungalow within 3 years of purchase. The premium is £70 for the 3-year period; you also have to pay for a surveyor's assessment report (£30) made at the time of the mortgage valuation and an 'investigation' deposit (£50) at the time of making a claim (returnable if the claim is found valid or reasonably made). There is an excess of £75 on a claim.

The maximum payment is £50,000 or the value of the house at the time of the claim, whichever is the lower. Only major defects are covered, and only those that were not revealed by the surveyor's initial assessment. Defects due to wear and tear or inadequate maintenance are excluded. No payment is made if another insurance policy covers the same defect (but the excess on a subsidence claim on a household policy can be claimed).

Household removal insurance

If your contents policy includes 'contents temporarily removed', do not assume that this covers a household removal: check with the insurers.

Insurance for your belongings while you move permanently to another house or flat is included in some, but not all, contents policies. If not, most insurers will extend an existing contents policy to take in the increased risks of a removal, at an additional premium. A few are willing to issue a separate household removal policy even if you have no existing insurance with them (rarely advertised but still available: you may need a broker to find it for you). Either way – extension or separate policy – there will be a minimum premium of at least £10.

Points to watch for

- cover should include all-risks or at least accidental damage (not be restricted to fire, explosion and theft, or restricted to damage only if caused by an accident to the removal van)
- the removal or the packing may have to be carried out by professional removers
- cover is usually only within the British Isles (sea transit is not included in all policies)
- cover can be for up to seven days (but with some policies limited to, say, 48 hours or 72 hours)
- overnight storage in the removal van or for a few days en route should be included (in some policies, this would need an extension; in some policies, property in storage is specifically excluded)
- storage in a depository (unpacked from the van) is not normally included; special insurance would have to be arranged
- if the section in a contents policy, says 'removal to another home', removal to a depository is not covered – not even the journey to the depository
- damage caused by scratching, denting or bruising may not be covered
- money, jewellery and similar valuables may not be covered
- china, glass, earthenware and other brittle articles are generally not covered unless packed by professional packers
- an excess usually applies; it may be £10 (or as much as £50)
- any loss or damage for which the removers are liable under their contract with you is likely to be excluded.

Removers' insurance

The removal firm may offer to arrange insurance under the British Association of Removers' block policy. This is on an all-risks basis and includes some cover for expenses directly arising as a result of delay.

But look first at your own household contents policy, to establish what cover, if any, it provides (ask your insurers or broker if it is not clear). If this cover seems adequate, it will not be necessary to pay for the insurance scheme offered by a removal firm.

If the quotation for the removal is an all-in price, including insurance, find out how much of it is for the insurance premium: it may be possible to obtain a lower quotation excluding insurance. (But some removal firms withdraw their quotation for the move when the customer does not take up the insurance offered.) If you need to extend your household contents insurance to cover the move, check that premium against the cost of the removal firm's insurance.

Moving is rarely a snap decision, so do not think about insurance cover just as the van is leaving: give the insurers time to arrange it.

The sum insured should be a realistic one because if you are under-insured, averaging would be applied if you have to claim.

claiming

It may be a condition of your removal insurance that you have to notify the insurers of an impending claim within 48 hours of the move. If you are not able to unpack everything at once, tell the insurers straightaway that you will be unable to comply with this time limit.

Alternatively, a way round this is to notify a claim – the first small damage you see – and tell them that you are checking through and will be in touch again as soon as all the details are known.

On the claim form you have to fill in, describe the circumstances as precisely as possible in the blank space provided, and list the lost or damaged items. Keep any bills or receipts for repairs or replacements to produce in support of your claim. For an extensive loss, the insurers will ask you for further details and are likely to take up the matter with the removers. For a relatively small sum, the insurers will probably send you a cheque rather than waste time and money with enquiries.

After the move

Even if your contents policy automatically covers the removal, you need to advise the insurers if you want to continue insurance with them. They must be told of your new permanent address and the date you move in.

You should give details of the new house and its construction, and who will be living there, and amend the sum insured if necessary.

When you have moved into your new house, there may be a number of people with keys to the previous locks, so change all the locks and fit good quality replacements.

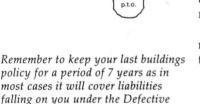

Remember to keep your last buildings policy for a period of 7 years as in most cases it will cover liabilities falling on you under the Defective Premises Act.

Letters you may need to write

These letters are for people who are dealing direct with the insurance company, rather than via a broker or agent.

Work on the principle that a short letter is more likely to be read and understood.

In none of them has a particular department or individual been identified to whom to address a letter – the post openers at the company's offices will identify by the policy number more quickly, so always quote this. Also quote the renewal date: many offices file in date order. Use the same heading as the insurers use if you have already had some correspondence on the matter; always quote their reference number.

If you are not certain which office is dealing with your policy, write to the insurance company's head office; the letter will be sent on to the right branch office.

---

letter no 1 *to notify change of address*

The British Flag Insurance Co
15 Heathgate
London EC6

The Copse
61 Southwood Close
Leafville
LZ3 7WW

Dear Sirs

POLICY NO. H 3893456 RENEWAL DATE: 28 FEBRUARY

Giving the postcode enables your insurance rating district to be easily identified.

I am about to buy a new house, and hope to exchange contracts on 3 June. I shall want buildings-only insurance from that date. The address will be: 24 The Gables, Minsterville, GA24 5BT.

It is a brick-built detached three-bedroom two-storey house, roofed with tiles, built around 1930. The purchase price is £50,000; my surveyor advises that the rebuilding cost would be nearer £62,000, and this should be the sum insured for the building.

You may be asked to pay an additional premium if you are moving from a rural area to a city or centre of town. You may be sent an endorsement to your present policy or, more likely, a fresh proposal form to complete (the insurers probably hoping that when you fill in the new proposal form you will increase most of the sums insured, and get attracted by some of the other insurances they offer).

We hope to move in on 14 July, and the full insurance for our present house should be transferred to the new one on that date. The sum insured for contents remains the same (£12,000).

The house will be occupied by myself, my husband and our teenage son, and our daughter during the university vacations.

Yours faithfully

U. N. Eye (Mrs)

You need only give enough information at this stage to enable the insurers to know what sort of claim form you need and to assess whether they want someone to call on you to look at the damage. If you put more detail into the letter, you will only have to repeat a lot on the claim form.

If it were a big emergency job, you should have telephoned the insurance company, and someone would definitely call.

Cannot include plumber's bill in claim

letter no 2a *to notify a claim*

The British Flag Insurance Co	*24 The Gables*
15 Heathgate	*Minsterville*
London EC6	*GA24 5BT*

Dear Sirs

POLICY NO. H 3893456 RENEWAL DATE: 28 FEBRUARY

Last night the water tank in my roof overflowed and the water caused damage to the ceiling and the furniture in the room underneath. I called in a plumber and he has fitted a new ball valve.

Please send the necessary form for me to claim under the above policy.

Yours faithfully

U. N. Eye (Mrs)

letter no 2b *to get repairs authorised*

Generally you can get the work done and send the receipted bill for repairs but for a large amount if you would like some assurance that the insurers are going to pay, write this kind of letter. It is an insured person's obligation to minimise further damage. Telling them that the damage is likely to get worse (and the claim higher) may hurry things along.

I enclose my claim form setting out details of the damage done by water overflowing from the storage tank to my ceilings and wallpaper. Attached is an estimate from Messrs Slagthorpe & Sons for the necessary repair and redecoration. The damage looks very unsightly and a fall of plaster may cause further damage so I should like to have the work done as soon as possible. If you want to send someone to inspect the damage before the repairs are done, please telephone me to make an appointment (Minsterville 190612).

Yours faithfully

U. N. Eye (Mrs)

letter no 3 *when not renewing*

There is no need to write a letter – the reason for your cancellation does not have to be explained: merely write across your renewal notice 'NOT BEING RENEWED' and sign it. You need not even do this, but it is a matter of courtesy and saves reminders and people's time generally. You can either send it back direct to the insurers or hand it to your broker or agent.

letter no 4 *to end a policy because you are selling house and contents*

The Peninsular Insurance Co	*Channel View*
Spice Dock	*The Cliffs*
London EC5	*Folkemouth*

Dear Sirs

POLICY NO. H 7270199 RENEWAL DATE: 4 OCTOBER

On 27th May 1984, I shall complete the sale of my house, Channel View. The contents are being sold with the house. As I shall be living permanently in France, I shall not require further insurance here and the policy should be cancelled from that date.

As far as I am aware, there are no claims pending on the policy and no incident has arisen likely to give rise to one.

Your cheque for the refund of premium should be sent to me c/o my solicitors in England – Messrs Blank and Nobody, 22 High Street, Folkemouth.

Yours faithfully

Frank O'Fyle

---

letter no 5 *to add to all-risks insurance*

The British Flag Insurance Co	*24 The Gables*
15 Heathgate	*Minsterville*
London EC6	*GA24 5BT*

Dear Sirs

POLICY NO. H 3893456 RENEWAL DATE: 28 FEBRUARY

Please add, with effect from today, the following items to my list of specified valuables for all-risks cover in the above policy. A copy of the valuation is enclosed for your records.

The insurers require proof of valuation for items over a certain value. If you inherit anything, you have to get it valued. If the article is a gift, you may be able to get hold of the receipt, which is just as good as a valuation, and free.

item 25: a two-stone diamond ring, with claw setting in 18ct gold – to be insured for £1,250

item 26: a brooch in a bird design with 14 diamonds and platinum setting – to be insured for £2,500

According to my calculations, this will increase the total sum insured under this section to £20,500.

Please send me an endorsement to the policy and let me know if any additional premium is due.

Yours faithfully

U. N. Eye (Mrs)

letter no 6 *when placing specified items in safe deposit*

The British Flag Insurance Co
15 Heathgate
London EC6

24 The Gables
Minsterville
GA24 5BT

Dear Sirs

POLICY NO. H 3893456 RENEWAL DATE: 28 FEBRUARY

Please note that I am today placing in my strong box at Lloyds Bank, The Parade, Minsterville, the following items listed in the 'all-risks' specification of my policy.

item 25: a two-stone diamond ring, with claw setting in 18ct gold – insured for £1,250

item 26: a brooch in a bird design with 14 diamonds and platinum setting – insured for £2,500

As far as I am aware at the moment, they will remain there for the foreseeable future.

Please send me an endorsement to my policy accordingly and let me know about the adjustment of premium.

If she wants to take them out of the bank to wear one evening, she should tell the insurers.

Yours faithfully

U. N. Eye (Mrs)

---

letter no 7 *when deleting items from all-risks insurance*

The British Flag Insurance Co
15 Heathgate
London EC6

24 The Gables
Minsterville
GA24 5BT

Dear Sirs

POLICY NO. H 3893456 RENEWAL DATE: 28 FEBRUARY

Please note that on 12th May, I sold the following item covered by my all-risks insurance for specified valuables:

item 25: two-stone diamond ring, with claw setting in 18ct gold – insured for £1,250

According to my calculations, this reduces the total sum insured under this section to £19,250. I presume a refund of premium is now due, and I await your cheque, together with an endorsement to the policy.

Yours faithfully

U. N. Eye (Mrs)

letter no 8 *when building not of standard construction*

The British Flag Insurance Co	*The Batchery*
15 Heathgate	*Ruralton*
London EC6	*RA25 1AZ*

Dear Sirs

I enclose a completed proposal form for the purpose of getting a quotation from you. Please note that my house does not conform to the normal construction as described in your form, and I would draw your attention to the following features.

The roof of the main building is thatched in Norfolk reed but all the outbuildings and the garage have traditional clay tiles. There is a substantial amount of wood in the construction of the main building, which is timber-framed filled with wattle and daub, but at least 50 per cent of the walls have now been replaced by ordinary brickwork. As far as I can ascertain, the building is about 300 years old. It is listed as grade 2 and is within a conservation area.

If you wish to inspect the premises before making a quotation, an appointment can be made by telephoning me any day on Ruralton 4849.

Yours faithfully

P. N. Reid-Strawe

---

letter no 9 *when information not given on policy schedule*

The British Flag Insurance Co	*24 The Batchery*
15 Heathgate	*Ruralton*
London EC6	*RA25 1AZ*

Dear Sirs

POLICY NO. H 9408932 RENEWAL DATE: 19 APRIL

This letter is only needed if the policy or schedule states the construction is 'BSST'. If construction is not mentioned at all, an endorsement is not needed.

I have today received the above policy, but can find no mention on the schedule that my property has a thatched roof. When I arranged the insurance with you, I notified you of this fact and was under the impression that your quotation had been prepared accordingly. Would you kindly send me an amended schedule so that no misunderstandings will occur at any future date.

Yours faithfully

P. N. Reid-Strawe

letter no 10 *to notify change of circumstances*

The British Flag Insurance Co
15 Heathgate
London EC6

24 The Gables
Minsterville
GA24 5BT

Dear Sirs

POLICY NO. H 3893456 RENEWAL DATE: 28 FEBRUARY

No need to mention premium: in most circumstances, there will not be an increase, but if you live in a high-theft area, the insurers may ask for details of your anti-burglar precautions or want to survey the premises to see what these are like – and no doubt recommend some more. This largely depends on the sum insured for your contents.

When the above policy was taken out in 1980, both my husband and I were working from home and our house was then hardly ever left without an occupant. The position has now reversed: the house is empty each day and occasionally left for up to 3 days at a time without an occupant. Would you kindly confirm that you have noted this change and that it does not affect the cover given by the policy.

Yours faithfully

U. N. Eye (Mrs)

---

letter no 11 *to notify change of circumstances*

The British Flag Insurance Co
15 Heathgate
London EC6

25 Broad Drive
Anytown
Midshire
AA77 1AA

Dear Sirs

POLICY NO. H2031570 RENEWAL DATE: 13 MARCH

When the above policy was taken out in 1976, the property was always left unoccupied during the day while I was out at work. I have now retired and, also because I have taken on some home typing, I am there for most part of every day.

Please let me know whether this reduces the amount of my premium.

Yours faithfully

I. M. Mee

letter no 12 *to challenge renewal premium*

The Bridstow Insurance Co
Tana Lane
Stowbridge
Tenshire

14 Twintree Avenue
Minford
Tenshire

Dear Sirs

POLICY NO. H 3408197 RENEWAL DATE: 7 JANUARY

I have received your renewal notice for the above policy and see that the sum insured for buildings and contents shows a considerable increase compared with last year's. I appreciate that the policy is index-linked, but was under the impression that the overall percentage increase in prices generally was now on the decrease. Nowhere on the renewal notice can I find details of the actual percentage used and I shall be grateful if you can advise me of this.

Yours faithfully

Matthew Seaton

---

letter no 13 *to change premium at renewal*

The Bridstow Insurance Co
Tana Lane
Stowbridge
Tenshire

14 Twintree Avenue
Minford
Tenshire

Dear Sirs

POLICY NO. H 3408197 RENEWAL DATE: 7 JANUARY

I have received my renewal notice for the above policy and find that both my buildings and contents sums insured have been considerably increased by virtue of index-linking. I do not think that these now reflect the true picture for my property.

Regarding the buildings, I have recently demolished several of the outbuildings, and having checked the position with the leaflet 'Guide to buildings insurance' which you sent with the renewal notice, I feel that £36,000 would now be a more realistic figure for the sum insured.

Regarding the contents, we have recently bought a new three-piece suite and replaced both our dishwasher and washing machine with larger, more up-to-date models, and have made several other purchases of household equipment during the year. The figure should therefore now be increased by £1,500, bringing the total sum insured for contents to £15,000.

Please let me know the new premium for these revised amounts so that I can send you my cheque to renew the policy.

Yours faithfully

Matthew Seaton

---

letter no 14 *when dealing with third party claim*

The British Flag Insurance Co
15 Heathgate
London EC6

24 *The Gables*
Minsterville
GA24 5BT

Dear Sirs

POLICY NO. H 3893456 RENEWAL DATE: 28 FEBRUARY

The insurers will almost certainly send a claim form which asks for a lot more detail than the brief outline which is all you need to give in the letter. The important thing is not to tell the 'third party' that your insurance will pay. (But you can say that you have passed the letter to your insurers.)

On 3rd January a visitor to my house, Miss A. D. Venture of 27 Broad Drive, Anytown, tore her coat on a nail protruding from my banisters. I did not think that any more would come of the incident, so did not advise you at the time. However, I have now received the enclosed letter from Miss Venture's solicitors and shall be grateful if you will deal with the matter under the terms of my policy.

Yours faithfully

U. N. Eye (Mrs)

---

letter no 15 *to report further losses after a theft*

The British Flag Insurance Co
15 Heathgate
London EC6

The Batchery
Ruralton
RA25 1AZ

Dear Sirs

The claim number is very important and should be quoted at all times; the ref. number is generally the telephone extension of the claims clerk.

CLAIM NO. H1/51/617 YOUR REF. ER/52

POLICY NO. H 9408932 RENEWAL DATE: 19 APRIL

When I sent my claim form to your office on 25th May, I said that the loss of further items might come to light. We have now discovered that the following are also missing and must be presumed to have been stolen at the same time:

a small Philips portable radio bought 2 years ago – current price of a similar model £25
a lady's suede coat, made by Zuedetex of Swainston, 5 years old – approximate value now £70
a gentleman's gold pocket watch, with chain, about 80 years old, not working but worth its weight in gold – approximately £50

Please add these items to my claim. I have advised Sgt Dixon at Ruralton police station. I am unfortunately unable to say with certainty that everything has yet been accounted for, but hope that this now represents the total amount taken.

Yours faithfully

P. N. Reid-Strawe

---

letter no 16 *when returning satisfaction note re claims payment*

The Bridstow Insurance Co
Tana Lane
Stowbridge
Tenshire

13 Knockit Down
Hazardville
Bumpshire

Dear Sirs

CLAIM NO. H2/03/157 YOUR REF. BH/23

POLICY NO. H 3713719 RENEWAL DATE: 3 MARCH

Thank you for your cheque for £167.50, in payment for my claim on the above policy. Although I am quite satisfied with the way the matter has been dealt with, I have deleted the last line of your satisfaction note (discharge receipt) because I am not in a position even yet to be certain that further evidence of damage from the explosion will not be detected at some later date; in such a case, I would want to reopen this claim.

Yours faithfully

Victor V. Careless

---

letter no 17 *to query delay in settlement of claim*

The Bridstow Insurance Co
Tana Lane
Stowbridge
Tenshire

14 Twintree Avenue
Minford
Tenshire

Dear Sirs

CLAIM NO. H8/52/028 YOUR REF. AL/14

POLICY NO. H 3408197 RENEWAL DATE: 7 JANUARY

On 30 March, I sent you a claim form for damage to my roof. Since that time, apart from an acknowledging postcard, I have heard nothing further from you. As I explained in my covering letter, in order to minimise the danger of further damage, I had the work undertaken at once, and enclosed a copy of Timeric & Co's receipted account with the claim form. Even taking into account the large number of properties damaged during that storm, I feel the time taken to deal with this matter is excessive and shall be glad if you will send me your cheque without further delay.

Yours faithfully

Matthew Seaton

---

letter no 18 *to query reduced claim settlement*

The Bridstow Insurance Co   14 *Twintree Avenue*
Tana Lane   *Minford*
Stowbridge   *Tenshire*
Tenshire

Dear Sirs

CLAIM NO. H8/52/028 YOUR REF. AL/14

POLICY NO. H 3408197 RENEWAL DATE: 7 JANUARY

I was most surprised by your offer of settlement in your letter of 25th May. This water could have entered my house only due to the damage to the parapet during the storm on the night of 28th March. The damage to the parapet was obviously caused by the storm and should therefore be paid for under the policy, as well as the damage caused by the water. The gutters had been cleared and the pointing made good by Messrs Timeric & Co in January. I enclose a copy of their account for carrying out this work, which proves that there was no lack of maintenance or any other 'gradually operating cause' that could have been responsible for the damage.

In most cases, insurers give an explanation for reducing a claim so you can use their jargon in challenging it.

I shall be glad therefore if you will reconsider my claim in the light of this evidence, and I look forward to receiving your cheque for the full amount of my claim.

Yours faithfully

Matthew Seaton

letter no 19 *to decline policy just received*

The Red House Insurance Co
22 Bank Street
London WC3

Bernice College
Osborne
Wordshire

Dear Sirs

POLICY NO. H 06722

Thank you for sending the above policy, herewith returned.

The insurers could be within their rights not to refund the full premium because a few days' insurance has existed. To avoid this, you would need to use the insurance terminology, and say 'Please treat the policy as not taken up'.

When I filled in your proposal form for insurance for my jewellery, I was not aware that I would be expected to bear the first £50 of all losses myself. I do not feel that this was made sufficiently clear in the proposal form. As I am not prepared to accept this, I am returning the policy. Please cancel your records and refund the premium of £84.50 which I paid.

Yours faithfully

Penny Wyse

Apart from the obvious reason of being able to buy another car if
you smash yours, you need insurance for your car because the law
says so.

Under the Road Traffic Act, all motorists have to insure for their
liability for injuries sustained by other people (including
passengers) caused by a road accident with their vehicle. But it is
only this 'Act-only' or RTA cover that is compulsory. You can drive
perfectly legally on the roads with no insurance for damage you may
do to other people's property, despite the fact that you could be
~~r~~~~d~~ legally liable for damages running into many thousands

---

c. 20   *Road Traffic Act 1972*

PART VI

THIRD-PARTY LIABILITIES

*Compulsory insurance or security against
third-party risks*

Users of motor
vehicles to be
insured or
secured
against
third-party
risks.

143.—(1) Subject to the provisions of this Part of this Act, it
shall not be lawful for a person to use, or to cause or permit
any other person to use, a motor vehicle on a road unless there
is in force in relation to the use of the vehicle by that person or
that other person, as the case may be, such a policy of insurance
or such a security in respect of third-party risks as complies
with the requirements of this Part of this Act; and if a person
acts in contravention of this section he shall be guilty of an
offence.

Types of policy

accidental damage
In the context of motor policies, this phrase usually covers all damage to the policyholder's vehicle which is not excluded from the policy and which does not come under a specific section of the policy. (The accidental damage section is what distinguishes a comprehensive motor policy from a third party, fire & theft policy.)
INSURANCE OMBUDSMAN BUREAU
annual report for 1982

- 'Act-only' (insurers do not encourage 'Act-only' policies)
- third party only (that is, liability for injuries caused to other people and to passengers in the car, liability of passengers in the car for accidents caused by them, liability for damage to other people's property)
- third party, fire and theft
- comprehensive

The British Insurance Association's leaflet *What you need to know about motor insurance* summarises the cover provided by the different types of policies:

1	**Act only** numbers 1 & 2		
2			
3		**Third party** numbers 1 to 5	**Third party fire and theft** numbers 1 to 6
4			
5			
6			
7			
8			
9			
10			**Comprehensive** numbers 1 to 10

1 Liability for injuries to other people, arising from accidents caused by your car on public roads or elsewhere.
Legal costs incurred with your insurers' consent in connection with a claim against you will also be paid.

2 Liability for injuries to passengers in your car.

3 Liability of passengers in your car in respect of accidents caused by them.
(For example, the careless opening of a door causing injury to a passer-by or damage to his property.)

4 Liability for damage to other people's property.
(For example, if you are involved in an accident which causes damage to another car, your insurance will pay all or part of the cost of repairs to the other car, depending on the extent to which you are legally to blame.)

5 Liability for injuries to other people or damage to their property caused by a trailer or caravan attached to your car.

6 Fire or theft.
(But if your car is not normally kept in a locked garage at night, your insurers may exclude theft or make theft cover subject to special conditions or charge an extra premium.)

7 Accidental damage to your car.
(But not wear and tear, depreciation, loss of use, mechanical or electrical breakdown, punctures.)

8 Accidents to yourself and perhaps your wife or husband, resulting in death or loss of sight and/or limbs, up to stated amounts.
(This applies to all journeys in your car or in any other private car not belonging to you, whether you are driving or not.)

9 Medical expenses up to a stated amount incurred by you or your passengers as a result of an accident involving your car.

10 Loss or damage to rugs, clothing and personal effects up to a stated amount while they are in the car.

There are a few comprehensive policies without cover for personal accident (no. 8) and without cover for personal effects (no. 10).

Driving another car

Most policies, whether comprehensive or not, cover the policyholder while driving a car belonging to someone else, with the owner's permission. But the cover is limited to third party liability: you are not insured for the damage that you do to the car that you have borrowed. However, if the owner of the borrowed car has comprehensive insurance on an any-driver basis, that covers you not only for third party claims, but for damage to the car as well. So, before driving another's car, check the other car owner's insurance cover rather than relying on the limited third party cover from your own policy.

Cover for driving other cars is sometimes deleted from a policy – for example, when a car is insured in a firm's name, or the policyholder has a bad driving record or is very young. This is meant to stop him borrowing a fast unfamiliar car and restricts him to driving only the car his insurers know about.

If you are covered by a comprehensive policy as 'spouse' on a 'named driver and spouse only' basis, that insurance does not cover you while driving anybody else's vehicle. So, unless the owner of the borrowed car has an 'any driver' policy, not only would you be personally liable for any damage or injuries in the event of an accident, you would also be driving unlawfully because you would not be covered by any insurance.

Maximum fine for driving without insurance is £1000.

The proposal form

The proposal form asks your name and age, address and where the car is normally kept (if not the same).

Driving experience and age

A young driver (up to the age of 25 in many policies) will have to pay a higher premium or bear an excess for damage to his car (or both). For example, a £25 excess on any claim for damage to the car may be increased to £50 or more for a driver under 21. The main reason for an excess is the driver being very young, inexperienced – or accident-prone.

Once you are of mature age, which may be anything from 30+ and up to 70, some insurers welcome you with open arms.

But after the age of 70 or so, it will be difficult to get taken on as a new policyholder, so you may have to stay with your existing insurers.

Most will keep you on normal terms over the age of 75 while you are able to keep your driving licence. Some insurers ask for a doctor's certificate every year (for which the doctor can charge a fee) or get you to sign a declaration of health each year and answer questions about the extent of driving in the year.

special policies

You may qualify for a 'mature driver's' policy, at a lower premium. The cover is normal comprehensive insurance but with restrictions. An excess on damage claims (£25 or £35 or £50) is usually incorporated.

A mature driver can be as young as 45 or even 30, and a spouse can be included in the policy even if less mature than the policyholder. These policies are usually limited to people with no claims or convictions over the last 5 years, and generally do not cover high group cars.

Some of these policies assume that everybody who is 'mature' is also retired, so all business use is excluded (but you can use the car to go to and from your place of employment). Most of these policies allow no young drivers at all or limit cover for them to RTA only, so if you later wish a younger person to drive your car, you will have to change to an ordinary comprehensive policy.

Address

Where you live and keep the car affects the premium you will have to pay. Rural areas are the lowest rated areas, London and the big towns the highest, where there are more accidents and higher repair costs and far more thefts.

Insurers divide Great Britain into areas (usually seven) which roughly reflect the amount of traffic – and incidence of motor claims. The higher the number (or letter) of the area you live in, the higher the premium you will have to pay. For example:

If at the time of an accident, your car is being driven by or is in the charge of someone who holds a provisional licence, or has held a full licence for less than a year, or who is under 25 years old, you will usually have to accept an excess (of £50 upwards) on a claim for damage to your car.

AREA 1
rural counties, offshore islands

AREA 2
semi-rural counties

AREA 3
counties of average population and medium-size towns

AREA 4
more densely populated counties and some large cities

AREA 5
certain large provincial cities and their surrounding areas

AREA 6
densely populated areas of the biggest cities

AREA 7
inner London

Not all companies quote for Northern Ireland; those that do, usually quote a higher premium than for area 7.

But insurers do not all delineate their areas in the same way. For instance, Brentford in Middlesex is in 'Central London' (the most expensive area) for one company, in an outer (no. 4) area for another.

So, if you live in an area that might be rated in two categories, it is worth finding an insurer who rates yours as a lower area. Some insurers list their areas in the brochure or prospectus; if not, ask. Your area may have been recently up or down-rated.

You have to state whether the car is kept on the street, or garaged; this may affect the premium.

page 134

The car

The details asked about the car include its cubic capacity, make and model, year of make, registration number and whether it has been converted, adapted, modified.

The current value has to be stated. This affects the premium if the value is high. It can also affect how much you will get following a total loss of the car because settlement will be for the market value at the time or the value you state, whichever is the less – so do not be too modest in your valuation: look around the secondhand car dealers and see what they are asking for a good similar model. If the car is brand new and you bought it at a discount, put in the full on-the-road price.

Insurers sort cars into up to 8 or 9 groups. Group 1 is the cheapest to insure.

Each model of every make of car is allocated to a group, but groups vary slightly from insurer to insurer. Most insurance companies list their grouping of the more popular models in brochures and proposal forms.

For example,

GROUP 1
Citroen 2CV, Fiat Panda, Mini City, Talbot Samba LE

GROUP 2
Austin Metro 1.3, Morris Ital 1.3L, Ford Fiesta 1100L, Vauxhall Astra 1.2L, VW Polo CL

GROUP 3
Datsun Sunny 1.2GL, Ford Escort 1300L, Renault 5TL, Vauxhall Cavalier 1.6GL Saloon, Ford Sierra 1600L.

GROUP 4
Austin Ambassador 1.7L, Citroen GSA Pallas, Ford Capri 1600GL, Renault 9GTL, Talbot Alpine 1.6GL

GROUP 5
Audi 80GL, Datsun Bluebird 1.8GL, Granada 2000L, Honda Accord, VW Golf GL, Vauxhall Carlton, Volvo 343DL

GROUP 6
Citroen CX Reflex, Renault Fuego GTX, Rover 2300, VW Scirocco GL, Talbot Tagora GLS

GROUP 7
BMW 520i, Colt Cordia Turbo, Rover 3500SE, Saab 900GLS, Mercedes 250

GROUP 8
Alfa Romeo Alfetta 1.8GT, MMW 728i, Daimler Sovereign XJ 4.2, Volvo 760 Turbo

GROUP 9
Aston Martin V8, Bentley Mulsanne, Jaguar XJS 4.6, Porsche 911SC.

Lloyd's syndicates use a similar system, placing most cars in 7 groups but with flexibility regarding specialist, sporting or expensive cars which are 'on application to the underwriters'.

Insurance companies issue motor rating guides to their brokers and agents, listing all makes and models of cars and the groups they put each into, and giving their premium rates for the different groups in the various areas. When you are thinking of buying a new car, you can check which premium group it will fall into.

age of the car
The age of the car affects the premium. The basic premium is often lower if the car is over a certain number of years old, which varies with different insurers. For example, 7$\frac{1}{2}$% off if the car is 4 to 6 years old; 15% off if it is 7 years old.

The drivers

The fewer the people allowed to drive your car, the lower the premium. Your policy can be for the car to be driven by

A young driver's policy may be restricted to named drivers only (without the named-driver discount).

- any driver
- named drivers only
- you and one other named driver
- you and husband/wife only
- you only (lowest premium)

You should think carefully before restricting driving to yourself alone. If you are the only named driver, it would be illegal for other people to drive your car, even in an emergency, unless they had their own insurance – which would normally give only third party cover while driving someone else's car.

You are asked to provide details of all the people, as well as yourself, who you expect will drive the car. This has to be completed even for an 'any driver' policy – you are expected to know who will be using it regularly, even if on some occasions you allow a comparative stranger to drive.

An underwriter may decide, on seeing a number of young or unsatisfactory drivers listed, to vary the policy terms in addition to the built-in excess for young drivers, which is part of all comprehensive policies.

Occupation

Insurers have deduced that some jobs seem, on average, to carry a higher risk of motor accidents; which these are varies from insurer to insurer.

A commercial traveller, insurance agent or suchlike, who uses the car for business, will have to pay up to 50% more for insurance than ordinary motorists. If you do this kind of job but have a trouble-free claims and driving record, there will be no difficulty about getting insurance – but it will cost you more.

People who are likely to have to pay more and may find it difficult to obtain insurance except from specialist insurers, and whose policy may be limited, include club proprietor, croupier, dance band or group musician, entertainer, hawker or market trader, horse or dog trainer, jockey, journalist, professional sportsman, publican, scrap merchant, student, turf commission agent, worker in holiday camps or fun fairs.

There can be problems even if the job is only part-time: for example, a bank clerk who also earns money as a member of a dance band in the evenings and at weekends.

On the other hand, some occupations such as teachers, office workers in government or local government, employees of banks or insurance companies, the police, may get preferential rates.

Driving experience

You will be asked about the type of driving licence you and the other drivers hold – full or provisional or international, and how long the licence has been held.

A person asking for comprehensive cover who is a provisional licence holder or has held a full licence for less than 12 months would have to accept an excess in the region of £50 to £70 of every claim for damage to the insured car.

Driving record

The proposal form will ask whether any of the drivers, including yourself, have
■ *been convicted during the past 5 years of an offence connected with a motor vehicle or have any prosecutions pending?*
■ *had a driving licence suspended at anytime?*
■ *had during the past 3 (or 4 or 5) years any accident, loss or claim (irrespective of who was at fault) in connection with any motor vehicle, whether covered by insurance or not?*

If you answer 'yes' to any of these questions, you will be asked for more details. For instance, the date of a conviction and the offence code (as endorsed on the licence); for accidents, the date of the incident, whether a third party was involved, any payment for damage, sometimes who was at fault and why (you are expected to give a simple description of the accident).

The premium is likely to be increased if you have a record of frequent accidents or have been convicted of a serious driving offence (such as dangerous driving) or a number of less serious ones (such as speeding) during the past few years.

Motoring convictions are rated on a points structure by the courts, and your premium will be increased according to the points allocated. If you have comprehensive insurance, a large excess may also be imposed.

If you have been convicted of driving with excess alcohol in your blood, your insurance cover is likely to be restricted to third party only, your premium loaded (by 100%, or more), driving other cars excluded, and the insurance limited to drivers named in the policy.

A young or a new driver with a number of convictions will find it difficult to get motor insurance with a normal insurer, and impossible at a reasonable price. Cover will be minimal and the cost very high, and the insurance may be given for three months at a time only. But some insurers specialise in this type of risk (see the report on car insurance in *Which?* January 1983).

Use of the car

In general, insurers specify 'classes' for the use of a car. Most insurers have similar classes but there are some differences, and some different ways in which they are referred to – class 1, 2, 3, or class A, B, C.

An average classification runs something like

CLASS 1 *Use for social, domestic and pleasure purposes, and use by the policyholder in person in connection with his business* (and, with some insurers, *that of his employer or partner*)
You and any other driver covered by the policy can go to and from a regular place of work in the car, but (except in certain occupations) only you can use it for making business calls.

Normally, it is the policyholder only who has cover for business use, but if he or she does not use the car for business, usually the wife or husband can do so instead, at no extra premium. But the insurers must be told who is doing so because this cover is generally restricted to use for business by one person only. Not many insurers allow business use by both the insured and spouse as normal without extra charge, so it is worth shopping around if that is what you require.

Excluded from this class of use is
- hiring out ('for hire or reward')
- racing, competitions
- trials, rallies (but road safety rallies or treasure hunts are not excluded)

People who are in their car all day and every day, often covering quite large distances, such as commercial travellers and sales representatives, are excluded.

premium:
about 30% more than class 1

CLASS 2 *Use for social, domestic and pleasure purposes, and use for the business of the policyholder and that of his employer or partner.*
The difference here is that not just the policyholder in person but other people can drive for business use. The exclusions are the same as for class 1.

premium:
about 60% more than class 1

CLASS 3 *Use for social, domestic and pleasure purposes, and use for the business of the policyholder and that of his employer or partner.*
The use is the same as for class 2 except that commercial travellers and sales representatives are not excluded.

The wording is so much alike that you need to make certain that you choose the correct class of use.

giving a lift
All the categories exclude use for 'carriage of passengers for hire and reward'. But if you give a lift to someone who then contributes to the cost of the journey (paying for the petrol, perhaps) your insurance will hold – provided that you do not make a profit from such payments.

What contribution you can accept depends on whether the journey would have been made in any event (in which case the passenger must pay not more than his proportion) or whether it is undertaken specially for the passenger (who can pay you for the whole of the running costs of that journey).

Other questions

The questions that are asked about every named driver may include

- *any period of residence outside the British Isles in the past three years?*
- *suffer from diabetes, epilepsy, heart condition, or any other physical (or mental) disability, infirmity or disease?*
- *subject to any condition necessitating the use of prescribed drugs or mechanical aids (except defective vision or hearing if corrected by a hearing aid or spectacles)?*

■ *ever had a motor insurance policy declined or cancelled, or been asked to pay an increased premium or had special conditions imposed?*

There may be other questions asked by a particular insurer. For example:

■ *have you owned any vehicles in the last 3 years?*

You may be asked to state total owned at any one time during the past 3 years. This is followed by three spaces:

1981 total owned . . .

1982 total owned . . .

1983 total owned . . .

This is meant to enable the insurers to assess your driving history, and whether you buy and sell cars frequently.

■ *do you own the car?*

Buying it on hire purchase is considered owning it, but a leasing agreement is not.

■ *do you own or have the use of any other vehicle?*

(This would include a company car.) If so, you have to give details and, with some insurers, the reasons for use of this car.

'You' includes members of your household, and if any of them are under 25 (or other young age), there may be further questions.

Declaration

As on any insurance proposal form, there is a warning about the duty to disclose all information that may be relevant to the insurance asked for.

Then comes the declaration that everything you have said is true, and the space for your signature.

Before signing, read through the answers given, especially if a broker or agent completed the form. An inaccurate answer could entitle the insurers to repudiate a claim.

A proposer who allows a broker or other intermediary to fill in blank spaces on a proposal form must realise that he cannot afterwards complain that the proposal was wrongly completed.
INSURANCE OMBUDSMAN BUREAU
annual report for 1982

The premium

The main factors that affect the premium are
- the rating group of the car
- the area where it is kept
- the class of use
- the main driver's age, occupation, experience and driving record
- the type of cover you choose (comprehensive costs more than third-party, fire and theft).

voluntary excess
If you want to save money on a comprehensive motor policy, you can elect to pay £xx of every claim for damage to your car. This may be anything from £20 (or £25) to get 7½% off, to an excess of £100, for which a 15% or 20% discount might be given.

The amount of the discount will not ever be more than the amount of the excess. For example, where a £50 voluntary excess would gain a 15% discount, if your non-discount premium is £446, the discount for the voluntary excess will be only £50 not £66.90.

A voluntary excess would be in addition to any compulsory excess in the policy.

restricting the drivers
You can get a reduction in premium for restricting driving to one named driver (in some cases, a greater reduction if a woman), to yourself and spouse, to two named drivers (no relationship required). Discounts for these are usually between 7½% and 12½% of the normal premium.

shorter period of insurance
Premiums for motor insurance policies are normally based on annual payment. If you require insurance for a shorter period, what you will be asked to pay is not normally a proportionate percentage of the annual premium, but special short period rates. The short period scale varies between insurers; generally a policy for more than 9 months will be charged at the full annual rate.

Short period policies do not normally carry an entitlement to a no-claim discount.

No-claim discount (NCD)

You should read your policy carefully to understand exactly what the position is regarding the earning and losing of a no-claim discount.

Nearly all insurers give substantial no-claim discounts (sometimes called bonuses). A common scale is
NCD after 1 year without a claim 30%
NCD after 2 years without a claim 40%
NCD after 3 years without a claim 50%
NCD after 4 years or more without a claim 60%.

With some insurers, the range starts at only 25%; with some, it goes up to 65%; with some, you do not get 65% until the 6th year.

If you make one claim during a year, you normally move back two steps. For example, if you have a 60% NCD now and make a claim, you will get only 40% NCD when you renew the policy. If you make more than one claim during the year, you usually lose all your NCD. It builds up again one step at a time as the number of consecutive claim-free years increases.

'Protected' NCD

A way to qualify for a protected NCD with some insurers is to insure the car as part of a householder's package policy.

Many insurers offer schemes or special policies which allow you to make some claims without your NCD being reduced: for example, two claims in any three-year (with some insurers, five-year) period, without loss of discount.

Most insurers tell you how many claims you can have before the protection runs out; others give veiled hints such as 'terms are likely to be amended only if there is evidence of bad driving, frequent claims or a conviction for a serious offence'.

In order to qualify for a protected NCD, you have to satisfy certain conditions, for example
- be within a certain age range (say, 25 to 65)
- able to prove that you have not made a claim for the last five years
- be free from motoring convictions.

You may have to pay an extra 6% or 10% premium for this 'protection' (or an extra £5 or £7) or accept an excess on damage claims (£25 to £50).

no NCD

A few insurers offer policies which do not have any no-claim discount at all but have low basic premiums instead. Because there is no NCD to lose, claims do not automatically affect the premium. Usually in order to qualify, you will have to satisfy similar conditions to those for protected NCD policies (appropriate age, good driving record) and there is an excess for accidental damage claims.

Introductory bonus

If you have been driving on someone else's insurance (perhaps as a named driver) or using a car (perhaps a company car) regularly on an any-driver basis, and now want to insure a car of your own, normally you would not be entitled to a no-claim discount. But a number of insurers acknowledge that people in this category, provided that they are claim-free and conviction-free, deserve a discount, and therefore have an 'introductory bonus' of anything from 25% to 50% off the premium, or the percentage of a normal first-year discount. This may be offered only for comprehensive cover.

The criteria for getting an introductory bonus vary between insurers. For instance
* that you are a son or daughter or spouse of an existing policyholder
* that you have held a licence for not less than two years

* that you have been a named driver on someone else's policy and can prove through their NCD that you have had no accident in previous years
* that you have had at least three years' insurance for a motor cycle in your own name without a claim
* that you learned to drive at a named driving school.

Transferring your NCD

page 129

If you want to transfer a current or previous no-claim discount when you are changing to another insurer, you have to send evidence, such as the latest renewal notice or a letter from previous insurers confirming that you have x number of years no-claim discount under a previous policy.

If it is the broker who is changing you to another insurer, he should automatically attach proof of NCD to the new proposal for you.

If that insurance had no no-claim discount system, ask the insurers to state that the policy had run for x number of years without claims; this will allow you to pick up on the new insurers' no-claim discount scheme.

How car premiums are calculated

The basic premium usually incorporates: type of car, age of driver and district of use (with some companies, 'basic' does not include the age of the driver, and a percentage is added for youth).

	BASIC PREMIUM	£xxx.xx
less	age of vehicle discount:	= _____
plus	excess value: (if the car is worth more than about £8000) flat charge per £100	= _____
plus	conviction* or accident loading: % of last total	= _____
plus	class of use loading: % of last total	= _____
less	restriction of driver: (*eg* insured only) % of last total	= _____
less	voluntary excess: % of last total (but discount not to exceed the excess)	= _____
less	bonus for occupation: % of last total	= _____
less	no-claim discount: % of last total	= _____
less	multi-car discount: (the cars do not have to be on the same policy but must be insured with the same company) % of last total	= _____
plus	NCD protection: % of last total	= _____
	what you finally pay:	= _____

* for certain convictions such as for drink-and-drive offences, the loading is a flat sum added at the end of this calculation: at least a three-figure load, which will be gradually reduced if no further problems arise

Example of premium calculation

```
MARY MINDFULL    age 28   local government officer in Somerset
one minor conviction   50% no-claim discount   insured-only driving
car 1977 Mini  value £1000   excess £75   comprehensive policy
Mr Mindfull has a Ford Escort insured with the same company
```

			£
BASIC PREMIUM			200·00
less age of vehicle discount:	10%		− 20·00
			180·00
plus excess value:	n/a		—
plus conviction loading: (+ £50 excess)	25%		+ 45·00
			225·00
plus class of use loading:	nil		—
less restriction of driver: (insured only- female)	10%		− 22·50
			202·50
less voluntary excess: (£25)*	5%		− 10·12
			192·38
less bonus for occupation:	10%		− 19·23
			173·15
less no-claim discount:	50%		− 86·57
			86·58
less multi-car discount: **	5%		− 4·32
			82·26
plus NCD protection:	n/a***		—
FINAL PREMIUM			£82·26

*   This makes an excess of £75, but £50 is compulsory because of the conviction, so one gets a discount only for the £25 which is voluntary

**   Mr Mindfull gets 5% off his as well

***   not eligible without full NCD

For the run-of-the-mill car and driver, the broker or agent can issue a temporary cover straightaway. But if there is something unusual – your car is very expensive or powerful, you have got a list of motoring convictions, you are in an unwelcome occupation – he would have to refer to the insurers.

Cover note

Once you have paid the premium or completed an instalment payments form and paid the deposit, if one is required, you will get a temporary cover note. This is usually for 30 days, but it may be for up to 60.

A cover note is evidence of motor insurance to meet the RTA requirements, and can be used for all purposes for which a certificate of motor insurance is required (registration of the car, showing to the police) until a permanent certificate is issued with the policy. If necessary, you will get a second temporary cover note.

Remember, if you drive without actually possessing a current certificate of motor insurance or a cover note, you are breaking the law.

Watch the expiry date: if you do not receive another cover note at least 2 days before your current one expires, ask that another cover note be sent to you at once. If you have had more than three cover notes without a very good reason, such as difficulty in getting proof of your past NCD, ask the broker or agent sternly to find out what has happened to your policy. Query a delay before it goes on too long. It could mean that the broker or agent has not passed the proposal to the insurers; in some cases, it is a fault on the part of the insurers or their computer system.

The policy

After an interval, long or short, you will receive your policy and certificate of motor insurance (the official document you need to show that you have the insurance required by law).

No two insurers' policies look alike. All contain a schedule showing details of your car, who may drive, class of use, the premium and the no-claim discount (if one applies). Check all these facts. If any are wrong, go back to where you bought the insurance and get them put right. Mostly (except perhaps for an incorrect spelling), it is not sufficient for the broker or agent to alter the schedule; it must be returned to the insurers.

A policy schedule is likely to be computer-produced, in that peculiar script, and have references to 'para A (iii)' and 'IV (a), (b)' and suchlike. Take the trouble to read not only the schedule but also the policy, so that you know what cover you have not got before you find out through having a claim rejected. If there is anything you do not understand (in policy or schedule) ask your broker, agent or the insurance company for an explanation.

Keep the policy and the certificate of motor insurance anywhere but in the car; if the certificate is stolen with it, the thief could use the car for quite a while before detection.

Put a note of the policy number and the name of the insurers with your driving licence, or in your diary, so that you can quote it at once, if required after an accident. With some policies, you get an accident report form, in readiness.

changing your car

If you change your car, you must give the insurers full details of the replacement car without delay. Your certificate of insurance may not specify the (old) car's registration number, in which case it may not be necessary for you to be sent a new certificate of insurance.

At the end of the year of insurance, your contract automatically expires.

Make a note of the date on which your policy falls due for renewal. No insurer is obliged to send you a renewal notice. In practice, most do send notices but if you hear nothing and wish to use the same insurers again, contact them.

This may be the moment to change insurers if you can get better terms elsewhere – fewer restrictions or lower premiums or less excess, or better discounts.

Your age may now be a reason for moving to another insurer. Some load the premium or the excess of a 'young' driver until the age of 25, whereas with others you can move out of this category at the age of 23.

Whatever your age, it may be worth getting alternative quotations because motor insurance is competitive, and insurers do not change their premium rates in concert at the same time by the same amounts. So, you may be able to take advantage of changes since you last renewed.

There is a little trick practised by some insurance agents (but strenuously denied) of holding back the issue of renewal papers just long enough to make shopping around for a better quotation difficult in the time remaining, so that the motorist tends to pay up rather than rush round madly looking for alternatives elsewhere. Such delaying tactics are more likely to be practised by single-company agents who have no alternatives to offer if their particular company is beginning to look a bit expensive. If you watch your renewal dates, this cannot be practised on you.

But if you suspect this, change your agent or go direct to the insurance company. An agent or broker dealing with more than one insurer should look at the position for you at each renewal, and if a better quotation can be had elsewhere, advise you in good time to consider a change. Alternatively, you should ask him to do so well in advance of the expiry date of your present policy.

If you have decided not to renew the policy with those insurers, you need do nothing – the insurance will automatically lapse. As a courtesy, however, you could inform the insurance company and/or the broker or agent.

Renewal notice

For someone insured at Lloyd's, the renewal notice will come from the broker. Many brokers issue their own form of renewal notice but should also send you the insurance company's renewal notice.

With the renewal notice, the insurers let you know about any changes in their terms for the coming year. Your previous contract is expiring, so now is the time that insurers can vary their terms, or impose conditions.

Endorsements may be sent with the renewal notice altering specific sections of your policy. If you have not been sent an endorsement for a section, you may safely conclude that that section is unaltered. Read the slips that accompany your renewal notice in conjunction with your policy.

To save money, insurers do not re-issue the policies each year but the invitation to renew, your payment, and their acceptance of a renewal premium constitutes a totally new contract between you and your insurers.

Changes to report

Remember the duty of disclosure. If, over the past year, you have had motoring accidents or convictions that you did not tell the insurers about immediately (as you ought to have done), tell them now.

You must also tell them if
- any new drivers have started to use the car (for example, a young son or daughter)
- any named drivers have been convicted of a motoring offence
- you or anyone regularly driving the car have changed jobs, or taken on a new part-time occupation
- the car is being garaged elsewhere
- you are now on prescribed drugs for some long-term illness
- you have become in any way disabled.

No action will necessarily be taken by the insurers but you must tell them of any changes in your or your car's circumstances that might be relevant to the insurance risk.

the premium

The renewal notice shows the amount of new basic premium minus the NCD deduction. If the premium is noticeably higher than last year, ask why, and make sure that any reduction in your NCD is justified.

If, at the time of renewal, there is a claim not yet settled or a third-party claim outstanding against you, your NCD may have been reduced in anticipation of a payment having to be made. If eventually your insurers do not pay out on the third party's claim, your NCD should be restored and the difference in money refunded to you.

no 'days of grace'

There are no days of grace with motor insurance.

The insurers' renewal notice includes a temporary cover note for 15 days of Road Traffic Act cover only, not your full policy cover. This period allows for you to send your premium by the date the old policy expires and for your new certificate of motor insurance to be issued. The temporary cover provided is only the minimum required by law and if you have an accident meanwhile, you could find that you are responsible for paying the cost of repairs to your car and anybody else's property.

15 days of RTA cover – but only provided you have not indicated by your actions that you did not intend to renew your policy.

It is a policy condition to notify the insurers of any accident, whether or not you are going to claim. But if you do not intend to claim, make it quite clear when notifying that you 'do not require indemnity'.

After an accident

Which? April 1983 also sets out what to do if you have an accident in your car.

After an accident, your first priority must be the safety and care of people involved. Injuries obviously need urgent attention.

The British Insurance Association's leaflet *When it comes to the crunch, do you know what to do next?* tells you to
- obtain name(s) and address(es) of other driver(s) involved
- note their vehicle registration number(s) and make of vehicle
- ask for the name of their insurers and their policy or certificate number
- note names and addresses of independent witnesses
- make a rough diagram of the accident

If not at the scene of the accident, produce it for the police as soon as possible and not later than 24 hours after the accident.

- if anybody is injured, produce your certificate of motor insurance
- if there is injury to any person or animal or damage to another vehicle or other property, give your name and address, the name and the address of the owner of the vehicle you are driving and its registration number, to anyone who has reasonable grounds for wanting them

Do not discuss whose fault it was as this may create difficulties for your insurers in their handling of your claim.

- note any statement made at the scene of the accident by any of the parties.

Also write down the exact location and the time the accident happened, and note (if you saw it) the registration number of any car whose occupants may have seen what happened.

What to do next

As soon as possible, inform your insurers of the accident even if you do not intend to make a claim. This is a condition of your policy.

If you are in your home district, immediately contact the branch of the insurance company you normally deal with or your broker.

When away from home, if there is a branch office of your insurance company (or broker) nearby, contact them. Explain the situation and quote your policy number if you can. If you cannot get in touch with a local branch, telephone or write immediately to your own branch office, or even the head office.

Anyone whose insurance is at Lloyd's should contact his broker. Most Lloyd's syndicates issue claims instructions with their policies, detailing the procedure to be followed after an accident.

Completing a claim form for information only does not affect a no-claim discount.

Always confirm any telephone conversation with a follow-up letter, giving the date of the accident, quoting your policy number and asking for an accident report form or a claim form.

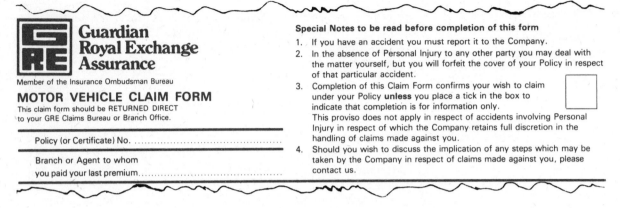

Guardian Royal Exchange Assurance

Member of the Insurance Ombudsman Bureau

MOTOR VEHICLE CLAIM FORM
This claim form should be RETURNED DIRECT
to your GRE Claims Bureau or Branch Office.

Policy (or Certificate) No. ....

Branch or Agent to whom
you paid your last premium...

Special Notes to be read before completion of this form

1. If you have an accident you must report it to the Company.
2. In the absence of Personal Injury to any other party you may deal with the matter yourself, but you will forfeit the cover of your Policy in respect of that particular accident.
3. Completion of this Claim Form confirms your wish to claim under your Policy **unless** you place a tick in the box to indicate that completion is for information only.
   This proviso does not apply in respect of accidents involving Personal Injury in respect of which the Company retains full discretion in the handling of claims made against you.
4. Should you wish to discuss the implication of any steps which may be taken by the Company in respect of claims made against you, please contact us.

Filling in the accident report or claim form

The form which you will be required to complete may be called claim form or motor accident report form. If you are not going to make a claim, fill in the form but make clear that you are not claiming, by writing 'report only' across it in red.

The form asks for

- policy number
- renewal date
- name and address of policyholder
- occupation
- details of the car, such as make and model, cubic capacity, year of manufacture, registration number
- approximate value of the car at the time of the accident

Is the vehicle owned by the policyholder? if not, state who is the owner
In the event of the car being a total write-off, this affects who gets the money. If the car is being acquired on hire purchase, you have to give the name and address of the finance company.

For what purpose was the vehicle being used at the time of the accident?
If the car was being used for a purpose which the policy does not cover, the insurers could refuse to meet the claim and the driver would have been driving uninsured.

Was the vehicle being used with the knowledge and consent of the policyholder?
If the answer is 'no', you have no claim on your policy – unless the car has been stolen.

If another person was driving with your permission, you have to give his or her name, address, age, usual occupation. (The age of the driver is relevant if the policy imposes an excess for drivers under a certain age.) The insurers normally want to get further details of the accident from the driver.

You are also asked to give full particulars of any previous accidents and any convictions for motoring offences, and whether you (or the driver) have had your licence endorsed or been disqualified – all of which should already have been declared to the insurers.

Be careful before doing this because the other party to the accident may make a substantial claim against you

page 133

A car dealer can give you a figure for any make and year of car, based on a trade publication.

Even if there is no excess on your policy, if the car is damaged while driven by a very young driver, the youth excess of £50 to £100 will be applied.

Your answers may be checked against the information you gave on the proposal form and at subsequent renewals, so if there are discrepancies they may make difficulties with your claim now.

There is also usually a question asking whether the driver, if he is not the policyholder, owns a vehicle of his own and, if so, to give the name and address of his insurers. Your insurers may try to involve the other insurers in sharing the claim. Even if the driver is not making any claim on his policy himself, he should tell his own insurers about the accident.

The remainder of the form asks questions about the accident, and you should be able to answer these from the notes you made at the time. If any of the questions do not appear relevant to the accident in which you have been involved, put 'not applicable'. If you are unable to answer any of the questions in this section of the form, say that you do not have the information available or that you cannot remember – do not guess at an answer.

Most policies contain a stipulation that the insured shall keep the vehicle in good condition, and an insurer could refuse to meet a claim, or reduce the amount paid, on the grounds that a car had not been maintained in a roadworthy condition. There is not a question of this nature on the accident report form: an engineer employed by the insurers is probably going to look at the car, to whose expert eye it will be obvious whether the car has been properly maintained or was unfit or unroadworthy – for instance, if the depth of tread on the tyres does not comply with the law.

Send the claim or accident report form off to the insurers as soon as you have completed it, even if you do not yet have an estimate for the cost of repairs.

If your policy is for third party, fire and theft only, you cannot claim for repairs to your car after an accident (unless it was damaged while it was stolen). You must nevertheless complete an accident report form, as a condition of your policy.

You may have the right to claim the cost of repairs from the third party.

Repairs

You have to let the insurers know where the damaged vehicle is. They may suggest that you take it to, or have it collected by, one of their recommended repairers – but you are not obliged to.

If the car is immobilised as a result of the accident and has to be towed to a garage or repairer, you can include in your claim the cost of towing to the nearest competent repairer.

– estimates

You have to ask for an estimate for the repairs to be provided for your insurers. Normally, the estimate is sent to you to pass on to them.

Usually an estimate shows the costs for labour; new parts needed for the repair are listed but not costed and shown as 'parts at manufacturer's retail prices' or words to that effect.

Even if the estimate comes to less than the amount of an excess on your policy, send it to the insurers – the total cost in the end will probably come to more and you may then want to claim.

If the repairs do cost less than the excess so that you have to pay in full for the work done, this cancels your claim for the damage. (Your no-claim discount will therefore not be reduced on that

'Motor insurance premiums are largely governed by the cost of accidental damage repairs. The insured is specially requested to obtain alternative estimates to ensure that the work is effected at as reasonable a cost as possible consistent with a satisfactory repair. Recent consumer surveys have overwhelmingly confirmed the value of doing this.'
from THE KGM (LLOYD'S) *accident report form*

account but it will be noted in your policy file that you have been involved in this accident.)

– getting the work done

Check with your insurers what you should do about getting the repairs done. You may find that the insurers give the instructions to the repairer direct.

Some insurers lay down in the policy a figure below which you can yourself give instructions to the garage to start the work. Others allow you to do so irrespective of the amount involved, provided an estimate is on its way and you give the insurers reasonable time to arrange to send someone to inspect the damage if they want to.

Any repairs carried out on your instructions are your responsibility until the insurers have agreed to indemnify you for the cost. The repairer may be reluctant to accept the authorisation from you in case the insurers later refuse to pay.

You may be asked to instruct the repairer to retain the damaged parts so that the insurers' engineer can inspect them afterwards. Alternatively, the insurers may arrange for their engineer to inspect the car at the repairer's before work is started.

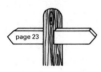
page 23

Usually, the engineer is someone employed by the insurers; some insurers use independent firms of motor claim assessors. The engineer writes a report about the damaged vehicle, including an assessment of its condition before the damage and whether this was contributory to the accident or reveals any lack of maintenance. He must also report whether any previous damage or wear and tear will be made good as a result of the repairs now required. (If you wish, you can arrange to be there when the engineer looks at your car so that you can ask him any questions or tell him anything relevant about the accident or the condition of the car.)

Once the engineer is satisfied that the car is repairable, he agrees the estimate with the repairer, authorises the repairs to be carried out, and sends his report to the insurers.

what you have to pay for

The insurers will tell you whether there are any items which the insurance does not cover and for which you may be asked to pay yourself. If it is considered that the parts that are to be replaced were already worn, damaged or rusted prior to the accident, you will be expected to pay a proportion of their replacement cost, because when you receive your car back, it will be better than it was before the accident.

Any question of betterment should be discussed with you after the insurers' engineer has seen your car. Normally, you can only be asked to pay a contribution towards a new battery, exhaust system or tyres. You should not be asked to contribute towards the cost of repairs to the bodywork if the total cost is within the market value of the car. Some insurers argue that a vehicle will be improved in value after repair. This is not so.

The question of any contribution towards the cost of respraying should be settled at this point. It is a matter which can potentially cause no end of trouble.

– when the work is done

When the car is ready, the repairer tells you. You should not at this stage be called upon to pay any contribution towards repairs if you had not previously agreed this in writing with your insurers.

If you have to pay any part of the bill yourself, because of betterment or an excess, you will have to pay this amount to the garage before you will be allowed to take the car away. The rest of the bill will be paid by the insurers to the garage direct or by reimbursement to you. The bill will have details of what was done to your car, so it is wise to ask for a copy of this.

You are expected to inspect the car yourself and may be asked to sign a collection or satisfaction note stating that the repairs have been carried out to your satisfaction, for the garage to send to the insurers with their bill.

Do not hesitate to refuse to sign the collection/satisfaction note if you think that the repairs may not be satisfactory. It may be difficult to tell just by looking at the car. So, when signing the note, write on it 'subject to no complaint being raised within 28 days of this date' (or some other reasonable period).

If you sign a satisfaction note and the repairs prove to be unsatisfactory, you are quite entitled to ask your insurers to sort the matter out. Notify the insurers of the situation straightaway and ask them to deal direct with the garage and ensure that the car is properly repaired to your satisfaction.

One insurance company covers hiring a car from a specified firm for up to 14 days while yours is being repaired. Another has an optional extension for 'loss of use' costs.

Another insurance company pays for one night's hotel accommodation (£25 for one person or £50 for all the occupants) if you cannot drive on home following accidental damage to the car.

It is up to the policyholder to list the defects at an early stage and for the company's engineer to deal with the repairer over putting them right.
INSURANCE OMBUDSMAN BUREAU *annual report 1983*

The cost of getting the car back to you is paid for by most policies. So, if the accident happened in Norwich and you live in London, you should claim for the cost of a single train ticket from London to Norwich.

Total loss

Their engineer's report may recommend that, from the insurers' point of view, it is not an economic proposition to repair the car. If this is the case, the insurers will offer you what they call a total loss settlement. This is usually the current market price for the car in the condition it was at the time of the crash. For longstanding policyholders – or a good broker – insurers may be prepared to pay the higher of the published figures for secondhand car prices. (But if the value of the car as stated by you when you took out the policy is less than the current price, that lower figure is usually all you will be offered.)

If the figure offered does not seem enough to you, do not hesitate to say so and discuss it with the broker, the engineer or your insurers direct. Suggest a figure you consider fair, and support your argument by giving prices of similar vehicles on sale in your locality.

The monthly publication *Motorist's guide to new and used car prices* costs 95p.

When a claim is settled on a total loss basis, the remains of the damaged vehicle – the salvage – becomes the property of the insurers. But you can agree a settlement on the basis that you retain the salvage.

Some policies offer to replace a car less than a certain number of months old and that will cost more than a certain amount to repair, with a new car of the same make and model, if available. There are some variations on this in different policies: for example, if the accident is six months from when you bought the car new and the repair would cost more than 60% of the recommended retail price at the time you bought it; or when the car is less than one year old and the repair cost would be more than 50% of its list price when new. You may have the option to ask for a cash settlement, if preferred.

Broken windscreen

With the policy, you may have received a windscreen replacement freefone number on a plastic disc that either sticks on to your windscreen (more sensible perhaps to put it on a side window) or hangs over one of the dashboard knobs, so that you can get quick replacement of a broken windscreen at any time of the day or night.

With nearly every comprehensive motor policy, a claim for windscreen or windows (with some, also sunroof), and for paintwork scratched owing to the breakage, does not affect a no-claim discount. (Some insurers do reduce an NCD if the cost of the replacement is more than a stated figure – so do not claim for more than that figure.)

You can get the windscreen or window replaced straightaway without having to check with the insurers first. With some, you have to pay for the repair and claim the cost back later; with others, provided you use the firm indicated by your insurers, you do not pay but just have to put in a claim to your insurers and they pay the firm direct.

Any excess on a claim for damage to the car does not apply if the only damage is the broken windscreen. But with some insurers, there is an upper limit to what will be paid.

A third party, fire and theft policy does not pay for broken windscreens. But some of the specialist repair firms offer a discount on the cost of replacement to all policyholders of some insurance companies.

Claims and discount

Motor claims are different from other claims: if you make one, it will affect your no-claim discount (or peel a layer of protection away from your protected NCD). If you have a small accident and would lose less by repairing the damage at your own expense, you can fill in the accident report form or claim form marking it '*For information only. 'No claim intended.*' If you do, you keep your NCD intact, but you are on your own, and may have to meet any claims made against you. It is sometimes worth it, but not always. Think carefully whether you want the insurers to handle the claim, at the cost of the NCD, or deal with it yourself. (If the other party was injured, you would be unwise not to let your insurers deal with the claim.)

Your insurers will reduce your discount at the first renewal following the settlement (or even the notification) of a claim under your policy, irrespective of who is to blame. If, for example, you come back to the car park and find your car has been ruined by a hit-and-run driver who is never traced and you claim on your policy, your discount is affected.

Some insurers reduce a maximum discount of, say, 60% to something like 40% when they have paid a claim, however large or small. And it may take you three years to catch up again with the percentage of discount.

When it comes to renewal and you see how much difference even a small claim has made to your discount on the premium, you can offer to 'buy back' the lost discount by paying to your insurers what they paid out for the claim. (They may, however, not agree.)

If, after the notification of an accident, you find that it is unnecessary to claim on your policy and no claim is upheld against you by a third party, your insurers should mark on your claims record that no claim was made so that your no-claim discount is not affected.

third-party claim on you
Often when an accident occurs, the two drivers are civil to each other, almost to the point of admitting liability, and agree to let their respective insurers deal with it, or even that it is not worth claiming for. Not long afterwards, one receives a letter accusing him of being at fault, having caused an accident through his negligence and that he is being held totally liable for the damage.

Send such a letter straight to your insurers, with your own account of the accident, and provide any witnesses' statements. Then pass any further correspondence from the other person unanswered to your insurers. (But if you do not want to invoke your policy, you can deal with the other person's claim yourself).

Knock-for-knock
There are so-called knock-for-knock agreements between insurers. If two people are involved in an accident, each having a comprehensive policy with different insurers who are participants in a knock-for-knock scheme, each insurer pays for its own policyholder's damage, regardless of liability and blame. From the insurers' point of view, this avoids the costs that would be involved in arguing about liability (and in theory this allows premiums to be lower than they would otherwise be). But as far as a no-claim discount is concerned, the question of liability is relevant: if liability is clear and a recovery could have been made

The knock-for-knock agreement is only supposed to govern matters of accounting between the companies concerned; nothing else. . . . It would be in the best interest of companies and their policyholders if insurers took the greatest care to ensure that the knock-for-knock agreement does not become the instrument of injustice many people think it to be.
INSURANCE OMBUDSMAN BUREAU
annual report 1983

from the other insurance company had it not been for the knock-for-knock agreement, your no-claim discount should be safe. But even if you are blameless, unless you can prove it (by getting some payment or other evidence of liability from the other driver), your insurers will reduce your no-claim discount after paying out under a knock-for-knock agreement.

Where there is doubt about who is liable, or there is shared liability for the damage, your no-claim discount will be reduced in the ordinary way.

Your insurers will not tell you as a matter of course whether they are going to settle under a knock-for-knock agreement.

preserving your NCD

If you feel convinced that you were not to blame for an accident where someone else was involved, you have to provide evidence to stop your insurers reducing your NCD – if possible, through witnesses.

If the police tell you that they are prosecuting the other driver, put that on your accident report form. If the other driver is convicted of a driving offence following the accident, that will certainly strengthen your case. Sometimes it takes so long to bring people to court that you could lose track of things, unless you have to appear as witness, but since you are an interested party, the police should be willing to tell you when the case is coming up, even if you are not involved with it.

If you can persuade the other driver (or his insurers) to pay you the amount of your 'uninsured losses' (excess, hire of other car), this will be taken by your insurers as evidence that the other driver was at fault (and should preserve your NCD). To get the proof necessary for the payment of your uninsured losses by the other person, and thus the preservation of your no-claim discount, may involve lots of letters and hassle.

uninsured losses

Even if you have a comprehensive policy, there may be some expenses arising from the accident for which you cannot claim on your policy. For example

- the amount of any excess you have to meet
- out-of-pocket expenses
- treatment or transport after an injury
- compensation for personal injury
- loss of earnings because of time off work
- alternative transport to work or the hire of a car while yours is out of action.

And if you do not have comprehensive insurance, the cost of repairing your car also is not covered.

Some insurers offer to arrange cover (for a premium of £2 to £5) for legal expenses (up to a set figure) incurred in pursuing a claim for uninsured losses against a third party and in dealing with another's claim and for representation on a prosecution.

claiming against a third party

If you are sure that the accident was the other driver's fault, send your claim for uninsured losses direct to the third party by

'first party' = you
'second party' = the insurers
'third party' = person who is injured or whose property is damaged

recorded delivery. He may pass your letter to his insurers who will undoubtedly write to you asking why you are holding their policyholder responsible, and the business of trying to establish liability for the accident will then begin.

If you succeed and the other party's insurers take on the payment of your claim, this should be reimbursement for everything the accident has cost you. But it may be a long time before everything is settled.

Without witnesses, you will not have much ground to stand on, just your word against his. If you get no satisfaction, consider threatening legal action (for an amount under £500 you can make your claim through the county court 'small claims' procedure; for a larger amount, or where there was serious personal injury, you will almost certainly have to employ a solicitor).

third-party claim on you
Often when an accident occurs, the two drivers are civil to each other, almost to the point of admitting liability, and agree to let their respective insurers deal with it, or even that it is not worth claiming for. Not long afterwards, one receives a letter accusing him of being at fault, having caused an accident through his negligence and that he is being held totally liable for the damage.

Send such a letter straight to your insurers, with your own account of the accident, and provide any witnesses' statements. Then pass any further correspondence from the other person unanswered to your insurers. (But if you do not want to invoke your policy, you can deal with the other person's claim yourself.)

Keep your eye on the progress of the claim. As you pass to your insurers all letters (unanswered) from the other party, make and keep a copy of each.

You must also submit to your insurers any notice of an intended prosecution or inquest.

Policyholders involved in minor accidents have lost a valuable no-claim discount because a third party claim against them has been settled by their company without their being consulted . . . The trouble stems from a basic misunderstanding. It is not always clear from a claim form that a policyholder involved in an accident has a right not to claim indemnity: he may, if he wishes, pay for his own damage and meet any claim made against him. Every policyholder is obliged by his policy conditions to report an accident but he need not claim indemnity. Where the position is not made clear, a policyholder may find that the claim form which he used to report the accident is treated by the claims department as automatic authority to settle a comparatively minor claim.
INSURANCE OMBUDSMAN BUREAU
annual report for 1982

Injuries

By law, your insurance policy must cover compensation for any injury caused to another person – a passenger in your or another car, a pedestrian, another driver – for which you are legally liable. The liability has to be proved: mere moral obligation plays no part.

The injured person's claim, supported by medical certificates and an itemised statement of expenses (including an amount for damages), should be sent to your insurers.

If you, the policyholder, have lost an eye or a limb as a result of the accident and you have a comprehensive motor policy, you can claim on the personal accident section for a lump sum payment – even if the fault was yours. (If the accident was fatal, the money will be paid to your estate; make sure your executors know of your policy so that they will claim after your death.)

Road Traffic Act 1972 s.155

Road Traffic Act 1972 s.154.

A doctor who gives immediate roadside treatment to someone injured as a result of a motor accident can require the person who was using the car at the time to pay an emergency treatment fee (of £10.90 per person so treated), plus a mileage allowance for getting to the scene. Similarly, a hospital can charge a fee for emergency treatment (even where the treatment is on the NHS). These fees will be paid by the insurers.

The insurers will also pay an additional amount (of up to £1525) for in-patient treatment and up to £152.50 for outpatient treatment.

If the bills come to you and not direct from the hospital to the insurers, pay and send the receipted bill to the insurers for reimbursement.

In addition, most comprehensive policies include a payment for medical expenses to anyone injured in your car, with a limit of £50 or £100 per person.

The Motor Insurers' Bureau

Motor Insurers' Bureau
Aldermary House
Queen Street
London EC4N 1TR

Notwithstanding the introduction of compulsory third party insurance in 1930, it became apparent that there were still circumstances in which people injured in road accidents were unable to obtain the compensation to which they were entitled, because the transgressor was unidentified, or had failed to insure or his insurers had become insolvent.

To overcome this, the Motor Insurers' Bureau was set up in 1946 by motor insurers who agreed to accept the responsibility for dealing with claims from third parties for death or bodily injuries where the culprit's insurance would not otherwise meet the claim. Where the driver was not insured at all, or, in the case of a hit-and-run accident, could not be traced, the Motor Insurers' Bureau itself pays the claim.

This compensation is for bodily injury or death only, not for damage to property or any other claim.

Theft

Your first action if you find that your car has been stolen should be to notify the police, and then your insurers.

Many cars are taken for joy-riding or for criminal purposes, and abandoned afterwards. Insurers therefore usually wait for four to six weeks before paying a claim for a stolen car, to allow for the car being recovered in the meantime. A policy that pays the cost of hiring a car for a fortnight while yours is out of action, would include when it is stolen (without loss of NCD if the car is recovered intact).

If the car is not recovered, an offer will be made to you by the insurers on a total loss basis. Should the car be recovered after the claim has been settled, it is the property of the insurers and you would have to negotiate if you wanted to buy it back. But if, on the other hand, the insurers suggest that they give you back the car if you return the claim money, you are under no obligation to agree.

Even if your car is recovered in a matter of hours, you should report its temporary loss to the insurers (and the police). You may need to claim subsequently on your policy as a result of some damage done while it was out of your possession (in this case, any excess on a claim for damage does not normally apply, but check your policy). Also, things may have been stolen from inside the car, for which you can claim.

– from the car

Theft from a car is not covered by a third-party, fire and theft policy.

There is usually a limit (£50 to £100) to the amount that will be paid by insurers for personal property stolen out of the car, such as a briefcase or camera.

Insurers ask on their claim forms whether you have any other policies which would cover the lost property. If you have a household contents policy, personal articles that you carry with you in your car may be covered by the 'temporarily removed' section or by all-risks insurance. But remember that
* the car policy pays only up to a set figure and will affect your no-claim discount
* the household policy pays only a percentage (usually 15%) of the total sum for which the contents of your home are insured; where it limits such claims to theft from a building and with forcible entry, theft from a car would not be covered;
* all-risks insurance will pay the full amount, subject to any excess.

Make it clear if you decide to claim on a household contents or all-risks policy for something stolen from a car that you are not claiming on your motor policy. Your no-claim discount should not be affected, even if the other insurers claim a contribution from the motor policy. But there is an agreement between insurers that in almost every case the household or all-risks insurers will pay if the claim is made against them, and not seek contribution from the motor insurers. This agreement is designed to minimise the possibility of arguments about no-claim discounts and improve public relations.

The British Insurance Association's leaflet about stolen cars says 'Whenever you leave it . . . lock it: a minute is long enough for a thief' and has a check list for whenever you leave your car
1 hide any property
2 close all windows
3 lock the doors, boot and tailgate
4 don't leave the ignition key in
5 use an anti-theft device.

A fitted-in car radio or a cassette player is part of the car and by most insurers is covered in full without the upper limit that applies to personal belongings. However, claiming for the loss of a radio or other in-car equipment would affect your no-claim discount.

Taking the car abroad

Your policy is effective in the United Kingdom, the Isle of Man and the Channel Islands. Additionally, motor insurance policies provide cover in accordance with the minimum legal requirements for third party insurance in all the EEC countries, plus Austria, Czechoslovakia, the German Democratic Republic, Finland, Hungary, Norway, Sweden and Switzerland. (This was agreed in order to enable frontier checks of insurance documents to be abolished.) But if you rely only on this automatic extension and you have an accident, minimum cover may well be inadequate. You can, however, get your full policy cover for driving in these countries by asking your insurers to extend your policy and to issue a 'green card' as evidence of the 'foreign use endorsement'.

The green card is an international certificate of motor insurance. As well as EEC and the other listed countries, it is also recognised in Bulgaria, Iceland, Iran, Iraq, Israel, Morocco, Poland, Portugal, Rumania, Spain, Tunisia, Turkey and Yugoslavia – although your insurers may not be willing to extend your policy cover fully in every one of these countries.

Most insurers charge a fee for issuing a green card. With some, you are charged only if you are going to be away for longer than a specified number of weeks or so-many times a year.

The charge for a green card may be a flat fee or according to your car group, and depending on the time you are to be abroad. Between £10 and £20 for a period of one month is about average. Some motor insurers offer a separate package deal which includes breakdown and recovery assistance and a combined continental claims service, at about double the cost of a green card.

You must sign the green card before you travel, in order to make it effective. By doing so, you also agre that the local green card bureau of each country visited may handle any claim arising out of an accident which is required to be covered by the country's compulsory insurance law.

Special territorial features

In some western european countries, particularly France, Belgium and Italy, a european accident statement of agreed facts has come into use. It is a standard form with spaces for details of the parties involved, their vehicles, the circumstances, and for a sketch plan. The statement contains the same questions in the same order, whatever language it is in. When applying for your green card, ask your insurers to be sure to send with it a copy of the english version of the european accident statement, with directions for use, so that if you should be faced with one of these forms in a foreign language, you can then refer to your english version to know what it says.

Spain
If you are travelling to or through Spain, get a bail bond (*fianza*). It is not essential except for your peace of mind: if you and your car

Make insurance arrangements before you are committed to a driving holiday abroad. Some countries – even one in the EEC – are not favoured by insurers and they may demand an off-puttingly high premium or refuse to issue a green card at all.

page 135

are detained by the spanish authorities following an accident, a deposit is payable against the possibility of your being found liable for the accident. A bail bond provides the necessary surety to release both you and your car. If, however, you are found liable and your insurers have to honour part or all of the bail bond by paying your fine, that amount must be paid back by you to your insurers on return to this country.

A bail bond comes free from some insurers with the green card; if not, expect to have to pay around £2 for one providing £500, £1000 or £1500 surety.

An accident abroad

Should you be involved in an accident with your car abroad, the same basic procedure should be adopted as for an accident in this country.

You may be required to show your passport and your insurance documents to the police and complete an accident statement. Doing so does not constitute an admission of liability on the part of either motorist; there is no harm in signing one of these forms provided the answers keep to undisputed facts.

You should make notes at the scene of the accident, take care not to admit liability and, in particular, not sign any form or statement made in a language with which you are not thoroughly familiar. If you feel obliged – perhaps because the police are so insistent – to sign a form that is in a language that you do not understand, sign it but add 'I do not understand greek' (or whatever the language happens to be).

You must notify your insurers in the UK as soon as possible, giving as much detail as possible, and telling them what is being done. If you telephone or send a telex, be certain to quote your policy number, your green card number if you have one, and give an address where they can get in touch with you.

Many insurers supply a list of the names and addresses of their branches abroad and of their agents in some countries who can be contacted in the event of an accident.

Strictly speaking, you should get authority from your insurers for any repairs to be done. Most insurers, however, state in their instructions to the traveller that reasonable repairs may be started, provided a detailed estimate is sent to the nearest branch office or their representative in the foreign country. They will probably not refuse to refund any reasonable payments made for on-the-spot repairs to enable you to continue your journey.

Even when you have their authority for repairs, your insurers are unlikely to send you money. Normally, you have to pay out and claim a refund on your return home. Do not forget to retain receipts for all payments you make.

The repairs may take longer than you can stay away. The extension of a comprehensive policy's cover abroad, with most policies includes the cost of getting the car back to your address in this country when the repairs are completed. Check whether this means the insurance will pay your fare for going back to collect the repaired car if this is the cheapest way of getting it home.

If the car cannot be repaired in the foreign country, the insurance will pay for bringing the damaged vehicle back home for repair. If the car is a total wreck, you would have to discuss with the insurers whether it should be brought back to this country or disposed of where it is.

If the car is not taken out of the country where the accident occurred, either because it is a total loss or is stolen, you may become liable for customs duty on it. Most policies cover this contingency automatically, but it is another aspect you should check when asking for your green card.

Third party claims

Under an international system operated by motor insurers, the green card bureau of the country in which an accident happens will handle any third party claim to which local compulsory insurance legislation applies involving personal injury or damage to property. (But damage to your own car should not be reported to the local bureau.) On the back of the green card is a list of the bureaux in the various countries within the system, to which notification of an accident should be made unless you have been requested by your insurer to report any accident to their representative in the country concerned. The police there, or some other authority, will help you to get in touch with the local green card bureau, or the representative.

Car breakdown service

Many people pay an annual subscription to a motoring organisation to cover the risk of breakdown and to provide a 'get you home' service while motoring within the UK. It is equally possible to arrange this type of cover for breakdown or failure of a vehicle while motoring in a foreign country. Both the AA and the RAC sell their overseas travel security and motoring protection plans to non-members.

Some insurers, along with the green card, offer a package arrangement for breakdown and accidents abroad. This covers breakdown and recovery assistance, and a combined continental claims service. All sorts of things are thrown in, such as vehicle recovery to the UK, hire car allowance, a chauffeur if the only driver is ill, repatriation of passengers, fares to continue the journey, transport of spare parts, a bail bond (for Spain). All this puts up the price of the green card to between £20 and £30 for a month's cover. This is fairly good value insurance-wise – unless all you wanted was a simple green card.

If you claim on an emergency breakdown service while abroad, your no-claim discount on your motor insurance is not affected.

Or you can take out similar 'insurance' from one of the emergency assistance companies used by insurers for their package deals but to whom you can apply direct. In many cases, the assistance provided relates not just to breakdowns but also operates in the event of an accident to or fire or theft of the vehicle.

The help you get

The breakdown assistance cover is additional to that provided by a standard motor insurance policy and will exclude any expenses which are normally recoverable under the motor policy.

The object is to provide help at the time of the breakdown (theft of the vehicle included) rather than to compensate you later for costs incurred. You are meant to call for assistance there and then, in the same way as if a serious illness or injury had occurred to yourself or to one of your party. The companies which provide a car breakdown facility handle both types of emergency situations.

These companies advertise either directly through specific publications and leaflets, or through agents, such as insurance brokers, tour operators, travel agents.

You are normally required to complete an application form. Premiums are calculated according to the age of vehicle (under 5 years, 5 to 10 years), number of days' cover required (up to 5 days, 6 to 12 days, 13 to 23 days, for example), number of passengers (up to 5, up to 8) and the amount of cover. With some policies, you have a choice of limited cover at a lower premium or wider cover which costs more. Or you may be offered a policy with benefits which cannot be varied.

There is usually a condition that the vehicle is serviced within a few weeks before the holiday or, if no service is due, that an inspection is carried out by the garage. This can add considerably to the cost of the breakdown insurance.

A summary of the cover you can expect to get is
- cost of towing the vehicle to the nearest garage
- spare parts

The cost of obtaining the parts is paid for by the assistance company, but you have to pay the cost of the actual parts. If you do not have enough money to pay for them at the time, the company will pay initially and recoup from you on your return home. Some companies provide credit vouchers, up to a limit of something like £200, to enable you to pay for repairs or other emergency costs on the spot, but on your return home you will have to repay the amounts spent.

- repatriation of the vehicle if it cannot be repaired abroad

- hotel expenses abroad while you are waiting for the vehicle to be repaired

Hotel expenses would normally include both driver and passengers. There is likely to be a limit of something like £50 to £100 per person in all, and there may also be a limit per night (up to £15, say).

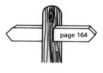

page 164

No cover for a car that is more than 10 years old (from the date of first registration).

If spare parts have to be flown in, you may be expected to make your own arrangements to collect them from the airport.

● cost of your fares to return home if the car breaks down abroad and you have to leave it behind

The type of transport is chosen by the company – for example, second class rail.

● cost of hiring an alternative vehicle if yours cannot be repaired within a stated number of hours (from 8 to 24 hours according to your particular scheme)

The total payable for this category is likely to be around £400 but there may also be a limit per day.

● provision of an alternative driver if the person driving the car falls ill and there is no one else in the party who can take over

These organisations have contacts in all the main holiday areas and an alternative driver can be whistled up even in the remoter areas to drive you back home.

● legal costs relating to the recovery of property or your defence where proceedings are brought against you following a motor offence overseas (but not fines or damages awarded against you)

● provision of customs indemnity

If your vehicle is a total loss as a result of an accident or has been stolen, you may become liable to pay customs duty and taxes.

when and where covered

As well as mainland Europe, some schemes also extend to countries bordering the Mediterranean Sea and mediterranean islands.

Most policies become operative at the moment you disembark on foreign soil; some from the moment you leave your own front gate. Some provide for the hire of a car if yours is stolen or involved in an accident in the week before your holiday and cannot be used for the trip.

What to do

Before you leave, check that you have the scheme's 24-hour emergency telephone number in this country. Keep all relevant documents with or on you. And do not forget to take with you any assistance advice booklet provided by the company. This gives detailed instructions on the action to be taken, and includes relevant telephone numbers and the forms that you may have to complete.

When the worst happens and your car is immobilised, some organisations provide facilities for emergency contact, others prefer you to contact them in the UK in all instances so that they can assess the situation and handle things wherever you are from the outset.

When contacting the emergency service, expect to be asked for the following information

- your policy or certificate number
- where you are (with telephone number at which you can be reached)
- where the vehicle is
- vehicle registration details
- make and model
- chassis number and engine number
- year of manufacture
- whether manual or automatic gears
- details of parts damaged.

Always make sure that you have your vehicle's registration document with you.

After your initial call, action should immediately be taken by the company or their local agent. If there are likely to be any delays, you should be contacted and told of the position. If this involves an overnight delay, and your cover includes hotel accommodation, this should be arranged on your behalf.

Any credit vouchers provided by the assistance company may not be valid for items such as hotel bills or car rental.

It is a policy condition that the vehicle must have been serviced regularly in accordance with the manufacturer's recommendations and be in good mechanical and roadworthy condition. If, on inspection, it appears that servicing in accordance with the manufacturer's recommendations has not been carried out, you may have to meet the cost of repairs yourself. If, however, you can give the details of the garage at which the car was last serviced, a quick check can be made to verify the situation.

Off-the-road plans

There are some separate schemes that pay out if disqualification from driving or an injury due to a car accident prevents you from driving your car. The schemes are for drivers over the age of 25 with no, or no more than a specified number of, penalty points on their driving licence when they apply to join. There is an annual subscription or premium.

subscription £30 to £75 a year
premium £64 to £175 a year

If you are disqualified (provided it is not because you refused to give a specimen or had twice the allowed level of alcohol in your bloodstream), you get either a weekly payment (£40 to £100, depending on the subscription you paid) for up to a year or a monthly sum (up to a total of £3,000 to £8,500 in the year, depending on the premium you paid). In addition, one scheme pays up to £100 for legal costs in defending a charge that might result in disqualification and also for out-of-pocket expenses if you do get disqualified; another pays up to £300 for financial loss due to an accident with the car.

If your car is off the road following an accident, or has been stolen, you will be paid £12 or £15 a day for 28 days (excluding the first three) towards the hire of a car, provided you are claiming on insurance for the damage or loss.

Motor cycle insurance

Mopeds are treated just the same as motor bikes but cost less to insure because of their limited speed; RTA obligations are the same.

Compulsory Road Traffic Act insurance is required for motor cycles in the same way as for cars.

Some leading insurers do not undertake motor cycle insurance. You may have to consult an insurance broker to get a policy. Some insurers restrict themselves to 'accommodation' risks only, which means that they accept only an individual or agent who has other valuable business with them.

Motor cycle policies may be comprehensive (but with more restricted cover than car policies), or third party, fire and theft, or third party, or Act-only. For young age groups, Act-only cover may be all that some insurers offer.

Proposal form and premium

GOING MOTOR CYCLING ABROAD? *Insurers say they will consider it, without committing themselves. So, before you make all the arrangements for a continental motor cycling holiday, find out whether your insurers will extend your cover for this.*

The proposal form for a motor cycle is similar to that for a car.

The bike can be insured for use by the policyholder for his business and for social, domestic and pleasure purposes. Racing, pace-making and speed testing are excluded, and so is carrying passengers for hire or reward.

Motor cycle policies rarely include the theft of accessories or spare parts, except when the motor cycle is stolen at the same time. And the insurance does not cover the loss of coats, any personal belongings or gear.

Although liability to passengers is fully covered, there is no personal accident cover for the insured driver/rider.

Premium

Where you live is not quite so important as with cars, so far as the premium is concerned, there being generally only two or three rating areas. Apart from this, the premium is based on the cubic capacity of the bike, the length of time that the driver has held a full driving licence for a motor cycle, and the age of the driver. Motor cycling tends to attract the young, and this is reflected in the fact that premiums for over 25-year-olds are considerably lower (but still high compared to car insurance). No-claim discounts, if given at all, are much lower – for instance, 10%, 15% and 20% over three claim-free years, and there is heavy loading of premiums after an accident.

There is a set short-period premium scale for policies taken out for less than a year, starting with, say, 17½% or 25% of annual premium for one month (depending on the type of policy and the insurers) to 90% of premium for ten months.

An excess on accidental damage claims is always imposed on motor cycle policies, and is higher for younger drivers. And on some motor cycle policies, unlike motor policies, the excess operates for fire and theft claims also.

the rider
An 'any driver' policy may be available only for a less powerful machine (under 100c.c.); for heavier machines, only named drivers are normally covered. If the name of another driver is to be included on the policy, the premium will be increased and the policy related to the age and premium applicable to the youngest driver, even if he is not the owner and the main driver of the bike.

There is a policy for one-rider only, but allowing the riding of any motor cycle up to a selected engine capacity.

Caravans

Before towing a caravan, make sure that your motor policy covers you for towing. Virtually all private motor policies give RTA or third party cover for the towing of a caravan provided it is properly attached to the car. A policy that excludes towing a caravan can be extended to include it.

Once the caravan is attached to the car, it counts as part of it, and so the third party liability cover of the car's insurance extends to it. However, no other sections of a motor policy automatically extend to a caravan. Even if you have a comprehensive motor policy, it will not cover accidental damage done to the caravan itself while being towed and while on a site.

Insurance for the caravan

A caravan can be insured by a specific caravan policy or as part of a package with household contents, or with sports equipment.

COVER REQUIRED	POLICY PROVIDING
damage done by *caravan*	
– while attached to car (for example, swaying out and hitting oncoming car)	towing vehicle's policy (third-party cover)
– while detached	specific caravan policy or package
damage done to *caravan*	
– while attached	
– while detached	specific caravan policy or package
loss of caravan (fire or theft)	specific caravan policy or package
damage to or loss of contents	specific caravan policy household contents policy ('temporarily removed' section)

A caravan policy usually provides cover for loss of or damage to the caravan and its equipment and fittings. But depreciation, mechanical breakdown, damage to tyres (by puncture) is not covered.

Contents

Personal possessions are not included in all caravan policies but can be covered by an optional extension.

Some of the contents of the caravan may already be covered by your household contents policy or all-risks insurance. But ask your household insurers to state exactly what cover you have for any of your possessions while these are in the caravan. For instance, check whether your household contents cover extends to television, video and audio equipment which you may want to have in the caravan for rainy days.

 There may be an excess on a caravan policy, so that you have to pay anything from £5 to £25 of any claim for loss or damage.

Some policies have a 'subject to average' clause for personal possessions in the caravan. If at the time of a claim you are found to be under-insured, the appropriate proportion of your claim will not be met.

The caravan itself

When completing the proposal form, remember that the sum insured for the caravan is the most you would get if the van were a total loss. The settlement you would be offered for a 'total loss' would be on the same principle as for a car. Caravan insurers use *Glass's guide to caravan values,* and base any offer on the figure shown there. But if you have done a lot of improvements since you bought the caravan, a higher figure should reflect this. Some insurers offer 'new for old' insurance for caravans less than a year old. Some insurers do not offer insurance at all for a caravan over 10 years old.

Not all policies cover damage to the caravan while it is being towed, so make sure you choose one that does. Only a few policies cover it or your possessions while the caravan is hired out to someone else.

Following any accidental damage, the policy covers the removal of the caravan to the nearest repairer, and, following the completed repairs, the reasonable cost of returning the caravan to your home address. For an extra premium, some policies will let you extend the caravan policy to cover the cost of alternative accommodation (usually limited to 5% of the sum insured) if you have to take temporary shelter elsewhere because the caravan is uninhabitable following an accident.

 The policy may cover the caravan if you take it abroad, for a limited period (usually 30 or 60 days). If yours does not, you can get it extended. Be sure to have the caravan shown on the car's green card for a holiday out of this country.

page 135

Theft of or from caravan

The Home Office's free leaflet *Caravan crimecut* (distributed through police stations) reminds you that
'Your caravan is your home – if only for a week-end. So protect it from thieves – just as you do your permanent home. It is exposed to a crime risk unique among dwellings: it can be uprooted and towed away. Yet it is simple and inexpensive to guard against this – fit a hitch-lock (make sure the padlock is strong enough not to be

wrenched off and that its shackle is so short that metal cutters can't grip it).'

The leaflet advises you to

- fit an alarm
- close all windows and lock the door
- fit the door with a good quality deadlock
- keep as few valuables as possible inside
- record serial numbers of the caravan and of valuable contents.

If you want to know how to protect your particular caravan, the crime prevention officer at the local police station can be asked to come and advise.

Letters you may need to write

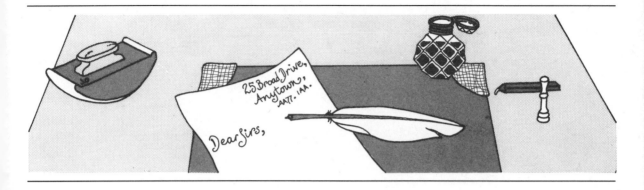

These letters are for people who are dealing direct with the insurance company, rather than via a broker or agent.

Work on the principle that a short letter is more likely to be read and understood.

In none of them has a particular department or individual been identified to whom to address a letter – the post openers at the company's offices will identify by the policy number more quickly, so always quote this. Also quote the renewal date: many offices file in date order. Use the same heading as the insurers use if you have already had some correspondence on the matter; always quote their reference number.

If you are not certain which office is dealing with your policy, write to the insurance company's head office; the letter will be sent on to the right branch office.

letter no 1 *to get confirmation from previous insurers of no-claim discount*

The British Flag Insurance Co   *25 Broad Drive*
15 Heathgate   *Anytown*
London EC6   *AA77 1AA*

Dear Sirs

POLICY NO. M 654321
NAME OF POLICYHOLDER: I. M. MEE
RENEWAL DATE: 25 NOVEMBER
AGENCY: RURAL BROKERS, ANYTOWN

Put in the number of years, not just the discount percentage: some policies' discounts extend above the normal 60%.

Would you please confirm that up to the date of cancellation, 2nd October 1984, I had a no-claim discount of 60% for six claim-free years.

Yours faithfully

I. M. Mee

if the policy was one without a no-claim discount scheme
after 'the date of cancellation . . .', continue:
. . . the above policy has been free of claims for 6 years.

letter no 2 *when changing cars*

The Peninsular Insurance Co   *25 Broad Drive*
Spice Dock   *Anytown*
London EC5   *AA77 1AA*

Dear Sirs

POLICY NO. M 123456   RENEWAL DATE: 25 NOVEMBER

On 3rd January 1985, I shall be buying the following car in exchange for
my Mini VHF 200G:

make and model	Austin Mini
cubic capacity	848cc
year of manufacture	1977
value	£1000
registration no.	NEU 123S

All other policy details, drivers etc, remain as at present. Please let me
have a cover note if necessary, and let me know if any additional
premium is required.

Yours faithfully

I. M. Mee

letter no 3 *when buying a second car*

The Peninsular Insurance Co   *25 Broad Drive*
Spice Dock   *Anytown*
London EC5   *AA77 1AA*

Dear Sirs

POLICY NO. M 123456   RENEWAL DATE: 25 NOVEMBER

On 3rd January 1985, I shall be buying the following, in addition to my
present car (VHF 200G):

make and model	Austin Mini
cubic capacity	848cc
year of manufacture	1977
value	£1000
registration no.	NEU 123S

If you have never owned two cars before, you may not get a no-claim discount for the second one, but most insurers do give what is known as a 'starter' discount (about 33$\frac{1}{3}$%); some insurers give two-car discounts. The insurers should volunteer these discounts but if they do not, ask.

The main driver of this car will be my wife (who is a named driver for
VHF 200G). All other policy details remain as at present.

I previously had a second car insured, your policy number M 24687, which
was cancelled in May last year when I sold that car, so I presume that the
no-claim discount of 50% earned on that car can now apply to this second
car (NEU 123S).

Please let me know what additional premium is required, and let me have
a certificate of insurance.

Yours faithfully

I. M. Mee

letter no 4 *when selling the car*

The Peninsular Insurance Co
Spice Dock
London EC5

25 Broad Drive
Anytown
AA77 1AA

Dear Sirs

POLICY NO. M 123456 RENEWAL DATE: 25 NOVEMBER

As a precaution, just in case the letter should go astray, write 'cancelled with effect from 12th June' (or whatever the date) in ink across the certificate of motor insurance.

I have today (12th June) sold my car (NEU 123S). The above policy should therefore now be cancelled. My certificate of motor insurance is enclosed. Please send your cheque for the unexpired part of my premium to me at the above address.

Yours faithfully

I. M. Mee

letter no 5a *when laying up car*

The Peninsular Insurance Co
Spice Dock
London EC5

25 Broad Drive
Anytown
AA77 1AA

Dear Sirs

POLICY NO. M 123456 RENEWAL DATE: 25 NOVEMBER

You have to send the certificate to show that you are not using the car, so that you can get any refund of premium, usually in the form of a credit at your next renewal.

Please note that my vehicle VHF 200G is off the road until further notice. I would like to remain insured for fire and theft risks only. My current certificate of motor insurance is enclosed.

Yours faithfully

I. M. Mee

letter no 5b *. . . and putting it on the road again*

Further to my letter of 2nd March, I will be starting to use my car VHF 200G again from 22nd June. Please resume full insurance cover from that date and let me have the certificate of motor insurance.

You never get this rebate by cheque.

No doubt you will let me know what adjustment will be made to my premium at next renewal to allow for this laid-up period.

Yours faithfully

I. M. Mee

letter no 6 *to reduce the insurance cover*

The Peninsular Insurance Co   25 Broad Drive
Spice Dock   Anytown
London EC5   AA77 1AA

Do not send back your certificate of motor insurance.
The insurers will issue either an endorsement to your current policy, or a new policy document; some may ask you to complete a fresh proposal form. (Insurers feel that when cover is reduced, it is important that the insured person is made doubly aware of it by completing a fresh proposal.)

Dear Sirs

POLICY NO. M 123456 RENEWAL DATE: 25 NOVEMBER

Please reduce the cover for my car VHF 200G from comprehensive to third party, fire and theft, from today. There are no changes to the car, or my use of it. Please let me know what the new annual premium will be and what refund of premium will be due.

Yours faithfully

I. M. Mee

---

letter no 7 *to ask for a voluntary excess*

The Peninsular Insurance Co   25 Broad Drive
Spice Dock   Anytown
London EC5   AA77 1AA

Dear Sirs

POLICY NO. M 123456 RENEWAL DATE: 25 NOVEMBER

It is always better to do this at renewal, as soon as you get your renewal notice. At any other time, you may be asked by the broker, or even the insurance company, to pay an endorsement charge.

Because of your recent increase in premiums, I would now like to offer to be responsible for some part of damage claims myself, in order to reduce my annual premium. Would you therefore let me know what the revised annual premium would be with an excess of £50 or £75 or £100.

My son has just had his 25th birthday, so the compulsory excess of £40 that operated while he was driving now no longer applies.

Yours faithfully

I. M. Mee

letter no 8 *when no third party is involved*

The Peninsular Insurance Co   *25 Broad Drive*
Spice Dock   *Anytown*
London EC5   *AA77 1AA*

Dear Sirs

POLICY NO. M 123456 RENEWAL DATE: 25 NOVEMBER

I know that under the terms of my policy, I have to notify you of any accident with my car. I have therefore completed the enclosed accident report form, but as the damage to my car was only slight, I propose to pay for the repair myself and not invoke the policy. No third party was involved in any way, and no one was injured.

Yours faithfully

I. M. Mee

---

letter no 9 *when no payment is to be made to third party*

The Peninsular Insurance Co   *25 Broad Drive*
Spice Dock   *Anytown*
London EC5   *AA77 1AA*

Dear Sirs

POLICY NO. M 123456 RENEWAL DATE: 25 NOVEMBER

It is also a good idea to write large, in red, across the top of the claim form, something like 'for information only – no payment to be made'. This is to prevent your insurers paying out on a third-party claim and to preserve your no-claim discount if the other party's insurers seek a contribution from yours.

On 3rd December 1984, I was involved in an accident with Mr V V Careless of 13 Knockit Down, Hazardville. Both our cars were damaged but no one was injured.

In compliance with the policy conditions, I have completed your accident report form, which is enclosed. But please note that I am not making a claim and do not wish to invoke my policy in this matter. I will myself pay for the repairs to my car.

Yours faithfully

I. M. Mee

letter no 10 *denying a third party's claim*

If you do not get this letter in quickly, the insurers may pay out and you lose your no-claim discount. Policy conditions give insurers the right to deal with claims as they see fit. If you told them you are not invoking your policy, the insurers should simply write to the third party and/or his insurers and say 'our insured will not make a claim under his policy with us and we suggest you deal with him direct'. If it gets as far as a court case, you will have to defend it without the backing of your insurers.

The Peninsular Insurance Co
Spice Dock
London EC5

25 Broad Drive
Anytown
AA77 1AA

Dear Sirs

POLICY NO. M 123456 RENEWAL DATE: 25 NOVEMBER

CLAIM NO. M2/3/405 YOUR REF JH/37

Thank you for your letter of 6 January, enclosing a copy of a letter you have received from Mr V V Careless. I can in no way agree with his version of the accident, for the reasons set out in my accident report form. I hold Mr Careless fully responsible for the incident.

You will remember that when I notified you of the accident, I said that I was not making a claim and did not wish to invoke my policy.

Yours faithfully

I. M. Mee

---

letter no 11 *to notify change of address*

The Peninsular Insurance Co
Spice Dock
London EC5

25 Broad Drive
Anytown
AA77 1AA

Dear Sirs

POLICY NO. M 123456 RENEWAL DATE: 25 NOVEMBER

Garaging affects both the premium and the cover, according to the district in which you live. Some insurers do not bother with an alteration in premium with anything under £5. Instead of getting a cheque returning part of your premium, a credit may be deducted from your next renewal premium.

Please note that from 24 February 1985, my permanent address will be

71 Long Road
Princehill Knavely
Barset
PZ88 0XY

My car will now not be garaged overnight, but be kept in the lane outside.

As Princehill is a very rural area, I presume there will be some adjustment to the premium. I look forward to hearing from you about this.

Yours faithfully

I. M. Mee

letter no 12 *to get a green card for motoring abroad*

Do not leave this letter until the last moment – give the insurance company at least 2 weeks' notice. If you do not know how much the cost will be when you write for a green card, you will be told when the card has been prepared and it will be sent to you once the insurance company has received your money. Check that the insurance for the caravan covers taking it abroad and extends for the planned length of time.

The Peninsular Insurance Co
Spice Dock
London EC5

71 Long Road
Princehill Knavely
Barset
PZ88 0XY

Dear Sirs

POLICY NO. M 123456 RENEWAL DATE: 25 NOVEMBER

I am taking my car abroad. Please extend the above policy as set out below. During this trip, my wife and I will be the drivers, and we shall be towing our caravan, which should be noted on the green card.

1) countries to be visited: France, Italy, Spain

2) Period (both dates inclusive): 21 July to 16 September

If you know the chassis number, state this but it is not absolutely necessary.

3) towing a Gnome Alpine caravan

Please let me have a Spanish bail bond.

I understand from our telephone conversation that the additional premium, including the issue of the green card and the bail bond, will be £30 and I enclose my cheque for this amount.

Yours faithfully

I. M. Mee

Miscellaneous insurances

Whatever you want to insure for, there is almost bound to be an insurance company somewhere or a syndicate of underwriters at Lloyd's willing to take you on.

There needs to be
* an insurable interest
* potential financial loss
* a fortuitous element to the event.

The insurance must not be against the public interest.

The Insurance Buyer's Guide to schemes, packages and unusual risks is published annually by Kluwer Publishing; 1984 edition (April) £9.95.

Insurance for an out-of-the-ordinary event that has to be individually underwritten would have to be arranged through a broker or other intermediary and there would be no printed proposal form or standard policy. Provided the insurer can make some estimate of the probability of having to pay out, and that this is not too great, and provided the cost of setting up the scheme for you is not too much, you should be able to get some form of insurance cover – at a price. There are usually substantial minimum premiums to cover 'one-off' specially prepared policies.

Many risks can be insured on a short-term basis, as and when a particular need arises. The premium rates for short-term insurances are generally relatively high.

You can, for instance, insure for expenses incurred by having to cancel a wedding reception (for good reason – not just because the bride has changed her mind); for missing documents (but generally not any relating to land); as executor of a will for having to pay out to a missing beneficiary who turns up after the money in the estate has been distributed.

Rain insurance

You can take out insurance to get some compensation if excessive rain spoils some outside event you are organising – such as a garden party, fête, charity fair, cricket match – where cancellation would mean financial loss.

Rain insurance is based on rainfall measurements taken at a

number of places throughout the country. The rainfall stipulations in a policy vary according to the location and the season of the year for which the insurance is required.

Policies are issued at Lloyd's and by the Eagle Star Insurance Company whose 'Pluvius' policy pays out the sum insured or a proportion of it (depending on the premium you pay) if more than stipulated amounts of rain fall in a certain number of hours.

The amount of rain needed for payment to be made may be as little as 0.03 of an inch (for 20% of the sum insured; 0.08 of an inch for the whole sum insured) or, for less rain-sensitive events, the range can be from one-tenth of an inch (for payment of 30% of the sum insured) to one-fifth of an inch for the full sum insured.

You have to arrange the insurance in advance, get a quotation and pay the premium at least 14 days before the date(s) you want covered.

Make sure if you take out rain insurance that it starts from about 3 hours before the opening of the garden party, charity fête or whatever event, because this is when people make their decision whether to come or not.

For having twins

A multiple birth policy will pay out if twins are born and both survive for more than 24 hours. (If triplets, quads or more are born, the policy pays out double.) The policy does not normally pay out if the babies are more than 6 weeks premature. Arrangements for the insurance must be completed six months before the expected date of birth.

You have to state on the proposal form whether there have been twins in either parent's family back to the grandparents' generation. There are also questions about the parents' ages, whether a fertility drug or treatment has been taken (no cover, if so), and whether a professional opinion has been expressed about the likelihood of twins.

The maximum sum you can insure for is £1000; there is a minimum premium of £10.

For contact lenses

Most opticians and lens manufacturers run their own schemes for replacing lost or damaged contact lenses. These schemes are generally cheaper than special insurance for contact lenses (especially for soft lenses).

A few insurance companies offer the option to insure your contact lenses as an extension to your household contents policy.

There are a few special insurance policies to cover loss or damage to contact lenses; you may need to go to a broker to find out about these.

The premiums for hard lenses are about a quarter of the sum for which you insure the lenses; for soft lenses, half as much again.

You have to attach the optician's receipt to your claim for reimbursement after a loss. There is no payment if hard lenses are replaced by soft lenses, or vice versa. The policies do not cover loss or damage to hard contact lenses when worn while you are swimming.

Musical instruments

A household contents policy covers most musical instruments but for limited amounts and only for damage done by the listed 'perils' unless the instrument is a 'specified valuable' on an all-risks schedule.

A few insurers issue special policies to cover musical instruments (classical and/or modern) on an all-risks basis. The exclusions on some policies are particularly pertinent to instruments – for instance, any process of cleaning, repairing or restoring, mechanical derangement, breakage of strings or reeds or valves, effects of climate (atmospheric conditions and extremes of temperature). An instrument left unattended in a vehicle will not be covered (unless you pay 25% more premium to have this exclusion deleted), or an excess (up to £75) is imposed for loss in such circumstances.

With one policy, you can insure for each type of instrument individually – from bassoons to zithers; others cover groups of instruments, differentiating only between classical and electrical equipment.

The insurance pays the replacement value of a lost or damaged instrument, but the policies are not index-linked so the sum insured should be regularly reviewed to take account of changing values.

Premium rates for individually insured instruments depend on the instrument and the sum insured, with lower premium rates for higher sums insured – for instance, $1^{1}/_{4}\%$ for a cello insured for up to £500, 1% up to £2000. There may be a minimum premium (for instance, £7.50) or a general excess (£10 or £25) on the whole policy. One policy offers a no-claim discount. There may be a higher premium for players under the age of 16, and also if you want to travel with your instrument farther afield than Europe.

Small boats

'On the hull' is the term for the boat itself and all its fixtures and fittings.

Marine insurance has slightly different rules and different jargon from other classes of insurance.

If your craft is not more than 5 metres long and, if power-driven, has a maximum speed of 17 knots, it can be covered by a basic 'small craft' insurance policy. If you take people out on fishing trips or sightseeing trips and get paid for it, even if only occasionally, you will have to insure in the commercial category.

where from

Most large insurers and Lloyd's offer small boats insurance policies. Cheaper cover because of the use of standard clauses is offered by brokers who arrange package deals for clubs. Similarly, sailing clubs and, particularly, class associations offer insurance to their members at comparatively low rates.

It is also possible to get a small boat insured as an extension on some household contents policies – no cheaper but easier. It would be a separate section and have its own conditions and exclusions.

If you keep your boat in the garage or shed when not in use, make sure that your household contents policy includes it.

how much

With some insurers, the premium is affected by how many months in the year the boat is 'in commission' – that is, on the water and ready for use – and where it will be laid up if you use it only in the summer months. You can insure for a limited period – for example, going on holiday for a month in the year.

By taking a voluntary excess, it is possible to reduce the premium. But there may be a minimum premium.

1st year 5%, rising to 15% after the 3rd or 4th claim-free year.

As with motor insurance, there are no-claim discounts on small craft policies. These do not amount to much but are worth enquiring about; they differ between insurers, unlike motor policies where NCDs are fairly standard, and they can be transferred between companies if you change your insurers.

for what

You can insure for
● loss of or damage to the craft (with its tackle, fittings and equipment) directly caused by accidental external means, including
– 'stress of weather'
– stranding, sinking or collision
– malicious acts
● theft of the boat
● theft of gear or equipment (but only following forcible entry or removal)
● fire, lightning, explosion
● breaking of propeller shaft
● the outboard motor dropping overboard

In marine insurance, salvage is the reward recoverable under maritime law by persons who, working independently of contract, render services to avert or minimise loss or to recover interest after loss.

● reasonable salvage charges – the costs charged by the professionals for pulling vessels off rocks and getting wrecks out of the way of other vessels
● liability at law to third parties and their property up to £250,000 (with some, £500,000) in any one accident; this would include
– damage to piers, docks, jetties
– claims made by passengers for death or bodily injuries and

damage to their property, while on the craft or boat or while embarking or disembarking
– legal costs incurred with the insurers' consent.

Third party liability cover does not include employees, so if you pay any of your crew, you must take out additional insurance.

exclusions
The main exclusions to these policies are
■ loss of or damage due to wear and tear, depreciation, war and riots
■ small damage (scratching, denting) while the boat is towed on a road trailer
■ the trailer itself
■ theft of an outboard motor that is not specially secured
■ breakage or damage to oars and paddles while in use

■ loss of or damage to personal property (except at an extra premium or with a £25 excess)
■ racing (with some policies, the cover while racing is reduced to two-thirds for damage to sails, masts, spars, standing or running rigging or blocks).

the proposal form
The proposal form requires information about the boat and its estimated present value and of the trailer and of any outboard motor. It also asks
* what you intend to use it for (private pleasure or racing)
* where it will be moored when it is not being used
* where it will be laid up
* what waters it will be in when it is being used.

The proposal form may also ask how many years' experience you have had in handling small craft. There are no compulsory sailing qualifications but some insurers may charge less if the owner holds a qualification or certificate. You are asked about any sailing accidents you were involved in during the last 3 (or 5) years.

page 17

The form includes the same reminder about duty of disclosure as all other insurances.

Cats and dogs

Domestic animals can be insured by a separate policy for pets. Some pet policies are specifically for dogs and cats, others are broader 'general livestock' policies, which cover a variety of non-farm animals. You may also be able to extend your household contents policy to insure your pet.

The policy can be transferred to a new owner if the dog or cat is sold or given away, and can be extended to insure the animal while it is boarded out.

There are lower and upper age limits for an animal to be insured (for instance, from 2 months to 8 years for a dog, up to 10 years for a cat).

A policy for a dog or cat may provide insurance for

– liability

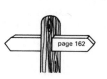
page 162

Injury it causes to other people (members of your family and employees are excluded) or their property for which you are legally liable as the dog's owner up to a set maximum (£100,000 or £500,000, depending on the policy) will be paid for.

– vet's fees

There are limits (up to £50, £100, or £200 for a dog) per incident on this section of a policy. The vet's travelling expenses may not be paid for and there is usually an excess of £5 to £10. Fees in any way connected with pregnancy or breeding are excluded, and so is the cost of routine protective inoculations. However, any inoculation that an animal needs after an accident can be claimed for. The fee for castration, unless certified by a veterinary surgeon to have been necessary following an accident, is excluded.

– lost, stolen or strayed

If the dog or cat is missing, the policy will pay the cost of any advertising or other expenses (such as a reward) incurred in trying to get it back, up to a set sum which may be £40 (dog), £20 (cat) or as much as £100. If the animal is not recovered after more than a set number of days, the policy pays for it as if it had died.

– death

On the animal's death by accident, or by a vet for humane reasons (with some policies, death from any cause), you will be paid its market value or purchase price, whichever is the less. (Some policies do not insure a cat's life even once, let alone nine times.) Some policies have a maximum (£150, say, or £200) that will be paid on the death of any animal.

Most domestic pets, however much they are cared about, have very little intrinsic monetary value so you cannot insure the animal for any great sum. However, if you have a pedigree pet which is worth money, you may insure its life for a specified sum.

the proposal form

The proposal form asks about the animal's health, sex, age, market value and the purpose for which it is kept. You have to put down separately its current market value and the sum for which you want to insure it.

The form asks if you have any other cat or dog not being insured – and if so, why not.

You may be asked whether the animal is known to have vicious tendencies. So, if you know that Fido has a nasty reaction to postmen, although you may not admit it to the post office, you must tell the insurers. You have to answer a question about any recent occurrences involving a claim or complaint.

A certificate may be attached to the proposal form to be signed by a veterinary surgeon if the value of the animal exceeds £100 (with most pedigree animals, it will). The vet has to state where and when he examined the animal and whether he has observed any signs of disease or injury (and give details of the condition, if so) and sign the form, showing his professional qualifications. His fee for doing this has to be paid by you. The insurance does not come into force unless and until this certificate is completed.

There is a minimum premium (£20 dog, £10 cat, or £25 for any animal, depending on the insurers); some will quote a premium only after seeing the proposal form.

claiming

When your animal has been injured in an accident or has developed a disease, the insurers do not take your word about what has happened: a veterinary surgeon's certificate (for which you have to pay the fee) is always required. You must provide the answers to questions about how the accident happened or when the animal first became ill, to be confirmed by the vet's certificate.

Horses and ponies

You can insure your child's pony and any horses you keep for riding and hunting and show events as an amateur, either on the same package policy as a dog and other livestock, or on a separate horse policy.

The premium is based on the sum insured, and the use of the animal. You have to pay more, for example, if you use a horse for point-to-points or hunter trials.

There may be an age limit for the horse to be insured (say, 15 years). A vet's certificate may be required when applying for insurance for a horse over, say, 12 years old, or for one to be insured for over a specified amount (anything from £1000 to £5000).

The basic cover is for the animal's death, and the damage it may do to people or their property (other than the owner or his family), up to a specified limit (£500,000 or £100,000).

In addition, a policy may cover (or can be extended to cover)
* vet's fees, up to a maximum (of £100 to £350 or even £750 per incident and for any one year of £500 to £1000), with an excess of £15 to £50
* theft or straying, for which you can claim the sum insured or the market value, whichever is lower, and the cost of advertising the loss and offering a reward (£50 or £100 maximum).

In addition to risks connected with the actual animal, the policy includes, or can be extended to include, loss of or damage to riding tack and saddlery, up to a specified limit; there may be an excess of up to £25.

The policy can include personal accident cover for the rider, up to £7,500 for total disablement or death (or as little as £500 or £1000).

The insurance pays the market value or the sum insured if the horse has to be destroyed following an accident or illness, provided the incapacity arose during the period of insurance.

You can claim if the horse has to be slaughtered because it is permanently incapacitated and unable to fulfil the function for which it is kept. (This is called economic slaughter and permanent loss of use.) If, however, the owner decides to keep the horse in retirement instead of having it slaughtered, the insurance pays out, but it may be a reduced amount (40% to 75% of the sum insured, depending on the policy).

claiming
The policy stipulates that
● if the horse is injured or contracts a disease, you must immediately get adequate attendance and treatment by a veterinary surgeon
● if the animal dies, the veterinary surgeon must certify the cause of death, after a post mortem if necessary
● if the horse has to be slaughtered for humane or 'economic' reasons, you must dispose of the carcass to best advantage; the amount obtained will belong to the insurers.

Firms specialising in the disposal of the carcasses of accidentally killed or slaughtered animals advertise in the local press in agricultural areas and in the Yellow Pages directory.

Look under 'abattoirs' or 'horse slaughterers' (referred to as a casualty service).

School fees

There are many variously complex schemes for parents to prepare for paying fees to schools if they think they may decide to send a child (or children) to a fee-paying school. Some schools have their own schemes for accepting a lump sum in advance from parents which is invested to prepare for funding the fees when the time comes. Or this can be done through an independent educational trust, taking advantage of tax concessions through its charitable status.

Life insurance can be used to anticipate the future expense by taking out an endowment policy timed to mature when the child is due to start school. A number of these can be taken out over the years, to spread the load. With-profits policies would be the best bet; unit-linked ones carry the risk that the price of the units may be low at the moment when you need to take the money. There is the tax advantage that the proceeds of a qualifying life insurance policy are not taxed. It is important that the policies are taken out well ahead – at least 10 years – of the first date when fees will become due. The Independent Schools Information Service (ISIS)

page 218

ISIS
56 Buckingham Gate
London SW1E 6AG

has a summarising leaflet about some ways of planning ahead to reduce the costs of school fees, including the names of some insurance companies and brokers who specialise in schemes for school fees.

Mortgage and other loans

The main purpose of protected mortgage or 'redundancy' insurance is to provide money to enable you to keep up your mortgage and other debt payments, school fees, if your income falls drastically due to your losing your job or becoming ill or incapacitated. It is a policy similar to personal accident/sickness and permanent health insurance.

Initially intended only for unemployment through statutorily defined redundancy, it is nowadays possible also to have this credit insurance for loss of job through any other cause – such as a straight sacking.

You can insure for the full amount of your monthly mortgage payments, or for less if you prefer – the premium is linked to the sum you want to have when the crisis occurs (the premium rate is between 3% and 5% of the monthly payment you want to get).

Premiums are payable monthly or annually with some policies, there is a single premium for the whole period of cover (say, 2 years).

These policies are offered by brokers, through some estate agents and builders, a few building societies and a number of banks. Redundancy insurance can be arranged on a group basis – for example, for members of a club.

There are quite stringent conditions and limitations, varying with the insurers. For example, to cover a mortgage
- the policy can only be taken out at the time you are starting a mortgage
- the mortgage must not be for more than, say, £30,000
- at that time, you must be in full employment, with no likelihood of your being made redundant (you may have to make a specific declaration about this)
- no payments are made until after so-many days off work, usually 30 days (for a lower premium, can be 60 days, with no payment for the first 30 days)
- payments are not made for more than 2 years – or less if you pay less premium
- the maximum age for this insurance is retirement age (60 for women, 65 for men).

Anyone who is self-employed, and cannot therefore be made redundant, may get a higher payment (50% or 100% more) to cover mortgage payments if unable to work because of illness or injury.

Earning money at home

page 51

You should inform your insurers if you start working from home. If no extra hazards, such as using flammable materials, are involved, the cover of your household insurance should not be affected. But if people call on you frequently because of your work, you will not be insured for theft of any of your possessions unless there has been forcible entry (or exit).

Only a few household contents policies can be extended to cover 'tools of a trade', so if through your work at home you are accumulating a number of valuable tools or other equipment, they will not be considered part of your personal possessions and will need special insurance cover.

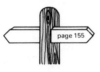

page 155

The area of insurance that is always affected when someone carries on a trade or business from home is legal liability for injury to others or damage to their property. Household policies (buildings and contents) specifically exclude liability arising from a business or profession, so you must insure separately for this, with a public liability policy appropriate to your trade – for example, for keeping kennels.

with paying guests

If you decide to take paying guests, you have to tell your insurers, get their agreement to continue your household insurance and ask for an endorsement on your policy.

The insurers will need to be given details of how many PGs you are taking and for how long (summer months only or all through the year). A number of paying guests may be allowed without additional premium – two, four or even six, also depending on the number of rooms being let.

Having lodgers may affect insurance for the building: the more people in a house, the more likely it is that some incident will arise due to carelessness, defects in apparatus, overloading of electrical wiring.

excess or higher premium

Specific exclusions will be applied to your household contents policy, such as no cover for theft or malicious damage by a person lawfully on the premises (that is the paying guest). There may be no insurance cover for the property the guests or lodgers bring with them. Although a few contents policies provide a small amount of cover for visitors' effects, paying guests and lodgers would not be considered as 'visitors'.

If you have paid an additional premium for accidental damage cover to the buildings or contents, you may find that the policy clearly states that claims for damage while any part of the house is let or sub-let will not be met.

page 159

You need to pay attention to the liability section of your contents policy. Your cover for liability to domestic servants may no longer apply if you employ them as part of your letting business (you would need employer's liability insurance). To cover liability for injury to your paying guests or damage to their property, you would need to get special insurance, as for a boarding house or hotel.

Legal expenses

There are policies which will pay for legal expenses, up to a certain limit (£5000, £10,000 or £25,000, depending on the policy). Most policies cover not only you but also the members of your family living with you.

This insurance is designed primarily for cases that go to court, but it will cover the bills if you settle without the case going to court. It covers you as plaintiff (when you sue somebody) or as defendant, and also for certain criminal prosecutions and appeals, mainly in connection with motoring offences; some policies cover tribunals such as employment and pensions but not tax or rent.

If you lose your case, you will have to find the money yourself for any compensation, damages or fine, but most of the policies pay for all other expenses – for example, your own solicitor's bill as well as any of the other side's costs awarded against you.

Most policies will cover you for events that were caused by circumstances which existed before you were insured, provided that you could not reasonably have known about the circumstances at that time.

Policies normally cover the legal expenses for cases of

- personal injury

claiming compensation if you or a member of your family get killed or injured in an accident caused by somebody else's negligence

- loss or damage to your property

caused by other people's negligence

- disputes over contracts

to buy or sell your house (but not other conveyancing matters), or about house repairs and decorations; if you live in rented accommodation, about tenancy agreements or notice to quit

- disputes with neighbours

about, for example, boundaries, noise, nuisance

- disputes arising from your job

such as unfair dismissal or an industrial accident

- consumer problems

over a contract to buy or hire goods, over loans, or for a service such as repairs or dry-cleaning

- motoring offences

defence costs if you are charged with certain driving offences such as speeding or driving with excess alcohol in your bloodstream. (Some schemes specialise in motorists' legal expenses, covering claims against a third party for uninsured losses, as well as prosecutions and disputes.)

page 114

exclusions
Routine legal work is excluded: conveyancing, divorce (with most schemes), making a will, normal probate work; also building work disputes.

Cases which are covered by any other insurance policy are excluded. For instance, a household contents policy normally provides personal liability cover to pay for your defence, and any damages you are ordered to pay. Similarly, a motor policy covers third party claims arising from a road accident.

Some schemes do not cover you for suing another insurance company over a claim on your policy with them. With others, you may be able to claim on your legal expenses policy for the expenses of taking a case to court to decide what an insurance policy does include – but generally not a dispute about how much it should pay.

taking out the insurance
This type of insurance is sold either as a separate policy or as an optional extra on another policy, such as a household contents or building insurance, via insurance brokers or solicitors or direct from the insuring companies.

The proposal form usually asks if you know of any circumstances which could give rise to a claim on the policy. If such circumstances exist, they may be specifically excluded from the cover.

If your proposal is accepted, you get cover for 12 months at a time. Premiums vary from approximately $\frac{1}{4}$% to $1\frac{1}{2}$% of the maximum that you would be able to claim.

claiming
You cannot just go to law and invoke the policy afterwards. Instead, you first have to give the insurers full details of the situation.

The insurers have the right to vet your choice of solicitor – and might turn him down if his fees are considered too high or if he practises too far away from where you are bringing the case.

The insurers stipulate that they can make their own investigations into your case or try to negotiate a settlement on your behalf. They can refuse to accept a case even if it appears to be covered by the policy if they think that you do not have a reasonable chance of success or if the person against whom you wish to claim would not be able to pay you compensation.

Most policies say that if you win and the other side has to pay your costs, these amounts are paid over to the insurers. But any expenses involved in whatever steps are needed to make the other side pay up, are covered by the policy.

Unrecovered damages

Some household contents policies and personal liability policies provide insurance for 'reverse liability'.

If you were the injured party, sued, and obtained a court judgment in your favour which the other party, the person who was found liable, cannot pay (because he is not insured or is a 'man of straw'), your own insurers will pay you the damages awarded to you if these have not been paid to you within three months of the date of the award. (They can then pursue your unsatisfied rights against the person responsible for your injuries.) This payment will only be made if the liability section of the policy would have insured you had the award been made against you rather than in your favour – the reverse situation.

This type of insurance is also referred to as 'reverse damages personal liability' or 'irrecoverable court awards' or 'unsatisfied court judgment' or 'reverse indemnity' insurance.

The most you will get, whatever the outstanding debt, is usually the limit for the personal liability section of the policy (in most policies, £500,000).

Private medical expenses

There are schemes designed specifically for people who want to have the option of having private medical consultations and hospital treatment instead of relying on the NHS, mostly provided by provident associations, who are specialist insurance companies in this field. A number of conventional insurance companies and Lloyd's syndicates are coming into this class of business.

Many people consider this type of insurance as a luxury but it may be thought essential by people who need to have medical treatment at a time that suits them and their business commitments, and need to be out of action for the shortest possible time and do not want to 'queue' for treatment. Also, having a private room may enable them to carry on their business from a hospital bed, and have visitors at all times.

The cover

If you fall ill, or are injured, and your general practitioner recommends that you see a specialist or go into hospital, the scheme will pay for the specialists' fees and hospital and nursing charges. The policy normally pays (up to certain limits) for
- specialists' consultation fees (as an in-patient or out-patient)
- hospital in-patient accommodation and nursing charges
- fees of surgeon, anaesthetist, radiographer, radiotherapist, pathologist, physiotherapist
- charges for drugs and other treatment while in hospital
- operating theatre fees
- charges for nursing at home up to a limited amount
- cost of treatment or nursing as an out-patient if the specialist recommends it.

But the charges of a private general practitioner are not included.

The insurance is designed to pay for treatment of surgical or acute medical conditions, on a short-term basis. Payment for long-term illnesses such as psychiatric or geriatric is therefore limited by some companies and excluded by others.

If you are treated under the NHS as a hospital in-patient, most policies pay a cash sum per day.

Exclusions

General exclusions vary from scheme to scheme. Typical ones with most of the schemes are
* any treatment of which the equivalent would not be provided by the NHS; but some schemes will pay ex gratia for treatment by an osteopath or chiropractor
* any claim for treatment outside the UK unless abroad only temporarily (*eg* on holiday)

* cosmetic treatment (but plastic surgery following an accident will be paid for)
* dental treatment unless as an in-patient for surgical treatment
* accommodation charges in mental or geriatric homes for longer than 180 days in any one period of insurance
* pregnancy and childbirth (unless there are any complications and it is more than 10 months since joining the scheme)
* charges at any health farm, hydro or nature cure clinic, convalescent homes, place for treatment of alcoholism or drug addiction
* injury or illness as a result of war, invasion, act of foreign enemy, hostilities (whether war be declared or not)
* preventive measures such as inoculations or vaccinations or routine checks such as sight testing (also, with most schemes, spectacles and hearing aids)
* health screening charges (but you may get a token discount off the normal scale of charges at a scheme's own medical centre)
* any physical or mental illness which was known to have existed prior to taking out the policy, unless it has been declared and was accepted by the insurers
* with some schemes, any treatment within the specified waiting period – for instance, during the 13 weeks after joining. Once the waiting period is over, you can claim for a condition which developed during that time for which you are still being treated. (There is no waiting period if you join through a group.)

Age limits

To take out a scheme in your own name, you must be 18 or over. Children under 18 (or even 21) can be included with parents.

With most schemes, you pay more the older you are at the start, and as you get older. But one scheme allows you to stay at the 30-year-old premium, provided you joined before that age.

Most schemes do not accept for full cover new subscribers who are over 65 (some, 70) when they apply, or charge a joining premium.

There is a scheme for older people, up to the age of 75 at the time of starting. But the cover is for private treatment only if NHS treatment is not available within a stipulated period (6 weeks). There is a similar scheme for people joining under the age of 65, paying for private treatment only if NHS treatment is delayed.

The cost

There may be a choice related to the accommodation charges made by the different types of NHS hospital. If you wish to be treated in a private hospital, the insurance will pay for accommodation up to the amount that would be charged by the NHS hospital on the scale of benefit that you have chosen.

Private treatment can be obtained in any NHS hospital which has pay beds. There are several types of NHS hospital; for the purpose of medical insurance, the most important are
– London postgraduate teaching hospital:
daily accommodation charge from £167
– provincial teaching hospital:
daily accommodation charge £115
– general hospital:
daily accommodation charge £110
(Charges are subject to annual review; these are the ones set by the DHSS from 1 April 1984.)

Private hospitals set their own charges; in practice, their accommodation charges tend to be grouped around the NHS levels.

Private medical expenses schemes are expensive, but if you claim, you may be paid large sums for the very high cost of private treatment. The schemes, and the scales within the schemes, differ considerably and you have to be careful not to commit yourself to expenses which are outside the cover of the scheme, and for which you will not get reimbursed. You should study the rules of the schemes and compare what each offers and excludes. A saving of £100 in subscription may be a false economy if you go in for this sort of scheme at all.

choice of scheme
● scheme pays up to an agreed amount for the specified benefits: accommodation, consultant's fees, theatre hire, anaesthetist's fee etc. (Certain limits may be increased for short periods when intensive care is required.) There is a limit to the amount claimable under each benefit but not to the aggregate amount claimable in any year for a combination of benefits.
● scheme has no limits on the scales for individual benefits, but there is an overall limit on the total amount that can be claimed in any one year.
    A slightly cheaper version is a scheme with limits on how much will be paid for any one benefit, and also an overall annual aggregate limit.
● scheme has no individual or aggregate limits.

lower cost
Some schemes reduce the cost (by about a third) if you accept a proviso that you have National Health Service treatment if it is available to you without an appreciable waiting time (more than six weeks, say). But the six weeks start only from the date of seeing the NHS specialist – and it can be quite a long time before that happens.
    You pay special lower rates for combined wife/husband schemes (but the subscription is based on the age of the older person). And there is normally also a wife/husband/children rate; the children must be unmarried and aged under 18 (with some schemes, under 21). After that, if the children subscribe in their own right, they may be allowed to pay a reduced subscription.
    Discounts are available on most schemes. For example, by joining
* as a group (which may be as few as 5 people)
* through an employer's group scheme
* as a member of a professional or trade association, or motoring organisation
* when under a certain age
* by paying through a credit card company, by direct debit or other non-cash transaction (but not if the subscription is paid by monthly instalments).
    One of the schemes offers a no-claim discount, rising to 40% after 5 claim-free years.

Claiming on a scheme

You have to have been referred to a specialist by your GP. Make sure that you are going to a hospital covered by your scale of benefit. Try to work out roughly how much the cost will be and whether the sums you have insured for are adequate. If, for any reason, the treatment or hospital would not be covered, it is better to find this out before incurring the cost.

You may be required to notify the insurers immediately at the beginning of any treatment, and will be sent a claim form.

Tell the specialists and hospital what scheme you are insured with. Normally, the hospital will give you bills as and when treatment and services are provided. But for a short stay only, you may receive a single itemised bill.

Separate bills will be submitted by consultants who do not work solely for the hospital.

Find out whether the bills will be paid direct by the insurers or whether you are expected to pay and then claim reimbursement.

You will have to complete a claim form. The insurers will check
- that you have been an in-patient as declared
- that the condition is not one that is specifically excluded
- that the charges are reasonable and 'necessarily incurred'
- that the length of your stay in hospital was not abnormally long
- where the amount payable for any benefit is limited, that you have not already used it up during the current period of insurance.

It may be possible for the hospital and insurers to deal direct. If treatment is at one of the schemes' private hospitals, you would not see any bills at all.

With the claim form, send bills or receipted accounts. Do not delay in sending in your claim even if you know further bills are to come – there may be a time limit (3 or 6 months) for an expenditure to be met.

Do not forget that if you have ordinary NHS in-patient treatment (without invoking the medical expenses scheme), you can claim a cash allowance – of anything from £10 to £25 a night, depending on the scheme.

Unless there is any doubt about your condition or treatment being covered, you should be reimbursed at once.

Hospital cash plans

With a hospital cash plan, you are paid a fixed amount for every day you spend in hospital, as a private or NHS in-patient. What you get would be nowhere near enough to pay for private treatment but could help to offset extra expenses, such as the cost of your family visiting you daily. One scheme pays separate amounts for specific expenses such as home help.

What you get is a fixed amount per day – from about £10 to about £40. Although there is no upper age limit with most of these plans, the payment made to people over 65 is only half that paid to younger ones – for the same premium.

Some schemes have a maximum number of days for which you can claim in a year, others a maximum amount. Some schemes pay for unlimited periods and unlimited amounts. Some will pay a lump sum if, following an accident, you lose the sight of an eye, or a limb.

Nothing will be paid unless you are getting active medical treatment in an 'acceptable' hospital – which does not include a mental or geriatric institution, a nursing home, old age home or, with most, any institution for drug addiction or alcoholism. One scheme pays a reduced amount for convalescence at home.

Exceptions may include
* self-inflicted injury or attempted suicide
* alcoholism, drug abuse
* mental illness
* pregnancy
* childbirth (but there may be a maternity grant).

There may be a waiting period, usually of 30 days (with one plan, six months) after joining the scheme before being able to claim, unless you have to be admitted to hospital following an accident. Also, with most schemes, no payments will be made for any condition or illness you suffered from at the time of or during the 12 months leading up to joining the scheme, until you have been a member for two years.

If you buy one of these plans through an advertisement in a newspaper, or through an offer which has been mailed to you, all you have to do is to complete a coupon with the basic details asked for. You do not have to give any medical details. There is rarely a separate proposal form to be completed. Acceptance is normally guaranteed, provided you are under the age of 65 when you apply.

Premiums vary from about £1.75 to £20 a month, depending on what the scheme offers and on your age when you first subscribe.

Claiming

The only requirements are that you obtain proof from the hospital that you were an in-patient for more than 24 hours, that the hospital is an eligible one, and that your medical condition is not one that is excluded by the terms of the scheme.

There may be a medical certificate to be completed by the hospital doctor who attended you. You will have to give your authority that any doctor who is, or has been, treating you may be approached.

If a prolonged stay in hospital is likely, some interim payment may be made. Otherwise, a single payment is made after you have been discharged. The payment is not taxable.

Liability to others

Your legal liability to others arises if they can show that you have been negligent. The word negligence has a more specific meaning in law than just careless: you must have failed in your duty of care to someone and be responsible for the injury or damage this caused.

Claims against you as a private individual for personal injury or damage to other people or their property may arise in many situations in your capacity as:
– owner of a house you do not live in
– occupier of your home
– tenant in somebody else's property
– an ordinary member of the public when not in your home
– employer of domestic servants
– owner or user of a private car or motor cycle
– owner or user of a bicycle
– owner or user of gardening or other equipment
– a sportsman
– owner or user of a caravan or boat
– owner of animals or rider of a horse or pony.

Most personal insurance policies give some liability cover in the context of the situations covered by the type of policy. For example, the majority of holiday insurance policies automatically include some personal liability cover.

One or two insurers still issue separate personal liability policies.

HOUSEHOLD BUILDINGS POLICY
insures for
– liability as owner of the building
– liability arising under the
  Defective Premises Act 1972

HOUSEHOLD CONTENTS POLICY
insures for
– liability as occupier
– liability to domestic servants
– personal or family liability
– liability of tenant as occupier
– liability of tenant to landlord

public or personal liability
'Public liability' relates to liability arising from commercial or business activities; personal liability relates only to liabilities arising in a personal and private capacity and specifically excludes business activities.

Public liability can arise from any 'business' activity for which you or your immediate family receive payment – for example, taking in lodgers or paying guests, minding other people's children at home, going out charring, gardening or doing other odd jobs for money. If you undertake such paid activities and want liability cover, you would have to get specific insurance.

Equally, if you employ others to do work for you (other than a domestic servant), you would have to take out a special form of liability insurance – employer's liability.

exclusion
Virtually all policies exclude liability you have taken on that would not normally be yours: for example, assuming the liability for any damage your builder may do to adjoining property. The moral is not to enter into any agreement to take over someone else's liability: your liability insurance will not cover this.

What personal liability insurance covers

Liability insurance is for the damages that could be awarded against you and legal costs incurred in fighting the case.

Even if you are not held liable for the injury or damage, legal and other expenses may be incurred in proving that it was not your responsibility. Insurers pay defence costs and expenses incurred with their written consent. Study the precise wording of the policy carefully: most insurers pay such costs over and above the limit of indemnity, but a few include such payments only within the limit of indemnity.

limit of indemnity: highest amount the insurer can be called upon to pay by the terms of the policy.

Damages awarded against you by the court may be in two parts: special and general. Special damages are a sum awarded for expenses and losses that resulted from the injury or damage, which can be proved and quantified at the time of the claim: for example, medical expenses incurred and earnings actually lost (as distinct from possible future medical expenses and prospective loss of earnings, which come under the heading of general damages). General damages are awarded as compensation for pain and suffering, future expenses and loss of earnings. You may also be ordered to pay the claimant's costs and legal expenses.

The maximum that policies pay out for personal liability claims varies from £250,000 to £1m. (Low limits can in most cases be increased for an additional premium.) Household policies may provide separate limits of £500,000 for each of property owner's liability, occupier's liability, personal liability.

■ as owner of a house
by: *household buildings policy*

This covers liability for incidents for which you are liable as owner of the building: for instance, if a slate off the roof injures somebody below when nobody is living in the house, or when tenants live there and you as landlord are responsible for maintenance and repairs.

Also you are covered for any liability which may arise under the Defective Premises Act in connection with a previous house you

The Act does not apply in Scotland.

You may need special cover for liability under the Defective Premises Act if you have never occupied the property.

owned and occupied. Under this Act, you may be legally liable for injury or damage as a result of repairs or alterations carried out by you or on your behalf while you owned the house, arising within 6 years from when you sold the property. The insurance cover for this liability usually continues for seven years after the date you sell the property, so hold on to your past buildings policy.

Many policies limit this indemnity to claims up to £500,000 – even lower in some.

■ as occupier of the home you own
by: *household contents policy*

As an occupier, you have a liability to passers-by and to visitors. Although many of the accidents resulting in damage or in injury are caused by the structure of the building (for example, guttering or roof tiles falling, loose floorboards), it is the household contents policy, not the buildings policy, that covers such claims, if you are the owner-occupier.

A buildings policy does not cover an owner-occupier for such liability: only a contents policy does.

Examples of possible liability on an owner-occupier:
– the canvasser breaks a leg as a result of falling due to an uneven flagstone in the path to your front door
– chimney pot falls on a visitor's car in your driveway
– big branch of a diseased tree in your garden falls on next door's greenhouse and breaks the glass.

■ as tenant
by: *household contents policy*

As occupier of the flat or house, you are covered by a contents policy in the same way as an owner-occupier.

In addition, most household contents policies provide a limited amount of cover for certain types of damage (but not, generally, that done by fire) to the landlord's property for which you are liable as tenant in accordance with the terms of your lease. So, look at your lease, find out what it makes you responsible for, then check that your contents policy covers this. Most contents policies limit this cover to 10% (up to 20% in a few policies) of the sum insured for the contents and an excess (*eg* £15) may apply.

■ as an individual or member of a family
by: *household contents policy*
or by: *personal liability policy*
or by: *holiday policy*

Insurers used to offer a separate policy for personal liability or, for an additional premium, to add an endorsement to a contents policy. Nowadays, most insurers include liability cover in their household contents policies without charging an additional premium. A handful of insurers still offer separate personal liability insurance policies.

As a general rule, not only the policyholder is covered but also members of his family who are permanently living with him. That is why a number of insurers call this section in a household policy 'family liability'.

Many policies define the term 'member of the family' – usually any member of the family who lives there permanently. Or the wording may refer to wife/husband, children, sisters, brothers, parents, grandparents.

Some policies do not include people who are living permanently in the house but who are not members of the family. If a couple live together who are not married to each other, a policy in the name of one will not give any protection to the other, so they would have to arrange liability cover specially. Insurers will issue a policy in joint names.

A son (or daughter) who is a student and who lives away from home for most of the year is still considered to be 'permanently resident' with the parents. But when the course of study finishes and he gets a job and continues to live away from home, he no longer counts as permanently resident with his parents and is on his own so far as insurance is concerned.

Examples of incidents which could give rise to a personal liability claim:
– your young daughter knocks down an old lady while riding her bicycle in the lane
– your young son casts his fishing line too wildly and injures a bystander's eye
– your carelessly dropped cigarette starts a fire
– your wife shuts someone's hand in a train door
– you cause a road accident by jay-walking.

exclusions

Liability is not covered if the damage is caused by an incident in connection with your occupation of your home (this is covered by your contents policy) or your ownership of any other building or land (for which liability cover is given by buildings insurance).

Not all personal liability insurance covers you if you temporarily look after and occupy some friends' house while they are away or rent holiday accommodation with your family and cause some damage – perhaps setting the place alight through your carelessness with a chip pan.

Damage caused by the use of certain mechanically driven equipment and mechanically propelled craft (car, speedboat), as specified in the policy, is also excluded.

If you or your family fly model aircraft or own and operate model steam trains, these are generally not covered by a household contents or personal liability policy, so check yours, and, if necessary, arrange to extend your policy to cover this activity.

■ as an employer in your home
by: *household contents policy*

Injury to employees is not covered by any personal liability insurance: anybody who employs even one other person has to take out employer's liability insurance. Domestic servants, however, are a different category.

domestic servants
Liability for injury to domestic servants while working for you is covered by a contents policy.

This applies not just to full-time domestic servants but also to part-time help in the home or the garden if they suffer injury due to your negligence. Most contents policies provide cover for claims made on you up to an unlimited amount, unlike other liability cover where there is a specified maximum. For example, if you provide your charlady with a stepladder to reach some of the windows and she has a fall due to a rung giving way and you are held liable for the injuries sustained, the policy would pay in full for the damages awarded.

odd-jobbers
There may be claims for injury or damage caused by someone you have taken on to carry out, for example, a one-off gardening job, tree lopping, painting, roofing.

As an example, if your jobbing gardener lights a bonfire which sets fire to and destroys your neighbour's hedge and fence, it could be held that you should have instructed the gardener to light the bonfire in a different place, bearing in mind your knowledge of the prevailing wind and general weather conditions. Your neighbour could well sue both you and the gardener jointly in any action for damages. You could find yourself having to make good, or contribute towards making good, the damage as well as having to pay any legal costs incurred by your neighbour and yourself. Your household contents policy would cover you for this liability, but not the jobbing gardener.

Many casual contractors claim to be 'fully insured' but this means different things to different people. So, when you engage any type of contractor, ask to see his insurance policy and check to see whether this does include full public liability cover which also protects you as 'employer' or 'principal'.

page 89

■ as owner or user of a private car or motor cycle
by: *motor policy*
or by: *motor cycle policy*

It is an offence under the Road Traffic Act to drive without insurance for your liability for injury to anyone else. All motor policies include this.

To cover liability for damage to other people's property, you need to have at least 'third-party' motor insurance cover.

■ as owner or user of a bicycle
by: *household contents policy (personal liability section)*
or by: *separate pedal cycle policy*
or by: *personal liability policy*

If you (or your children) when riding a bicycle carelessly knock someone down or ride into a parked car, or cause a car to swerve to avoid you resulting in a multiple crash, your insurance will pay if you are faced with a claim for injuries or damages.

If your children use their bikes to deliver newspapers, the policy's personal liability cover does not operate (the newsagent should arrange the necessary cover).

■ as owner or user of gardening or other equipment
by: *household contents policy (occupier's liability section or personal liability section)*
or by: *personal liability policy*

Policies usually have a phrase excluding liability for injury caused by ownership or use of any mechanically propelled vehicles. But if 'pedestrian-controlled' (as most motor lawn mowers are), they are covered. And with some policies, so would be a ride-on lawn mower on which the pedestrian gardener sits, so long as it is used in your own garden or grounds and not on the public road.

If you leave the electric hedgecutter connected to the supply and unattended and a neighbour's child is injured, the policy can be invoked to pay damages awarded against you.

And if you lend to a neighbour your ladder that has a defective rung which you fail to point out, you may be held liable if he is injured. The household contents policy would pay under the personal liability section (not the occupier's liability, because the incident was off your territory).

■ as a sportsman
by: *household contents policy (personal liability section)*
or by: *special sportsmans policy*
or by: *personal liability policy*

Many contents policies cover you, and members of your family living with you, while participating in sporting activities. You may injure another person while you are angling, playing golf,

squash, hockey, and you could be held liable at law for their injury.

Most household policies make no reference to firearms, so any liability arising out of their use would be covered. Some exclude firearms generally but allow airguns and sporting guns.

There are a number of sporting activities where associations or clubs offer special insurance cover – for instance, for yachting, water skiing, sail or surf boarding, sub-aqua diving, gliding, hang-gliding, model aircraft flying. Some clubs provide members with cover automatically and add the premium to the annual subscription. Check that the association's scheme gives you adequate liability cover; if not, it is essential to arrange your own.

As a general rule, contents and personal liability policies do not cover the use of mechanically propelled vehicles, aircraft, hovercraft, boats or caravans.

■ as owner or user of a caravan
by: *caravan policy*
or by: *caravan extension to household contents policy*
(plus motor policy)

HOUSEHOLD POLICY

If you have your caravan insured as an extension to your household contents policy, liability cover for the caravan may appear to be omitted from the extension but you will find caravans specifically mentioned in the liability section of the household policy.

MOTOR POLICY

Compulsory insurance under the Road Traffic Act applies to all mechanically propelled road vehicles. Cover for liability for injury to third parties while the caravan is being towed is therefore compulsory because it is part of a mechanically propelled vehicle and is covered by the car's policy – provided that the motor policy allows the towing of a caravan. (Most do this automatically, but if your motor policy does exclude towing a caravan, you must get the restriction removed; if necessary, change insurers.) Also, liability for damage to other people's property done by the caravan is covered by the car's policy while the caravan is attached to the car, provided that the motor policy is third-party or comprehensive.

page 126

Since the caravan itself is not mechanically propelled, the RTA requirements do not apply when the caravan is detached from the towing vehicle. A caravan policy does not include RTA liability (because that is covered by the car's policy while the caravan is attached).

Legal liability for accidental injury to someone or damage to their property (your third-party liability) in connection with the caravan when it is not attached to the car will be met by a caravan policy. For example, if you manually manoeuvre the caravan on site and push it into a parked car, the caravan policy operates.

If you hire out your caravan and have declared this to the insurers, the premium you pay also includes cover for claims by the hirer for injuries as a result of defects in the caravan.

page 138

■ **as owner or user of a boat**
by: *household contents policy (personal liability section)*
or by: *small craft policy*
or by: *small craft extension to household contents policy*

What is included in the personal liability section of a household contents policy varies with different policies. For example, some restrict cover to liability arising out of the use of
hand-propelled boats
or manually operated rowing boats, punts or canoes
or boats not propelled by power or sail
or rowing boats, model boats and windsurfers.

   If your policy does not cover your type of vessel, you would need a separate small craft policy with an adequate sum for liability cover. Some insurers offer a small craft extension to their household contents policies to cover sailing dinghies and motor boats, but in most cases, you need a separate policy for these.

■ **as owner of animals or rider of a horse or pony**
by: *some household contents policies (personal liability section)*
or by: *special animal insurance policy*

'where a dog causes damage by killing or injuring livestock (which is not only cattle, sheep and horses, but includes hens, geese, ducks and other poultry), any person who is a keeper of the dog is liable for the damage'
from the ANIMALS ACT 1971

Many contents policies will pay out if your domestic pets cause injury for which you can be held liable, and some extend to cover you or your family while riding a horse or pony for pleasure. Damage caused or injury done during point-to-point racing, hunting, polo is not covered and would need a special equestrian insurance policy.

   If insurance for injury caused by your dog is an optional extra to a policy, or part of a package policy, make sure that the amount for which you would be covered for any such claim is high enough (with some policies, it is £500,000; with another, only £250,000).

   Anyone who keeps wild animals on his property must comply with the requirements of the Dangerous Wild Animals Act 1976. Some insurance companies specifically exclude any animal which has to be licensed under the Act. In such cases, it may be difficult to get liability insurance, so you would need to consult a broker.

Claims

Generally a claim can arise only if someone (a third party) makes a claim against you. But if as a tenant you are liable for certain types of damage to your landlord's property and the damage that has been done is covered under your policy, the claim would be dealt with by your insurers without the landlord having to claim on you.

   Most policies set out what you have to do if a claim is made against you or a member of your family. As a general guide

Warning: you should not admit liability even if you think it was your fault, otherwise the insurers could refuse the claim.

● at the time the injury or damage occurs, do not admit any negligence or fault to the injured party or anyone else, and on no account sign anything

● you must not
– negotiate
– offer
– pay
– settle
– reject
a claim without your insurers' agreement.

For example, if you were to offer £50 to the injured neighbour in the hope that he will forget the matter, you would be in breach of your policy conditions and the insurers would be entitled to refuse to deal with the claim. (Moreover, the neighbour may use your payment to show that you had admitted liability – and then go for much more.)

● notify your insurers immediately you are aware of any incident which could give rise to a claim against you

● give your insurers full details in writing as soon as possible

● send your insurers without delay any letter, claim, writ, summons or other legal document sent to or served on you or your family

● do not dispose of the 'evidence' of what caused the injury or damage (though you should take immediate steps to prevent a recurrence).

Some insurers use a general claims advice form; most insurers have their own liability claim form.

The insurers will want to know the plain unvarnished facts, for better or worse – not opinions whether you are liable or not. By signing the declaration on the form, you give your authority for the information to be used by a solicitor in any litigation arising from the incident.

The insurers will deal with the claim direct with the injured party or his solicitor. Unless a dispute arises over the question of liability, you may not be required to give evidence, and may even never be told the outcome of the third party's claim.

When two policies are in force that cover the same incident, you must inform both insurers and each of the other. You can claim on two policies for the same incident, but they will pay only what the claim costs, up to the limit of each. For example: damages awarded are £400,000; policy A's limit is £250,000, policy B's limit is £250,000 – each pays £200,000.

In addition to the amount paid to the injured party, the insurers will meet your legal expenses incurred with their written consent, and costs awarded by the court.

If the amount of the award is more than the limit of the policy, the insurers pay up to this limit and leave you to settle the rest on your own.

✳ Holiday insurance

Anyone travelling abroad who wants insurance should have adequate cover for the circumstances and know the procedures for making a claim. Do not overlook the possible need for insurance also when holidaying in the UK.

24-hour emergency assistance

Most holiday insurance policies now include an emergency service for use by policyholders abroad. This is mainly for circumstances where there will be a claim for injury or sickness. Emergency assistance companies exist in their own right and you can subscribe to the service direct, irrespective of any insurance policy.

These emergency services aim to get you prompt and efficient attention, on the assumption that a speedier recovery will reduce your claim and avoid extortionate hospital or other fees.

transferred charge call:
téléphoner en PCV
a cuenta del destinatario
al carico del ricevente
pagavel no destino

Most of the major assistance companies operate a 24-hour service 365 days of the year. Be sure to note the appropriate telex or telephone number of the assistance service before you go on holiday and keep this in an accessible place. You can make a call reversing the charges.

The territorial coverage varies. The major organisations operate in all the main commercial and holiday centres of the world. But it is as well to check and to get a prospectus detailing the activities and extent of the assistance organisation.

Some assistance organisations are set up to deal only with serious medical and accident situations; others can offer help if, for instance, all of your money is stolen and you need further funds to be sent from home. The assistance company will lend you a suitable amount to tide you over but you will have to repay this money on your return home.

As with all insurance, you can go direct to an insurance company.

Through a tour operator

The brochures issued by most tour operators include details of the insurance cover available as an optional addition to the basic holiday price or, sometimes, as an integral part of it.

Many tour operators automatically assume that you require insurance to be included unless you specifically state otherwise on the booking form. In some booking forms, you are given a simple choice of whether you require their package insurance scheme or not and a tick against 'yes' or 'no' is all that is needed. With others, insurance is automatically included unless you write 'no' in the appropriate place.

For some tours if you do not take their insurance, you must state the name of the insurance company with whom you have arranged cover yourself. Tour operators want to avoid being left in a situation where one of their clients suffers a mishap and has no insurance provision to meet the consequent expenses.

Where a tour operator includes insurance within the holiday price, there may be no special mention of it on the booking form, but the fact that the insurance automatically exists should be made clear elsewhere in the brochure. (If you are in any doubt about whether insurance is included, ask.)

Normally, the insurance is underwritten by a company which is a member of the British Insurance Association or by underwriters at Lloyd's. The name of the insurers may not be stated in the brochure, but you can ask.

The brochure should contain a summary of the insurance cover provided by a tour operator's scheme. You may find that only a small space in the brochure has been allocated to describe the insurance cover: just the premium and the sums insured, with perhaps a reference to 'Principal Exclusions' – but other exclusions which are not specified may be equally important to you. So, ask the tour operator or the insurers themselves for a copy of the full policy if there is insufficient detail in the brochure, in case you think you need some extra insurance.

If these details are on the reverse side of the booking form, you will lose them once you complete the form and return it to the tour operator or agent. So, take a copy first or ask for another brochure to keep intact.

A policy is normally sent by the tour operator with their confirmation of the booking. This may be no more than a sheet of paper, setting out the cover provided and the exclusions in small print on the back.

Through a travel agent

Most travel agents offer to arrange holiday insurance for their clients.

Some agents deal exclusively with one insurance company.

But most travel agents are able to offer a choice of two or three schemes. The agent will have been provided with a pad of policies by the insurers and, once the premium has been paid, will issue a 'certificate of insurance' on the spot. This is also the policy and contains full details of the cover and conditions. You do not get any other document.

Through a broker or agent

Some people prefer to get an insurance broker to arrange their travel insurance, especially where a broker handles the rest of their insurances.

Some insurers issue their standard 'pad' policies to certain brokers. But any broker should be able to arrange an individual policy to suit your requirements.

Other full-time insurance agents are able to arrange holiday insurance in this way, too, with a particular company. Ask to see full details of the cover before committing yourself.

Some banks can arrange holiday insurance. Banks with an insurance division may issue their own policy; others, acting as agents, will have an arrangement with an insurance company to do so.

By other means

There are insurance slot meters at some airports which provide personal accident and death compensation. There is no restriction on the amount of cover you can take for a journey up to a limited number of hours – provided that you can afford the premium. If you buy such insurance, post the card or folder (to yourself or someone you can trust), otherwise in the event of your death, no one would know to make a claim.

At railway stations, you can buy together with your train ticket 'shilling insurance' (for 5p) which pays up to £2000 if you are killed or suffer severe bodily injury as a result of an accident while travelling in any public conveyance on the journey for which you bought the ticket.

Applying for insurance

You will not be asked to complete a proposal form if you are taking the cover offered in a tour operator's brochure, nor where a travel agent issues a pad policy.

Where there is a simple proposal form to complete, the information requested is minimal: names, addresses and possibly ages of all the people in the party, the period of the holiday and the area to be visited. Most insurers have no age limits for holiday policies. A few do not insure anyone over 75; some ask for a doctor's certificate for someone over 80.

All agents – tour operator, travel agent, insurance agent, bank, broker, motoring organisation and other intermediaries – receive commission from the insurers for placing business with them.

Claims for cancellation, medical expenses and accidents will not be met by most policies if it turns out that travel was undertaken against a doctor's advice or had been for the purpose of obtaining medical treatment abroad.

The person completing the form can include other people with whom he or she is travelling and may be required to sign a declaration 'that the persons to be insured are in good health and have no physical or mental defect or infirmity and are not receiving or awaiting medical or surgical treatment'.

On some forms, there is also a warranty that 'no insured person is travelling contrary to the advice of a medical practitioner or for the purpose of obtaining medical treatment'.

You will also be required to sign a declaration confirming that, to the best of your knowledge and belief, the information which you have provided is true and that there are no other facts affecting the proposal which should have been disclosed.

If you are taking out holiday insurance to cover, for example, a school holiday or scouts camp or OAP outing, ask the participants to let you have written details about their state of health. Photocopy any details of 'defects or infirmities' (*eg* diabetes, epilepsy, angina) and attach them to the proposal form. The wording of the declaration on the form should be amended by adding '. . . except as detailed in the attached photocopy'.

You are expected to tell the insurers of any circumstances which may affect their assessment of the risk to them of insuring you. If there is information which would affect the risk but of which are you unaware at the time of arranging the insurance, you would not be penalised – for example, the illness of a close relative which you did not know about and which later causes you to cancel your holiday.

It is important to read the policy carefully when you get it, especially where you have not seen a brochure or prospectus beforehand, so that you know what claims you can make and what is excluded.

Types of policy

For people who travel regularly, such as businessmen, there are annual travel policies where a flat premium is charged irrespective of the number and type of trips undertaken.

Insurance for holidays is nowadays either
● a package policy which includes cover for many different contingencies with fixed limits, all of which you have to take
or
● selective – you can choose how much of the different sections you want.

With some policies, you can take out additional cover for one particular section; with others, in order to improve the cover under one section, you have to buy more cover under all other sections of the policy.

PACKAGE

The 'packaging' of policies takes different forms. Some policies offer very limited cover at relatively low cost, plus a 'top-up' option to the basic cover. 'Top-up' means that you can choose to take more cover under one or more specific sections to suit your own particular requirements – for example, two units instead of one for loss of baggage.

SELECTIVE

Some insurers offer a 'selective benefits' holiday policy, where you can select and pay for specific risks only – for example, medical expenses and loss of money. This type of policy is generally more expensive than a package type. You will probably find that you are paying as much to insure for just, say, cancellation under this type of policy as you would for all sections on a package policy. But when you have to claim, payments may be for higher amounts than with the package policy.

Do not pay for the same cover twice: under most sections, you will not be paid twice. You may already have adequate cover for your personal belongings under the all-risks section of your household contents policy or for medical expenses under a medical bills insurance scheme, in which case a package holiday policy may be inappropriate.

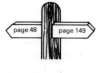

page 48   page 149

The cover

The cover you can expect to find in a holiday policy includes the following

For cancellation

This cover comes into operation as soon as the premium has been paid. Either a maximum sum insured will be specified or the cover will be for 'irrecoverable holiday costs' – which means any amounts you have already paid, or have contracted to pay, for the booked holiday and which are not refunded to you (up to a specified maximum of between £1000 and £3500, depending on the policy).

You will have to satisfy the insurers that the reason for cancelling is necessary and unavoidable – not merely that you now do not feel like going on that holiday or cannot afford it or are too busy to go.

The causes for cancellation that are normally covered are

● injury to, illness or death of yourself, husband/wife or other relative, your travelling companion, a close business associate.

If you are an unmarried orphan brought up by an aunt, her death would not normally count for cancellation.

Relatives may be specified as children, siblings, parents and (sometimes) in-laws.

Some policies cover all relatives, but most specify them so that the position is quite clear. Fiancé(e) may be included in some policies, not others.

Check whether there is an age limit or other restriction which would apply – for example, a parent over the age of 75.

'Close business associate' is not defined and, in the case of a claim, you would have to show that there would be a loss of business if both you and the business associate were absent at the same time. Cancelling because of a sudden business crisis or excessive workload would not be an allowable reason for claiming, nor would a travelling companion cancelling for business reasons. But if your companion cancelled due to the death or illness of a close relative, you could yourself claim for cancelling.

If you should die after taking out the insurance, your estate can claim for holiday costs which had been incurred and were not recoverable.

- being called for jury service, or as a witness in a court of law
- being made redundant (only with some policies – and not just being thrown out of a job for other reasons)
- becoming pregnant after the policy had been taken out

If you know you are pregnant at the time of booking, you will probably not be able to claim if you have to cancel due to your pregnancy. If you become pregnant after you have booked but before the start of the holiday, some insurers pay out if you cancel for this reason; some do not.

- being put in quarantine
- a fire or burglary at your own home, if you can show that because of it you have to be at home.
- tour operator's failure

A few policies allow as a cause for cancellation of a holiday, the failure of the tour operator, provided the company is a member of ABTA (Association of British Travel Agents), or a licensed coach operator or transport line.

So, if the firm you booked with goes bankrupt or into liquidation, the insurance will pay you up to a maximum of £1000 (or, with another policy, up to £3000) of the deposit or charges paid for the tour if this is cancelled before you go, and half that amount if you have set out and it is the return journey that is cancelled.

ABTA
55–57 Newman Street
London W1P 4AH

For curtailment

Valid reasons for claiming when you have to cut short your holiday are broadly the same as for cancellation, and in addition are likely to include

- having to return home because a relative (defined in the policy) in the UK has been taken seriously ill or has received a severe injury or has died.

This section will cover items such as additional travel costs: for example, travelling home early by scheduled flight rather than on the booked charter flight.

For personal accident

A specified lump sum will be paid if as a result of an accident you should die, or lose a limb or an eye, or suffer permanent total disablement.

'Loss of limb' may be limited to actual physical severance of an arm or a leg but some policies include in this definition the loss of use of the limb. Similarly, 'loss of an eye' may mean not only actual physical loss of the eye itself but also loss of sight.

'Permanent total disablement' means that you are injured so severely that twelve months after the accident you still cannot return to work in any form and there is no reasonable prospect of your condition improving. With some policies, the wording is more generous in that you can claim if you cannot return to an occupation for which you are suited by knowledge and training.

With some policies, the lump sum can be as low as £5000; some pay £15,000, and some as much as £25,000. If the person is under 16 years of age, the lump sum payment is generally limited to £500 or £1000; some insurers halve the lump sum for people over 70.

Some insurers (but not with most package policies) provide a weekly payment for temporary total disablement for up to 2 years; others for temporary partial disablement. A weekly payment for temporary total disablement may vary from £10 to £50 per week; for temporary partial disablement, it is generally 40% or 50% of the payment for temporary total disablement.

A weekly payment is normally made only to someone who is gainfully employed. This includes self-employed people, but not students, housewives, pensioners or children.

For loss of baggage

There is a limit on the total sum you can claim for loss or damage to your luggage and its contents, and also a limit to the amount that will be paid for any one single item. If the total value of the belongings you are taking with you is more than the sum provided for by the policy, ask the insurers for additional cover.

The single item limit varies from one policy to another and is likely to be between £150 and £250. Some policies may not pay anything at all on a claim for an item whose value is greater than that figure, most restrict payment to that amount. If you intend to take with you any items whose value is more than that, make sure that they are covered by an all-risks extension to your household contents policy. If they are not already specified there, add them. But remember that cover abroad under household contents insurance for all-risks is generally restricted to a set number of days (30 or 60) unless you ask to increase it.

In the event of a claim, some policies pay on a replacement-as-new basis for articles less than 2 years old; others on an 'intrinsic value' or indemnity basis (generally, current cost less an amount for wear and tear).

If luggage is lost in transit or delayed, your policy may pay for essentials which you had to buy, up to a certain amount – say, £50 or £100. This amount is deducted from any claim which you may subsequently make if the luggage proves to be permanently lost.

For loss of money

Some policies treat money as part of baggage but on other policies it is dealt with separately.

Most policies define what they include as 'money' – for example, passport, coupons and vouchers, tickets, green card. Keep a record of the numbers of travellers cheques, passport and the like in a different place from the actual documents. There is usually a limit on the amount of money that will be refunded, varying from perhaps £150 up to, say, £300.

There is an excess in most policies (£10 or £20) to prevent people making claims for small sums lost.

Personal liability

Some policies do not pay for damages awarded in courts outside the UK.

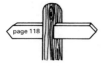

Your liability at law as a private individual is covered. The policy will meet claims for damages against you in respect of any accident for which you are responsible which resulted in bodily injury to, or loss or damage to the property of, anybody (except members of your own family). Legal costs are paid if they are incurred with the written consent of the insurers.

Liability arising from the use, ownership or control of a motor vehicle or boat is excluded. Separate arrangements must be made for liability insurance where a car or motor bike is to be driven abroad.

Compensation for delayed departure

Where there is delay due to no fault of the passenger, a 'delay benefit' payment (up to a specified limit per day, usually £60 or £100 in all) is generally available. With some insurers, this is an optional extension.

Most policies provide this cover for both the outward and the return journey – but check this. The cover does not usually operate until the delay exceeds 12 hours. It is for delays caused by
* strike or industrial action
* mechanical breakdown of an aircraft or vessel; a train with some policies (but not a coach or car)
* adverse weather.

Delay cover is not included as part of every 'pad' policy, but is available as an optional extension from a travel agent or broker. Many tour operators include delay cover automatically, costing it in under their 'airport charges'. If you paid twice, you can claim on both.

After a specified period of delay (normally 12 hours), you have the alternative option to cancel your holiday entirely and claim for the sums you have paid which are not recoverable (as under the 'cancellation' section).

delayed en route
With some policies, you can claim an amount (varying from £50 to £300) if you miss your flight or boat because failure of public transport (not private car) prevented you from getting to the port.

hijacking
Some policies pay (£100 per 24-hour period) if you are prevented from reaching your planned destination because the aircraft is hijacked, and will also reimburse reasonable expenses (unspecified) that you incur as a result of the hijacking.

staying on
Most policies remain in force beyond the normal expiry time if you are prevented from returning home by transport delay, illness or any other events beyond your control. With some, extension is automatic for one week, with others for up to a month.

For medical expenses

Dental treatment may be excluded unless it becomes necessary as the result of an accident.

One of the reasons why some people take out insurance for their holiday is the possibility of incurring large medical bills for illness or an accident while in a foreign country. Hospital treatment is particularly expensive in the USA and Canada; with some policies, you pay more if that is where you are going.

Some policies do not cover claims arising from a pre-existing medical condition, particularly for elderly people. 'Pre-existing' may refer to a period of six months or longer. But by no means all policies exclude pre-existing conditions, so you can shop around.

The cover includes not only the cost of medical treatment, hospital and nursing charges, but also any additional travel and/or accommodation expenses because of your illness. And most policies also cover the cost of the additional travel and hotel expenses of one member of your party who is needed on medical grounds to stay with you and escort you home. However, the additional travelling costs of a relative to come to you in these circumstances is generally not covered.

when in hospital
If you have to go into hospital, provided that your complaint is not one excluded by the policy, some policies pay a set sum per day (perhaps £10 for up to 20 or 30 days maximum), irrespective of, and additional to, other hospital charges incurred. Normally, insurers who provide this cover do not include any weekly disablement benefit under the personal accident section of the policy.

getting home
Where someone is seriously ill or severely injured, it may be considered best to get that person back to this country for treatment. The necessary expenses of such repatriation are normally included under the medical expenses section of a policy. As such costs can run into thousands of pounds, the sum insured for medical expenses should be adequate to cover such a situation.

on death

In the event of the death of an insured person, the cost of transporting the body or ashes back to the UK will be paid for. If the deceased person is buried abroad, the funeral expenses in that country are covered, but some insurers specify a limit.

Alternative arrangements

In EEC countries and some others, you are entitled to urgent medical treatment free or partly subsidised by the health or welfare scheme of that country.

An E111 issued after 1 September 1984 is valid for two years.

In order to take advantage of this reciprocal arrangement, you have to obtain a document known as 'form E111' from your local DHSS office before leaving the UK. This should be applied for at least a month in advance; you may be able to get one straightaway if you go in person to the office, with all the details required for the application.

Leaflet SA30, issued by the DHSS, contains the application form (CM1) for an E111. It also provides details about medical treatment you get free or have to pay for in the countries of Europe, what you need to know before you go and the documents needed to get concessionary medical treatment in each of the countries.

Repatriation costs, or the cost of somebody to stay on with you, are not covered.

If you are unable to get an E111 before you go abroad and you need medical treatment while you are away, you can apply through the local health insurance authorities in the country you are visiting, but this may be a complicated or protracted procedure.

What is not paid

Under most sections of a holiday policy, you have to pay for part of each claim. The amount of this excess varies from section to section and differs from one policy to another, and not all impose an excess on the same sections.

For example	EXCESS
loss of deposit only	nil to £10
cancellation	£5 to £20
medical expenses	£10 to £25
baggage	£10 to £20
money	£10 to £20

It is not possible to delete an excess by paying an extra premium.

There is no excess on the personal liability or personal accident sections nor, with most insurers, on payments for delayed departure.

Standard exclusions

No policy provides cover for the effects of war 'and kindred risks', not always specified – it may be any consequence of war, whether war be declared or not, civil war, rebellion, revolution, insurrection, military or usurped power. (But a Lloyd's policy may include these risks – except within the UK.) If you decide to cancel your holiday on the grounds that hostilities have broken out in or near the country you are travelling to, the costs of cancellation for that reason will not be met by your insurance.

Specific exceptions apply to individual sections of the policy. Many of these exceptions are common to all policies; some vary from one insurer to another. If the policy excludes a risk for which you specifically want cover the insurers may be prepared to extend the policy to meet your fears, for an extra premium.

Insurance brokers and travel agents who are selling package policies are not normally authorised to amend them in any way and if you make a particular request, they will have to refer it to the insurers for individual attention. Some insurers will not alter their package policy in any circumstances; others may consider a request on its merits.

Below is a brief summary of exclusions you may expect to find in different sections:

Cancellation, curtailment, personal accident, medical expenses
– own suicide, intentional self-injury
– pregnancy known about at the time the policy was taken out
– the effect of alcohol or drugs
– insanity
– air travel other than as a fare-paying passenger on a regular scheduled airline or licensed charter aircraft
– winter sports
– racing
– hazardous pursuits (as itemised by the insurers; may even include motor cycling)

Loss of baggage
– wear and tear
– damage by moths or vermin
– mechanical breakdown or derangement (which means malfunctioning or not working properly, perhaps a wrist watch being overwound)
– brittle or fragile articles (such as glass, china, ornaments, objets d'art)
– money (in policies where it is a separate section)

– confiscation by customs or other officials or authorities
– property otherwise insured

Loss of money
– any shortages due to error or omission (for example, changing money at a worse rate than is available elsewhere or being short-changed by a local trader)

Personal liability
– ownership or use of any aircraft, vessel, mechanically propelled vehicle (any means of transportation driven by mechanical power could be construed as coming within this wording)
– acts of an animal owned by you or under your control
– activities carried out under any contractual agreement or in connection with your business

Delay
– any circumstances that could have been anticipated at the time of taking out the policy

winter sports
Many holiday policies can be extended to include cover for winter sports at a multiple of the premium – usually 2 or 2½ or even 3 times the normal premium.

Winter sports tour operators usually have their own package schemes (with some, compulsory when you book the holiday).

The maximum amount payable under the medical expenses section may be reduced and you may find that no weekly benefit is payable under the personal accident section. Even when you have paid an additional premium, there will still be an exclusion relating to such activities as ski-racing, ski-jumping, ice-hockey and the use of bob-sleighs. You will have to make a special approach to your insurers if you wish to have cover for these particular risks.

Some of the definitions are different from ordinary policies. For example, the money section may include loss of ski-lift passes.

Some tour operators' policies have special extras, such as lack-of-snow compensation (payment of, say, £15 a day or free transport to a nearby resort with snow); or for an accident preventing you from skiing (a specified sum for each day you cannot ski).

How much, for how long, where

Look around at the choice of holiday policies each year: you may be able to get better cover or higher amounts from a different policy to the one you had last year.

Insurance companies generally change the terms of their contracts once a year. If you take out insurance shortly before such a change takes place, you may benefit by a pre-increase premium but, on the other hand, your cover may not be quite so good.

With a package policy, the length of time for which you want insurance and the countries to be visited determine the premium.

Some insurers offer reduced premium rates for children, and others even provide cover free of charge for very young children (such as up to 2 years old). Generally, the term 'children' means anyone under sixteen at the time of taking out the insurance; with others, this age may be twelve or fourteen.

where
Normally, the three basic territorial rating areas in order of cost are
  I United Kingdom
 II Europe
III World-wide (highest premium).

There are differences between insurers in the territories encompassed by their rating areas. For instance, Jordan and Iceland and the Canary Islands may be included in 'Europe' with one company, 'world-wide' by another.

The Channel Islands and the Republic of Ireland may fall into rating area (I) or (II). The world-wide rated area may be sub-divided between USA/Canada and the rest of the world. And different sections may have different territorial categories – for

example, world-wide may include Europe and the USA under one section (for instance, loss of money) but separate them under another (for instance, personal liability).

how long

Premiums vary according to the period of insurance. But the term 'two weeks' may mean 14, 15, 16 or 17 days, according to the insurers. It is worth checking what time-spans each policy offers: the minimum may be 3 or 4 or 5 days, then up to 8 or 9 days or up to 17 days.

One company may charge one premium for trips up to, say, 7 days and if you are going on an 8-day trip, you will fall into the next premium category. With another company, eight days may come at the top end of the lowest premium scale.

Make sure you count in the first and last day: saturday to saturday is eight days, not seven; 2nd to 10th November needs nine days' cover.

If you find that your holiday is one or two days longer than one insurance period – for instance, you are not coming back until the 9th day and the insurers' period ends on the 7th day – it might be unwise to stint by not paying up to be covered for the extra period.

But the insurance cover stops on completion of the direct journey home. Even if a 17-day premium was paid and the actual trip was for only 15 days, no claims would be met for any incident that happened once you are back home on the 16th or 17th day.

One company offers a per diem rating for holidays between 4 and 17 days: you pay a set premium for each day of cover (for longer than 17 days, the premium is on a weekly basis).

Most policies provide that if, as a result of circumstances beyond your control, your holiday is extended for longer than the period of insurance, the cover continues until the completion of the return journey or for a set number of days (from 7 to 31, depending on the policy).

Making a claim

Except for serious incidents, you are not expected to report a claim to the insurers while you are still away on holiday but should do so in writing as soon as practicable on your return. Where companies do not stipulate a specific time limit in which you have to claim, they state that you should do so as soon as reasonably possible.

The policy document normally gives some guidelines regarding the action to take; some have a tear-off coupon for claim notification.

You may be instructed to contact the insurance company direct or a named firm of loss adjusters or brokers. You will be sent a claim form and an acknowledgement quoting a claim number. Always quote this number in further correspondence, and also, if you can, the original policy or certificate number.

The claim form may be a composite one or specific to the type of claim you are making.

You will be told what documents you must submit in support of your claim. Return the completed form, with the required documents, quoting the reference numbers, as soon as possible.

The insurers may have an arrangement for an independent loss adjuster to handle the claim, negotiate and pay out on their behalf. He will contact you direct and may want to arrange a meeting to discuss the circumstances of the claim in further detail. Where the settlement is likely to be not straightforward, he will report back to the insurers in due course with his recommendation about whether they should meet the claim.

If you have two policies which cover the same claim – for example, a claim for a lost camera under holiday baggage and household contents all-risks – you should inform both insurers. One of the insurers will settle the loss direct with you and they then sort the matter out between themselves. You will not be indemnified twice for the same loss. But for a personal accident claim, you may get payment from the two policies.

Action required

Keep all bills and receipts. If you produce medical bills or police reports in a foreign language, the insurers will make arrangements for translation. But where there is some doubt about the authenticity of any document, the insurers may make further enquiries of their own.

For cancellation

Obtain documentary evidence of your reason for cancelling (such as a doctor's certificate). The closer your cancellation date to the date when the holiday was due to start, the higher will be the cancellation penalty charged by the tour operator. Send the form notifying you of the amount due (the cancellation invoice from the tour operator) to your insurers with your claim form.

For delay in departure (on outward or return journey)

'Fog' and the amended airline ticket may be enough if it is just a day's delay.

You have to give the reason for the delay and get written confirmation from the carrier (airline or shipping company) of the delay and its duration. You may have to wait to get confirmation from the carrier until you are home again rather than in the midst of chaos at the port or airport. What you get from the insurance is a fixed sum depending on the number of hours' delay, not related to any expenses you may have incurred.

For medical expenses

Where there is the likelihood of major expenses – such as hospital charges or repatriation costs – keep in touch with the insurers (or the emergency service) and if in doubt about any expenses, ask if they will authorise them.

With your claim form, send all receipts, invoices or bills from the hospital, medical attendant(s), ambulance, taxi, pharmacist, hotel. (Send the original documents if possible, and keep a copy yourself.) The insurers may want your permission to contact your own doctor.

For consequences of accident

Describe the circumstances of the accident and extent of the injury on the claim form as fully as possible and send in a doctor's report.

If as a result of an injury on holiday, you are off work for a lengthy period, the insurers are likely to arrange for you to be medically examined from time to time in order to check that your claim is genuine and to assess what progress you are making and whether payment for total disablement is due to you. The costs of such examinations are met by the insurers.

For curtailment

Provide documentary evidence (such as medical note, death certificate) to show that curtailment was necessary, and how much extra you had to pay to get home.

For loss of baggage and loss of money

It may be a policy condition that if your belongings have been stolen or lost, you must inform the police within 24 hours. Some companies insist that you report to the police anything you have lost; others require this for theft only. Insurers do not necessarily ask you to produce a police report, but if you can get one, that will save time when you claim.

In certain countries, you may find that the police are less than co-operative when you try to obtain a report from them. If all attempts fail, get the travel operator's representative or, failing that, the proprietor of the hotel at which you are staying, to confirm (in writing) details of the circumstances of the loss and that you reported it to the police.

If property is lost or damaged while in the custody of a carrier such as an airline, ask the airline company for a 'property irregularity report' as soon as you discover the loss or damage; send this to your insurers with your claim. (It is a standard form which the airline has to complete if loss or damage of property occurs during the course of transit while in the custody of the carrier.) The form will provide some detail of the nature of the damage and of the articles which have been lost or stolen.

You have to give a full description of the circumstances of the loss. It is a policy condition that you take reasonable care of your property so your claim may not be met if you left a valuable article unguarded on the beach while going into the water for a swim, for example.

You are required to send, where possible, receipts or valuations for items which have been lost or stolen.

for lost money

Insurers scrutinise claims for loss of money very closely and check up on the circumstances of the loss.

The loss has to be reported to the local police within 24 hours and a certified copy of the report or similar confirmation obtained from them.

Personal liability (for damage or injury done to another)

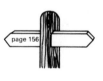

Notify your insurers as soon as the possibility of a claim arises (it is a condition of the policy to do this). The insurers will handle the whole matter on your behalf, so send all relevant correspondence to them unanswered, and without delay.

Do not make any payments yourself to anyone involved and do not admit any liability (this also is a policy condition). But it is all right to give your own or your insurers' name and address.

Give details of any witnesses. The insurers may wish to interview some or all of the people involved in the incident as soon as possible in order to obtain statements while memories of what happened are still fresh in the mind.

Some holiday policies specifically state that they will not meet claims where you have another policy covering personal liability (*eg* in a household contents policy). But a holiday policy may pay the part of any damages that come to more than the amount payable under the other policy.

After a claim

A claim will not be settled until all necessary documents have been submitted. There may be delays where these have to be obtained from abroad or where additional enquiries need to be made. If you feel that it is all taking too long, check with the person handling your claim, remembering to quote reference numbers.

When you make a claim, the onus is on you to prove your loss. If the insurers turn down your claim, they must clearly explain why and should refer to the precise wording in the policy which supports their statement.

Ill health and accident insurance

Not many people could cope with losing their main income by having to be off work through serious illness, injury or disability for more than a few months. What is euphemistically called 'health insurance' can provide some income in such a situation.

The sums (monthly payments, lump sum) for which you insure are not related to what the accident or sickness costs you: the amount has to be decided by you before it all happens.

What being ill may cost

To assess how vulnerable you would be if a sudden accident or illness prevented you from earning, ask yourself
* how much income would I lose each week if I were injured or fell ill tomorrow?
* what sort of extra expenses would I have to meet?
* how much money would I save as a result of being confined to the house every day?
* how much would I get from my employer, and for how long?
* will I receive any income from the state? and for how long?

statutory payments

Rates from April 1984
(subject to annual review)

STATUTORY SICK PAY (SSP)
from employer for up to 8 weeks; based on salary bands; minimum £28.55 pw, maximum £42.25 pw; taxable
DHSS leaflets NI 244, 208 and 16

Rates from November 1983
(subject to annual review)

SICKNESS BENEFIT
if self-employed or non-employed or after 8 weeks of SSP; subject to minimum NI contributions; £25.95 pw plus increase for dependants; for up to 28 weeks; not taxable
DHSS leaflet NI 16

INVALIDITY BENEFIT
after 28 weeks of sickness benefit; subject to minimum number of NI contributions; minimum £34.90 pw, maximum £39.75, depending on age, plus increase for dependants; paid up to pensionable age; not taxable
DHSS leaflet NI 16A

NON-CONTRIBUTORY INVALIDITY PENSION
after 28 weeks off work if not qualifying for sickness benefit; £20.45 pw plus increase for dependants; paid up to pensionable age; not taxable
DHSS leaflets NI 210 (214 for married women)

You may be due an income tax rebate when your employer stops paying you.

If you are an employee, your firm may continue to pay you your basic salary for some weeks or months while you are ill. Check what would happen in your case.

If you are self-employed, you may lose income immediately, and the impact of a continuing disability could be serious. The problem is two-fold: the need to maintain your own income and the need to pay someone else to do your job.

If you are ill in hospital, there may be extra transport costs: greater use of car, someone else driving, taxis, buses to visit hospital, and for any journey where you would be unable to walk after a serious disability. But you will save the cost of travelling to and from work.

If you are being looked after at home, you may need to pay for nursing attention. You may also have to pay for extra domestic help.

What insurance

If you decide you want to have insurance for when you are not able to work, there are various types of policy you can take out:

personal accident:
weekly payment for a limited period and/or lump sum
personal accident and sickness:
weekly payment for a limited period and/or lump sum
permanent health:
weekly payment until retirement age or death.
   (Permanent health insurance is usually dealt with by life insurance companies; personal accident and sickness insurance usually by the accident department of a general insurance company.)
   They are not mutually exclusive: theoretically, you can have as many of them as you like, and also the slightly different 'insurance' of
medical expenses:
reimbursement for private treatment
cash while in hospital:
set sum per day, up to a set limit.

page 149   page 153

   For most types, you have to give detailed information about yourself on a proposal form, particularly about your past and present state of health and (for accident insurance) your occupation. These may affect what you can be insured for and how much you have to pay for it.

Medical information

All proposal forms ask for your age, height, weight, previous illnesses and accidents. They also ask whether you have been turned down, or had special terms imposed, for any health insurance.

You are expected to reveal all the relevant details about your health.

You must tell the insurers about past illnesses and accidents which are in any way likely to cause problems in the future. Otherwise, if you should have a claim due to, or aggravated by, any illness or accident which you were aware of but failed to tell the insurers about, they may not pay.

You can ignore ordinary coughs and colds and childhood diseases such as chickenpox or measles, but you must mention diseases such as rheumatic fever or tuberculosis which can result in permanent changes in the body, and any operations you have had.

If you have had a serious accident or illness in the last few years, you are expected to give full details (if this needs more space than the limited area allocated on the proposal form, add a separate sheet of paper). It may indicate an increased likelihood of having a recurrence or may mean that when you have an accident, your recovery will take longer than expected, and so your claim will cost the insurers more.

If you have any disorder which is controlled by drugs – for example, angina, asthma, high blood pressure, depression – you must tell the insurers, even if the drugs result in your being able to lead a perfectly normal life, and the condition has never caused you to be off work.

You must also mention accidents resulting in a 'slipped disc', cartilage trouble or broken limbs where the body may not have fully recovered, or some weakness may persist.

If you have been feeling generally unwell recently and have consulted your doctor but have not been given a firm diagnosis, this should be mentioned.

You may be asked specifically if you have had any of the following conditions (condition is a medical euphemism for something being physically abnormal):
heart conditions
mental conditions
respiratory conditions
digestive conditions.

These questions are designed to find out if you have had any health problems which are likely to recur and cause you to claim more frequently than a healthy person.

If you have consulted a doctor or had any absence from work in the last five years (or other length of time specified on the proposal form), you will be expected to give some details of each event. The answer will be taken as a guide to how much of a 'risk' you will be in the future. The insurers need your agreement to their writing to ask your GP to give them information about you.

more details

If the insurers need more detailed information about a medical condition revealed on the proposal form (or even after the policy is in force), this may be done by

● special questionnaire

A printed form (which you can return to the insurers in a sealed envelope if you prefer) is used to obtain extra information from you about diseases such as asthma, diabetes, epilepsy.

The insurers may decide without any further evidence what terms to impose. If the answers are ambiguous, or reveal that yours is a severe case, you will be asked to authorise a doctor's report.

● doctor's report

You have to authorise the insurers to approach your own doctor, or any specialist who has treated you, to obtain a professional assessment of how ill you are. These reports are known as 'private medical attendants' reports (PMA).

You may or may not have to pay the fee for this; the report is sent direct to the insurers' chief medical officer.

● physical examination

Where the GP's report does not give enough detailed information, you may be asked to attend for a physical examination. This does not necessarily mean that you are seriously ill.

Medical examinations are automatic for many permanent health insurances, particularly if you are over 40 or want to insure for high weekly payments. Paying the fee for a medical report or examination does not commit the insurers to accepting your proposal.

Height and weight

You will be asked how tall you are and how much you weigh.

If the ratio of your height to your weight is significantly out of line, the insurers will want to check on your general state of health and may impose a higher premium.

Although some women's magazines, and medical dictionaries, quote an ideal weight for height, nobody should expect to meet the magic combination exactly. A guide to ideal weight comes from american insurance companies who pooled their data on about 5 million of their customers.

An insurance company will not be concerned unless your weight is at least 20% to 25% above or below the ideal combination. For example, if a 6-foot tall man should ideally weigh 11 st 6 lb (73 kg), insurers would not be greatly concerned unless he weighed more than 14 stone (about 90 kg).

Being underweight is rarely a problem unless there is a significant loss of weight – which may be associated with some condition such as cancer or anorexia nervosa. There is usually a question on the form about recent change in weight.

HEIGHT/WEIGHT RATIOS   *metric version*

men

weight without clothes	height without shoes (ft in)	ideal weight (st lb)	height without shoes (cm)	ideal weight (kg)
	5 1	8 5	155	53
	5 2	8 8	157	54
	5 3	8 11	160	56
	5 4	9 0	162	57
	5 5	9 4	165	59
	5 6	9 8	167	61
	5 7	9 12	170	63
	5 8	10 2	172	64
	5 9	10 6	175	66
	5 10	10 11	177	68
	5 11	11 1	180	70
	6 0	11 6	183	73
	6 1	11 10	186	74
	6 2	12 1	188	77
	6 3	12 6	191	79

HEIGHT/WEIGHT RATIOS   *metric version*

women

weight without clothes	height without shoes (ft in)	ideal weight (st lb)	height without shoes (cm)	ideal weight (kg)
	4 8	6 13	142	44
	4 9	7 1	145	45
	4 10	7 4	147	46
	4 11	7 7	150	48
	5 0	7 10	152	49
	5 1	7 13	155	50
	5 2	8 3	157	52
	5 3	8 6	160	54
	5 4	8 11	162	56
	5 5	9 1	165	58
	5 6	9 5	167	60
	5 7	9 9	170	62
	5 8	9 13	172	63
	5 9	10 3	175	65
	5 10	10 7	177	67

Age limits

You can normally take out this type of insurance only if you are within a specified age group. With most insurers, this is between the ages of 16 and 55 or 60. The lower age limit is set to coincide with school-leaving age when people can start full-time paid work.

Although most insurance companies will not take on someone who is over their age limit (say, 60), most continue to offer renewal to existing policyholders for as long as they remain in reasonable health. Permanent health insurance and sickness insurance comes to an end when you retire.

Occupation

Certain occupations are seen by insurers as poor risks for health insurance because of the greater likelihood of accident or illness resulting from the work, or because of the longer time needed before being fit enough to resume that job.

For some occupations, such as airline pilot or jockey, for which ordinary standard policies are not available, there are special schemes about which a broker should know.

Insurance companies classify jobs according to their hazards. These classes relate more to the risk of having an accident than to the risk of illness because relatively few jobs result directly in illness.

For personal accident insurance, separate rates are charged for each class. For other types of health insurance, a slight increase in premium may be required for people in occupations classified as more hazardous.

Some insurers have generalised groupings, such as

class 1 administrative, clerical, executive, retailing
class 2 supervisory
class 3 light manual
class 4 use of light machinery
class 5 use of heavy machinery

Alternatively, occupations which are generally acceptable to the insurers may be specified in classes, such as

class 1

accountant
architect
auctioneer
beautician
clergyman
estate agent
dentist
doctor
pharmacist
social worker
solicitor
teacher
typist

class 2

baker
cafe owner
chauffeur
cook
florist
furrier
greengrocer
ironmonger
nurse
shop staff
tobacconist
veterinary surgeon

class 3

ambulance driver
boat builder
bricklayer
bus driver
butcher
driving instructor
dry cleaner
electrician
farmer
gardener
glazier
motor mechanic
plumber
shopfitter
taxi driver

class 4

abbattoir worker
blacksmith
boilermaker
coal merchant
dustman
fireman
foundry worker
furniture remover
security guard

Some insurers publish a very detailed list of many more jobs, going up to eight categories.

Your occupation is a key factor in determining how much the cover will cost you. On the proposal form, you must give a clear description of precisely what you do. Not even 'accountant' is self-explanatory – it could be turf or chartered; 'company director'

or 'supervisor' also needs more detail. Some proposal forms ask what industry you work in, whether you are employed or self-employed, whether you use machinery in your job; others expect you to tell them.

If your occupation is not listed in the categories on the proposal form, ask. Most companies have a more detailed list, in addition to their standard published list of job categories, and will refer to this if your job does not fall obviously into a particular class.

When you will be paid and for what

The insurance will pay if you are too disabled to continue working, either temporarily or ever.

Total disablement

The most restrictive policy wording says that you must be *permanently disabled from gainful employment of any and every kind*. This means that if you can do any job at all after your accident or illness, nothing will be paid.

Slightly wider is *permanently disabled from usual occupation or any other occupation for which the insured person is fitted by knowledge and training*. If you are a heavy goods vehicle driver who can no longer drive a heavy lorry after an accident, you would not be paid if you could still drive a much smaller vehicle. But you would be paid if you could not drive any vehicle but could get an unskilled job in, say, a factory.

The best policy wording says *permanent disablement from the insured person's usual occupation*. So, if you are permanently unable to do your current job, you will be paid regardless of whether you can take alternative paid employment.

The insurers do not want the total you receive in weekly benefits to be more than your normal income. If you were to buy a number of such policies which together provide you with £500 per week when your normal gross pay is only £250 per week, there might be a temptation to stay off work for longer than necessary. Therefore, a proposal form asks if you have any other personal accident or sickness policies, and would limit the total benefit from all of the policies you have taken out. (Policies providing only lump sum payments can, however, be bought from as many companies as you wish – provided that you can afford to pay the premiums.)

partial disablement

You can choose a policy which also provides a weekly payment (at a lower level) if you can return to work part-time, or do part of your job only.

Exclusions

Generally, the insurance will not pay if the injury or disablement is wholly or in part due to, or recovery is delayed as a result of, any of the following

* self-inflicted injury
* wilful exposure to needless peril
* insanity (which, however, is not defined)
* alcoholism/intoxication
* drugs, unless taken under the direction of a qualified medical practitioner
* pregnancy or childbirth
* pre-existing health defects which have not been declared to the insurers
* any criminal act on your part (except a Road Traffic Act offence)
* flying other than as a fare-paying passenger on a scheduled or charter flight
* suicide or attempted suicide
* war, invasion, act of foreign enemy, hostilities (whether war be declared or not), civil war, rebellion, revolution, insurrection, military or usurped power. So, if you travel to an area where fighting is in progress or likely (the Middle East, for example) and you want insurance that covers for any injuries from bullets or bomb damage, you will have to tell the insurers exactly where you are going, and for how long. An extra premium will probably be charged.

Most of these exclusions cannot normally be removed. But there are a number of exclusions, mostly relating to sports and hazardous leisure activities, which can be removed to give you full cover if you pay a higher premium or accept a deferment period for claims arising out of the activity.

Deferment period or franchise

A deferment period means that for the first few weeks when you are unable to work, the insurance will not pay you anything.

For instance, if the deferment period is two weeks, you will be paid only from the 15th day of disablement. If you go back to work after 13 days off, you will receive nothing. If you go back to work after three weeks off, you will receive one week's-worth of benefit.

A franchise, like a deferment period, cuts out claims for very short periods of disablement. Unlike a deferment period, however, if the length of time off work is longer than the franchise period, you will be paid for every day off work.

A typical franchise wording would say *The company shall not be liable for any period of disablement which does not exceed 7 days.*

Comparing a seven-day deferment period and a seven-day franchise: three days off work would result in no payment under either wording, fourteen days off work would result in a payment for seven days under a deferment period wording but the full fourteen days under a franchise wording.

longer deferment

Apart from any deferment period stipulated in the policy, you can choose to have a longer period, which will reduce your premium. Ask the insurers to issue the policy with a deferment period that coincides with the time at which your employer would cease to pay you when you are off work.

The insurers may insist on a longer than usual deferment period because of your occupation or hazardous activities. There would then not be any reduction in premium.

Waiting period

A waiting period or qualifying period is equivalent to a policy not being in force. A policy, for example, may not pay a benefit for any illness which occurs within three weeks of the policy being issued; another may not pay claims arising from existing health defects until after the policy has been in force for two years.

Once the waiting period is over, every claim is subject to the appropriate deferment period or franchise.

Not all insurers spell out how much cheaper it would be if you accepted a longer deferment period.

Permanent health insurance

Some insurers call this, more realistically, 'disability' insurance.

The permanent element is the insurance, not your health: a 'permanent health' (PHI) policy cannot be cancelled by the insurers and is the only type of insurance that provides long-term income for sickness or injury.

Once the policy has been issued, the insurers cannot refuse to renew the policy even if your health has become poor and you have claimed. Similarly, the premium cannot be increased on these grounds.

PHI cover

A permanent health insurance policy will pay you an income while you are disabled following an accident or illness, if necessary until you reach normal retirement age. If you are severely injured, or contract some incapacitating disease at the age of 25 and you can never work again, the policy will pay you a monthly income until you reach the age of 65 if a man, 60 if a woman.

All policies have a deferment period: 4 or 13 or 26 week periods are typical. The longer the period, the lower is the premium.

What you will be paid

The policy pays out if you are 'totally unable to follow your usual occupation as stated in the schedule'.

If you go back to any kind of work other than full-time to your pre-illness one, you will get either rehabilitation or proportionate benefit to fill the gap between your previous earnings and what you can get now. The difference is that 'rehabilitation' benefit is paid for a limited period (of six months or 12 months), 'proportionate' benefit will be paid, if necessary, until retirement age.

Rehabilitation is meant to encourage you to return to your old job (although still entitled to benefit) on a part-time basis. What you will get is the difference between what you earn now part-time and the average of what you were earning full-time during the year before you became ill.

Increase in benefit

Because it may be a long time before you want to make a claim, and when you do, the payment may go on for a long time, make sure that your policy offers some inflation protection both before a claim and by increasing the amount paid to you during the period of the claim.

Look for this in the brochure or prospectus as: *guaranteed benefit increase, optional increasing policy, index-linked policy, claims escalator, increasing cover policy, escalation of benefit, increasing benefit option.*

Most insurers offer some kind of automatic increase in payments you will get. For this, you pay at a higher-than-normal rate, or the premium is increased each year.

A few policies allow you at a later date to increase the amounts that will become payable, provided you pay the appropriate additional premium.

The increases may be by fixed percentages either each year or every so-many years. With some insurers, the percentage increase is compound; with others, the simple percentage increase is higher every 5 or 10 years. Most policies have a limit on what the amounts can increase to.

With some policies, the increases are linked to the retail price index. Different insurers offer different schemes, and they are not easily comparable. For example:

cover before illness increases by	*income while claiming increases by*
30% simple every 3 years for first 15 years before age 55	5% compound a year
increases each year in line with RPI; maximum 3 times initial cover	7% simple a year
20% simple every 5 years; no increase in last 10 years of policy	20% simple every 5 years; no increase in last 10 years of policy
25% simple every 4 years before age 56 (or by rise in RPI if this is less)	7½% compound a year plus 25% simple every 4 years before age 56 (or by rise in RPI if this is less)
25% simple every 4 years	4% compound a year

What it costs

Premiums are quoted individually. Basically, the rate will depend on
*   whether you are a man or a woman
*   your age next birthday
*   number of years for which cover is required up to retirement age
*   your occupation
*   length of deferment period
*   whether the amounts payable are to increase automatically over the years
*   whether premium does not have to be paid while you are receiving payment.

Insurance companies give different weightings to these factors, so it is worth going to a number of different companies for quotations, or getting a broker to do so, so that you can choose the best one for you. The lowest premium is not necessarily the criterion because there are so many other factors to take into account.

In addition to the premium, you have to pay an 'administration' charge every year. It may be called a policy fee and ranges from £3 to £15, most likely around £10, irrespective of how much the

The Permanent Health Insurance Review, published annually by Kluwer Publishing, lists the premiums, terms and benefits of all PHI policies currently available (1984 edition £8.95); most brokers have access to it.

premium is. This annual charge is likely to be increased from time to time.

You can pay premiums monthly or annually, but work out what the extra cost is: the monthly premium will be more than one-twelfth of the annual premium.

With most policies, there is a 'waiver of premium' clause. This means that while you are being paid on a claim, you do not have to continue to pay premiums. With some policies, you have to pay extra for this option.

With some policies, the final year or years of insurance are premium-free.

Information you have to give

The proposal form is fairly searching in the questions it asks.

Name and address

A woman has to pay more than a man, generally up to 50% more.

Not many companies will insure a housewife, unless she took out the policy while she had a job, because of the difficulty of assessing the financial loss when she is unable to do her normal household tasks. Those that do accept a housewife usually insist on a 13-week deferment period, and pay not more than a set maximum in a year. Payments are normally made only if the housewife is 'confined to the house'.

If you live or intend to live outside the United Kingdom (with some companies, outside a member country of the EEC, North America, Australia) for more than three months, an additional premium will be required, or a longer deferment period imposed.

If you regularly travel to tropical areas, you have to declare this. You would have to pay an additional premium and accept a longer deferment period to get cover for disablement due to illness contracted in the tropics.

Age

The age you are now affects the premium you will be asked to pay, which will be based on the maximum number of years (i.e. retirement age less age now) for which benefit may have to be paid. 'Retirement' is either the beginning of state pensionable age (65 for men, 60 for women) or any earlier age you choose – generally, whenever payments from your occupational pension or self-employed pension scheme start.

Occupation

Different companies have different criteria for grouping occupations into categories. They also differ in what they consider

unacceptable: not only occupations that carry a high accident risk, but also those which are put in jeopardy by illness or disorder such as the ones needing great manual skill or great physical exertion.

You are also asked if you engage in any hazardous leisure activities. If so, some additional premium is almost bound to be payable.

And if yours is an occupation with seasonal or irregular income, whether freelance or employed, you will have to pay a higher premium or accept a longer deferment period. Insurers want to discourage people from using a PHI policy when their income has become reduced for any reason.

The maximum you will be paid

To make sure that no one is better off by staying away from work, all insurers put a limit on the income they will pay out if you claim.

Proposal forms ask if you are insured elsewhere for accidents and sickness.

The most common rule is that the income paid out by the policy, plus income from any similar policies, plus the 'benefits' you get from the state, must not come to more than three-quarters of your average earnings over the previous twelve months. Some companies set lower limits (two-thirds rather than three-quarters) for earnings above a certain amount (£15,000 or £10,000, say, or even £6,000).

For very high earnings, the limit may be 55% of earnings above a specified level.

So, before you take out a policy, make sure you understand what the maximum limit is based on. Beware of over-insurance, because if you are above the policy limits when the time comes, you will not be paid the full amount you have been paying premiums for. Work out what the relevant percentage of your current gross weekly or monthly earnings comes to and insure for no more than that. (With a few policies, you can increase the amount at renewal time to keep pace with your earnings in the future.)

deferment

For as long as your employer continues to pay your full salary, the insurance will not pay out.

The deferment period you choose should be related to the time at which other sources of income will cease: for example, the number of weeks for which your employer goes on paying while you are ill.

If you are self-employed, all income may cease immediately you are ill, so you will want the shortest possible deferment period and will therefore have to pay a higher premium.

Renewal

The insurers are obliged to offer to renew your policy. They can cancel the policy only if
■ you change your occupation to one which is unacceptably hazardous (most occupations are acceptable, but you may have to pay a higher premium)
■ you move abroad permanently (for more than 1 year).

You must pay the premium within a specified number of days (anything from 7 to 30) of the renewal date; otherwise, your policy will lapse at the end of these 'days of grace'.

You may be able to reinstate it, provided that you do so within a set number of months (3 or 6 or 12 months) of the renewal date. You will have to pay the premium for the whole of the intervening period and may have to give evidence of continued good health. This brings the policy back into action but only from the date of payment, so any disablement that arose during the intervening months will not be covered.

Premium at renewal

Unless yours is an index-linked policy or one with an automatic increase in benefits (and premium), the premium remains unaltered throughout the life of the policy, irrespective of any claims you may have made in the year.

If you want to increase your level of benefits payable, some insurers allow you to do this.

Because the premium is fixed for the life of the policy and is averaged out over those years, if you decide after some years not to renew, you will have been paying premiums well above the level that would have been charged for the number of years to your retirement age.

If you retire earlier than anticipated, you will not get any refund of premium.

at the end

The policy comes to an end when you reach the age you agreed at the outset – normally, your retirement age. With some policies, you do not have to pay the premium for the last years – one, two or three years.

When you retire, do not forget to cancel the standing order or direct debit mandate.

Making a claim

Normally, the insurers specify how many weeks (say, four) before the end of the deferment period you must notify them if you think your disablement is going to last longer. The deferment period starts with the first day you are unable to work because of the illness or injury.

You can, if you want, 'prove age' by showing your birth certificate when you take out the policy. The policy then says that this has been done, and you do not have to do it again.

DATE OF BIRTH

DATE OF DISABILITY

NAME AND ADDRESS OF GP

OTHER POLICIES

Usually, the 75% limit is taken into account at the proposal stage not the payment stage.

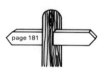

page 181

STATE BENEFITS

'weekly benefit' = monthly payment

You will be sent a claim form to complete which will ask for details of the illness or injury.

You may be required to provide proof of your age if you had not done so when taking out the insurance, or if there is a discrepancy between the age you quote now and that stated when the policy was issued.

You have to give the date on which you last worked (this is the date from which the deferment period starts to run), and the date on which you consulted the doctor. These two dates should normally be close together – if not, you may have to explain what happened.

The claim form includes an authorisation for the insurers to approach your GP for full details. Payment of your claim is subject to your providing any medical evidence the insurers may require. They will not necessarily get in touch with your doctor, but if you do not sign this authorisation, they will not pay out on your claim.

You will be asked if there is any other sickness or accident policy in force because the insurers want to be alerted about possible extra income while you are disabled. Generally, the monthly payment from the insurance plus any other accident or sickness policy and any National Insurance benefit and any continuing income from the employer must not come to more than 75% of your average gross monthly earnings in the last 12 months.

So, if you get any payment from other sources, you may then not get paid the full amounts that your premiums would entitle you to.

The policy clearly states that the benefit payable is calculated after deduction of any National Insurance benefits, or the statutory sick pay (SSP) that comes via your employer for 8 weeks. If you are eligible to claim sickness benefit from the DHSS but have not done so, the insurers will assume that you have.

Being paid

Once the deferment period is over, you get payments monthly (unless there is any special reason to pay fortnightly) – but in arrears, so you will have to wait another month before you get anything.

While you are getting payments, you have to produce monthly a medical certificate from your doctor.

The insurers may also check with your GP on the reasons for your continuing disablement and the latest estimate on when a return to work is anticipated. If the GP's evidence is sketchy or ambiguous, or disablement seems to be lasting too long, an examination and a report by an independent doctor may be required; if so, this will be arranged and paid for by the insurers.

Where it is very unlikely that you will return to work, the insurers may accept medical certificates at quarterly intervals – and eventually, annually.

If within 13 weeks of being back at work full-time and no longer getting any payment from the insurance company, you again become disabled from the same cause to the extent of not being able to do your job, this second period of incapacity is treated as if it were a continuation of the original disablement. The deferment period does not, therefore, apply and you can start receiving payments straightaway.

Income tax

Any benefit from an insurance policy which is paid regularly as income is subject to income tax. However, the Inland Revenue allow a 'tax holiday': no income tax is payable until you have been receiving the payments for more than one complete tax year (6 April to 5 April).

When your payments go on into a second tax year, you have to start paying income tax on the payments you receive.

disability starts	disability ceases	income tax payable
1 Feb 1984	31 Dec 1984	nil
1 Feb 1984	31 Dec 1985	for period 6 April 1985 to 31 Dec 1985
1 May 1984	31 Dec 1986	for period 6 April 1986 to 31 Dec 1986

Back to work

The payment ceases if you are eventually able to return to your old job full-time. If either you return to your old job on a part-time basis or you take up a less lucrative job full-time, the policy will pay an amount to make up the income you are losing. This is intended as an incentive to return to work as soon as it is reasonable to do so.

The amount of partial 'rehabilitation' or 'proportionate' payment is: the full payment minus the proportion that the new, reduced earnings bear to what you earned before the illness. For example, if you had been earning £900 per month and during the months of sickness received £600 from the insurance and when you are well enough to go back to your old job part-time, or to some lesser-paid job, paying you £300 a month (that is, one-third of the previous salary), the insurance payment is reduced by one-third and you will get £400 as rehabilitation or proportionate payment.

If, while totally disabled from the occupation stated in the schedule, the insured engages in another occupation, there shall be payable such proportion of the sum insured as is represented by the proportion which the insured's monthly loss of earned income resulting from this disablement bears to the average monthly income for a period of one year prior to the commencement of such disbility.

Sequence of claim payment

unable to work:
after deferment period, receive full payments
(maximum according to your policy and other income)
increases in payments if policy provides this
until retirement age if necessary
you do not pay premiums

working again:
back to old job full-time
payments to you cease
you start paying premiums again

or: back part-time to your old job
receive partial payments (rehabilitation)
for up to 12 months

or: back full-time or part-time to another, lower-paid job
receive partial payments (proportionate)
until retirement age if necessary.

Accident and sickness insurance

Personal accident insurance is often part of, or an extension of, another policy – motor, household, travel/holiday, sportsmans, redundancy, equestrian. None of these policies provides a high level of payments.

Personal accident and sickness insurance can be taken out on its own and is cheap. But consider instead a life insurance policy to get a lump sum for your dependants if you should die, and a permanent health insurance policy to pay you if you are disabled as a result of an accident or sickness.

Accident insurance pays an immediate lump sum on death. But what would be paid is not a significant sum compared to an appropriate life insurance policy.

Summary of cover

If you are accidentally injured, the policy will pay you a lump sum if the injury results within a specified period (anything from 3 months to $2^1/_2$ years) in

LUMP SUM

* death, or
* loss of one or both arms, or
* loss of one or both legs, or
* loss of one or both eyes, or
* permanent and total disablement.

(A few policies also give a lump sum payment if total deafness or total loss of the power of speech follows an accident.)

If, as a result of the injury, you are unable to do your normal job, a weekly amount will be paid normally for up to two years – 'temporary total disablement benefit'.

WEEKLY PAYMENTS

If you can do some but only a small part of your usual work, you are paid about half this amount with some policies – 'temporary partial disablement benefit'.

MEDICAL EXPENSES

Some policies also offer a small amount (say, 10% of the claim payment) to pay for treatment and associated costs which arise directly from the injuries – 'medical expenses benefit'.

Alternatively, some policies pay an amount for each day or week you have to stay in hospital more than 24 hours following an accident.

sickness insurance

Cover for being off work sick (sometimes called 'illness' insurance) is also available, generally linked to a personal accident insurance policy. Some insurers offer the cover on its own, but this is generally not worth buying.

If you are unable to go to work because of illness, the policy will pay you a set amount (based on so-much per day) up to a maximum of one year (with some policies, two years). Unlike personal accident insurance, there is no payment if you are able to do part of your job, and no lump sum payment if illness results in death.

Premiums

Premiums are directly related to your occupation, and occupations are grouped according to the risk of having an accident. Not all occupations are acceptable. Insurers put occupations into groups. Those listed in the proposal form are benchmarks or specimens; occupations not listed are allocated to one of these groups, by comparison of degree of risk.

For sickness cover, occupation does not significantly affect the premium rate charged unless you are engaged in an occupation where there is a specially high level of work-related disease.

Because it is assumed that women have more days off work for illness than men, some insurers exclude 'ailments peculiar to the female sex'. Others charge higher premiums for sickness insurance for women (typically, an extra 50%).

But some accident policies offer a discount when both husband and wife are insured, and a family discount for children.

A deferment period of a week is usually standard for a sickness claim. Premiums can be reduced by volunteering to have a longer deferment period.

Also, premiums are reduced if you agree to be paid for a shorter time than the policy's standard period (which is normally 104 weeks).

page 188

For sickness, there may be a franchise rather than a deferment period. And there will be a waiting period: usually 30 days. That means not only that you will not get any payment until the policy has been in effect for a month, but you will not get anything for any illness that started during that period.

your health

Insurers may ask for extra premium if they consider any health defect is significant, but are more likely to exclude cover for any sickness arising from a pre-existing condition, or a recurrent one – for example, back trouble.

hazardous activities

Accidents arising from sports or other activities known to involve a high risk of accidental injury will normally be excluded. If you want to be insured for these activities, you will have to pay an additional premium or accept a lesser payment for accidents arising from such activities.

The prospectus or proposal form gives a list of what the insurers consider hazardous activities. For example:

'No payment will be made for illness or injury caused by or resulting from accidents occurring through the Insured's engaging in winter sports (except sledging within the UK, curling or skating), hunting, horse racing or training or breaking, show jumping, polo, mountaineering or rock climbing, pot-holing or caving, any type of football, motor cycling (including as a passenger), motor racing competitions or trials, aerial activity, boxing, wrestling (including judo,

Special schemes are available for most sports, often via the sporting association or a specialist broker.

karate and unarmed combat), fencing, squash, hockey, power boating, yachting or boating (except on inland waters or within three miles of land), water skiing, use of underwater breathing apparatus, professional sport of any kind.

At the request of the proposer, the Company will consider amending exclusions. . . .'

You may have to declare that you 'do not contemplate entering upon any hazardous undertaking'.

other insurances

On the proposal form you are asked if you have ever had special terms imposed on a life, sickness or personal accident insurance. If so, the insurers you are now applying to will want to find out the full reasons.

You will also be asked if you are covered for accidents or sickness by any other policy. The answer may be 'yes' – under a motor policy, travel or holiday policy, sportsmans policy. But there is no reason why a lump sum should not be paid to you (or to your dependants) from each policy you have been paying premiums on.

How much to be paid

A personal accident policy does not pay for actual loss in earnings: it pays out the 'benefit' you have decided to buy.

Proposal forms set out quite clearly, generally in tabular form, what units of payment (benefit) you can have and how much each will cost you. But these units are not obligatory and if you have worked out exactly what sum you need, ask for that, and what the premium will be. If, however, the insurers consider that what you have chosen is out of proportion to your likely earnings, they may ask a few searching questions about your circumstances.

Where there is a minimum premium (perhaps £10 or £20), make sure you take insurance for enough units of cover (weekly payments or lump sum) to make maximum use of the minimum premium.

age limits

The normal age limits for taking out accident and sickness insurance are 16 to 55 or 60.

Someone under 18 does not normally have any dependants, and most insurers will not allow a large sum to be insured for the death of a minor: £1000 is the normal lump sum limit.

Once the policyholder has retired, the insurers will probably restrict the cover to a lump sum on loss of a limb or eye or on death following an accident and no other disablement payments. When you reach retirement age and the cover then becomes so restricted, it may not be worth your while renewing.

When you will not get paid

Before taking out a policy, check
● that there is '24-hour cover', for accidents at any time of day, anywhere
(Some insurance companies provide cover for accidents only while in a car or in the home: such restricted policies are invariably poor value.)
● that you do not have to wait until you return to work before being paid
● that the amount of any 'weekly benefit' you receive will not be deducted from a lump sum paid eventually for permanent disablement
● that the resulting disability can occur up to two years after the accident
(Some companies limit this to a much shorter time.)
● that injury is not restricted to being by 'external violent and visible means'
(Such a wording could mean that no payment would be made, for example, following accidental gas poisoning. The exclusion of 'gradually operating causes' also means that there is no cover for anything that has not arisen from an obvious specific incident but is the result of a degenerative process or an accumulation of assaults on the body such as deafness not following an explosion but after working in a factory with continuous high noise levels.)
● the wording of the criterion for permanent total disablement
(Where the wording says 'permanent total disablement from gainful employment of any and every kind', you would need to show, in order to get payment, that you cannot ever again expect to be fit enough to be employed in any kind of job.)
● that 'loss of eye' means loss of sight
● that 'loss of limb' means not only loss by amputation but includes loss of use (by paralysis, for instance)
● that the defined point of amputation is not too high up the limb
● that the insurance pays on the 'continental' scale.

If you should lose the sight of one eye and the use of one arm and one leg as the result of an accident, only one lump sum will be paid, not three.

Scale for lump sum payments

For a slightly higher premium, some policies pay out a lump sum following disablement on what is called the 'continental' scale. What will be paid is a percentage of the full sum insured for permanent disablement, appropriate to the degree of disablement.
   For example:

* permanent total disablement   100%
* loss of sight in one or both eyes   100%
* permanent total loss of hearing
   in both ears   40%
   in one ear   10%
* loss by amputation or permanent total loss of use of
   one or more limbs   100%

one big toe   10%
any other toe   5%
one thumb   25% right, 20% left
one forefinger   20% right, 15% left
any other finger   10% right, 6% left
(all reversed if person is left handed)
* permanent loss of use of
shoulder or elbow   25%
wrist   20% right, 15% left
hip or knee or ankle   20% right, 20% left
* removal of lower jaw by surgical operation   30%

Without such a scale, for example, you would get 100% of the lump sum if you had your hand amputated, but nothing for the loss of your thumb. A policy on the continental scale would pay 25% for such a partial disability.

You can never get more than 100% in total for injuries resulting from one accident. If you lose the total use of one arm and also two fingers from the other hand, you get only the one lump sum, not the extra percentage for the lost fingers.

'hands insurance'
A variation of an accident and sickness policy is one designed specially for people whose living depends on their manual dexterity – surgeons, musicians, engravers, dressmakers, draughtsmen and suchlike.

You can insure for increased percentages to be payable for injuries to parts of your hand or arm, if these would severely limit your ability to continue in your particular job. For instance, a dentist or violinist might want to receive 100% of the lump sum for permanent damage to the ends of a thumb or forefinger.

Payment is made on a modified continental scale. More is payable for injuries to the right hand (unless you are left handed).

You can insure any part of the body you gain income from: for example, a model her legs. Policies are usually written at Lloyd's, but at least one insurance company also does so.

Premium rates are not generally published and you would have to ask for an individual quotation.

Claiming

You can claim if an illness or injury has resulted in your being unable to work for a period longer than the deferment period, and more than the specified number of weeks after the policy was issued (the waiting period). The claim must be within the stipulated period (1 year or 2 years). For example, if as a result of falling downstairs you start getting very severe headaches which become progressively more disabling, you may have to give up work some time after the accident occurred. Such a gap between

For example, a blow on the ankle may seem trivial at the time but as days go by, the swelling and pain increase and after a week struggling into work, you find that you have, in fact, cracked a bone and have to be off work for eight weeks.

injury and disablement would not preclude a claim unless the gap exceeds the period stipulated in the policy.

Tell the insurers as soon as reasonably possible of any circumstances that may give rise to a claim. The results of some injuries take time to show their full effects. Even if in doubt about whether an injury is going to be serious enough to merit a claim, notify the insurers and ask for a claim form.

The claim form

The claim form which the insurers will send you requires certain information about the accident or sickness, about the consequences of the accident, about you and your current occupation. Before meeting a claim, the insurers will want to find out whether
* you have suffered from the same condition in the past without telling them
* you really are totally unable to work.

Typical questions on an accident claim form would be

what were you doing when the accident happened?
This is to find out whether you were doing anything particularly hazardous or any excluded activity, such as water-skiing, racing.

what is the extent of your injuries?
This allows the insurers to assess whether it is reasonable that these injuries resulted solely from the accident as described and allows them to estimate the cost of the claim.

name and address of witnesses
Witnesses may help you prove that your injury was due to a genuine accident. Tell them that you are giving their names to your insurers.

when did disability start?
This is not necessarily when the accident happened (you may not have had to stop work immediately), but the date when you became unable to work.

medical certificate
Insurers will not consider a claim without medical corroboration. All claim forms come with a medical certificate to be completed. Your GP or consultant will have to sign the form saying
* what is wrong with you
* whether the injury is solely the result of the accident as stated
* when you became disabled
* how long your recovery should take
* when you are likely to be capable of doing your job again.
You will have to pay any fee asked by the doctor for completing this form.

Claiming a lump sum

A claim can be made for death within 12 months of the accident (with some policies, 2 years). Your personal representatives must prove that your death resulted from the accidental injury, not from natural causes, sickness or disease. The main evidence will be the death certificate which must be produced before payment will be made.

A claim will not be accepted if the death was due to suicide or resulted from intentional self-injury, or was due to 'wilful exposure to needless peril' (perhaps doing something for a dare – driving up the wrong carriageway on a motorway – or leaping from a moving train on purpose) or to any of the other exclusions.

A lump sum from a personal accident policy paid on death will be subject to capital transfer tax, as part of the estate. CTT can be avoided if the lump sum is held in trust for the benefit of named persons.

Income tax is not payable on a lump sum payment received following, for example, the loss of eyesight or of a limb.

for loss of eye

If you have lost the sight of an eye, the doctor's report will have to confirm that the loss of sight was due solely to the accident, that you have no useful sight left and that there is no hope of eventual recovery.

Payment of a lump sum for loss of sight in an eye or the use of a hand or leg, exhausts the policy, and if you still want to be insured for accidents, you have to start afresh with a new policy.

for loss of limb

If you lose a limb or the use of a limb, you can claim a lump sum even if you can continue to do your job and it does not affect your earning power.

Amputation must have been necessary solely as a result of the accident. The policy will specify the point of amputation for a claim to be met: at or above the wrist, at or above the point where the fingers join the palm, at or above the ankle.

You can pay for your own specialist to prepare an alternative assessment if you want to – but the insurance company does not have to take note if it does not want to.

For loss of use of a limb, it will take longer for the lump sum payment to be made because the insurers will wait until all the medical evidence shows that the loss of use is permanent, and without reasonable hope of recovery. The insurers may want you to be examined by an independent specialist (at their expense). The specialist will determine the degree of lost use.

for permanent total disablement

A policy normally states that disablement must have lasted for 104 weeks before this lump sum payment is made. This long wait is because the insurers want to see whether recovery is possible. Before paying the lump sum, the insurers will obtain a specialist's opinion (at their expense).

Most accident policies provide a weekly payment for total disablement, giving you an income in the intervening months.

Claiming a weekly benefit

'weekly benefit' = monthly payment

You get a weekly payment if you are unable to do your own job as a result of the accident or illness.

Your doctor will be asked to say how long he expects you to be unable to work. While the GP certifies your continued absence from work, you should receive regular payments.

No income tax has to be paid on weekly payments for one tax year.

If the disablement lasts significantly longer than the doctor expected, the insurers will ask him if there are medical reasons for your slow recovery.

Where a claimant could have been expected to return to work earlier, a claims inspector may come round unannounced to check that the person is not doing any work and is still fully disabled.

For a sickness claim, too, the insurers will check that your recovery is as speedy as possible and that there is no malingering.

Unless you have a policy which provides for temporary partial disablement, no payment will be made once you return to work part-time.

A policy normally pays a weekly amount for a maximum of 104 weeks. After that, the criterion for getting the lump sum for total disablement will be whether there is any possibility of your doing a paid job of any kind again, even if up to then monthly payments were made because you could not carry on with your own job.

medical expenses

Some policies pay out for medical expenses arising directly as a result of an accident, provided that accident is sufficiently severe to result in a claim for weekly payments. You can claim for private consultation and treatment, drugs and transport to and from doctors and hospitals.

The amount you can claim for these expenses is limited to a set percentage of the total amount you have received in weekly payments. Receipts will usually have to be produced to support your claim, so make sure you keep them because it may be some time before you can make this claim.

Guaranteed acceptance policies

Some insurers sell their accident policies through newspaper advertisements and direct mailing lists. Such offers usually guarantee to accept you provided you return the simple application form before a given date. The attraction of such offers is that no questions are asked about your state of health, there may be no age limits and renewal is normally guaranteed.

But premiums for such schemes are pitched at a level related to the number of poor risks who are likely to apply, so if you are young and in good health, you would be able to obtain a better deal elsewhere.

Is it worth it?

The conditions and exclusions of these policies are stringent and restrictive, so consider very carefully whether the likelihood of your having an injury or illness that falls within the policy limits is sufficient to justify the premiums.

The insurers can refuse to renew anyone's policy at any age, and they are likely to do so if your health becomes poor or you have had a number of long periods off work. If you want a policy which is renewable regardless of deteriorating health, you would need to buy a 'permanent health' insurance policy. This, however, would be virtually impossible if insurers had declined to renew your ordinary sickness policy.

But if personal accident cover is included as part of another policy, you can take advantage of this.

third party claim
It may be that your injury was caused by somebody else's negligence or lack of proper care. If so, you may have a civil claim against that person or official body. It may be worth starting proceedings – but consult a solicitor first. The other party may, in turn, be able to invoke a personal (or public) liability insurance or motor policy to pay your claim.

Life insurance

What could be simpler than the concept of a group of people getting together, putting some money into a pool, and sharing out that pool to the dependants of those of them who die? That was how life insurance operated in the early years of the 18th century. The share-out normally took place at the end of each year, and then the survivors, and perhaps a few new members, would put money into the pool for the following year.

There was, of course, a flaw in the system. If a man died in a year when none of the others in that particular group died, his dependants would be handsomely looked after. If, on the other hand, he died in a year when several of the others also died, the pool would have to be split several ways, and his dependants would not do so well.

Naturally, a man thinking of joining one of the groups would have a look at the other members, and form a rough idea of whether they were likely to live or die. If many of them looked likely to die, he would join a different group. So, anybody young and fit would have no difficulty in joining a group and staying there; anyone in middle age would find himself less welcome.

It was his inability, on account of his middle age, to obtain membership of any such group that so enraged a mathematician called James Dodson that in 1756 he sat down and invented life insurance as we know it today. His reasoning was that, whatever one's age, there must be the right price to pay for life insurance. It was simply a question of working out what people of different ages should pay for the same amount of life insurance 'protection' in the form of a set amount paid on death. James Dodson did his sums, and drew up some tables.

James Dodson had to use such information as was then available about the life expectancy of people of different ages. That information was not terribly accurate, so, although his arithmetic was perfectly sound, the premiums he calculated turned out to be too high – the members were not dying as early as the information about life expectancy had suggested they would. The people running the group realised that there was more money than they needed. So, they called the members together to decide what to do with it. Some were in favour of cash

James Dodson's original tables are still in the offices of The Equitable Life Assurance Society, which his work was instrumental in founding in 1762.

The amount the individual was securing on death became known as the 'sum assured' - in contrast to the previous pool system, where no particular sum was assured because it depended on how many members died during the particular year. The amount which each individual had to pay in order to secure a given sum assured became known as the premium.

Policies issued by foreign insurance companies are not 'qualifying' unless issued and administered by a UK branch.

refunds, but the view which prevailed was that the spare money should be used to make additions, known as bonuses, to the sums assured for all the members. That was the start of what is now known as 'with-profits' life insurance.

Life insurance today

Over the years, many variations on the theme of an amount payable on death have gradually built up.
● a whole-life policy
is a policy which produces a specified lump sum (the sum assured) when you die, whenever that is – tomorrow or when you are in your nineties
● an endowment policy
pays a specified lump sum after however many years you specify or if you die in the meantime
● term insurance
pays the amount in question only if you die within a specified period of years (cheaper than the other types because there is a chance that nothing will ever be paid at all)
    Nowadays, many policies are available in which the savings element is the object of the exercise and the life insurance element is small.
    The reason for adopting one particular arrangement, rather than an alternative course which might appear to lead to a similar result, has often been the taxation treatment: the question of income tax, capital gains tax and capital transfer tax when a lump sum is paid (and for policies taken out before the changes proposed in the Chancellor's March 1984 budget, the availability of tax relief on premiums was another important factor).

Tax and qualifying policies

As far as income tax is concerned, the crucial factor is whether the policy is a 'qualifying' one.
    The main requirements for a qualifying policy are that
* premiums are paid at regular intervals
* premiums are payable for at least 10 years (unless term insurance)
* the amount of premium paid in any one year must not be more than double that paid in any other year
* the amount payable on death or at the end of the term must be at least a certain minimum (normally three-quarters of the total amount paid in premiums if death occurred at the age of 75)

premiums and tax
If you have a qualifying life insurance policy taken out before 14 March 1984, you get 15% tax relief on the eligible premiums you pay. In most cases, the relief is given by deduction from the premium you pay, rather than through PAYE or direct assessment.

So, if the premium is £100, you pay only £85 to the life insurance company and the company gets the other £15, the tax relief, from the Inland Revenue. This is also done for non-taxpayers.

The limitation on eligible premiums is that in any tax year they cannot exceed whichever is the greater of
* £1,500 in all (for all the life policies you have) or
* one-sixth of your total gross income (joint income and the premiums both pay, for husband and wife living together, even if taxed separately).

Assuming that the March 1984 budget proposals are carried through into the Finance Act 1984, no tax relief is allowed on the premiums of a life insurance policy taken out since 13 March 1984 or varied after that date so as to increase the benefits secured or to extend the term.

final lump sum and tax

If your policy is qualifying, broadly the proceeds at the end of its term will be free of income tax. This applies whether you take the proceeds as one lump sum or whether, as you can do with certain types of policy, you take the proceeds in instalments instead.

There is an exception to the rule about the proceeds being tax free. If you cash-in the policy or make it paid-up during the first 10 years or, if shorter, during the first three-quarters of the originally intended term, whatever gain you make is subject to tax at your highest rate less basic rate. For example, if you are paying tax at 55% while the basic rate is 30%, you will suffer tax at 25% on your gain from the policy (if you pay tax at no more than basic rate, tax free).

A single-premium policy (otherwise known as a bond) is usually a non-qualifying policy: any gain you make at any time from such a policy will be subject to tax in excess of the basic rate.

Generally speaking, the proceeds of a life insurance policy are free of capital gains tax.

Insurable interest

In 1774, an Act of Parliament laid down specific rules about who could insure whose life, in order to put a stop to wild bouts of gambling from insuring the lives of famous people – or of anyone whose death could then be conveniently arranged.

Unlike most other types of insurance, such as motor or household, life insurance is not technically a contract of indemnity; that is to say, a life insurance policy will produce whatever are the proceeds of it, not cover you only for a 'loss'. Correspondingly, under the terms of the Life Assurance Act 1774, sometimes known as the Gambling Act, you have to have an insurable interest in the life of anybody on whose life you wish to take out an insurance.

An individual has an unlimited insurable interest in his own life and also in the life of his or her spouse and can insure it for any amount he or she chooses. (But if the amount for which you wish to insure seems excessive in relation to your means and prospects so that you or your spouse would be worth more dead than alive, the insurers are unlikely to accept this risk.)

Apart from yourself and your spouse, you have an insurable

interest in somebody only if his or her death would cause you financial loss. You can insure for the amount of money you would lose if he or she dies. You cannot insure for more. Examples would include business partners and an employer wishing to insure the life of a key employee.

In life insurance, the insurable interest must be present when the policy is taken out, and subsequent events (divorce, dissolution of partnership) do not invalidate the policy. In general insurance, the question of insurable interest as such does not arise but you can only be indemnfied if you suffer loss at the time the insured event occurs – you could insure the crown jewels but would only be paid if you owned them at the time of their theft.

Women ought to have their lives insured as they are expensive to substitute for by paid housekeepers etc. Even so, my husband never took seriously my suggestion of insuring my life, which is probably because men see themselves as providers.
Which? reader A 90

We asked a number of *Which?* readers, some of whom ('B') already had a life insurance policy and some ('A') who did not, to tell us what they knew or wanted to know about life insurance and to let us have their comments generally. We are quoting from some of their responses.

Different classes of life insurance

The premium for a life insurance policy depends on the age of the policyholder, the amount that the policy has to cover (that is the sum assured), and the length of the period to be covered.

The broadest classification is into two types: temporary and permanent.

A temporary policy is roughly what it says: it exists for only a limited period of years. You will find it called temporary insurance or term insurance and sometimes it is called level term. The expression 'term' is used to describe a policy where if you die within a specified number of years – the term – a set sum is paid. The contract is that the amount insured is payable only if death occurs within the specified period. If you survive, nothing is payable.

A permanent policy is one which does not simply expire at the end of a specified term: a benefit will definitely be paid either on death whenever it occurs or at the end of a specified period.

Temporary insurance

Which? calls temporary insurance 'protection-only' life insurance.

Largely because of the possibility that nothing will ever be payable, the premiums for a term policy are always much lower than the premiums for a permanent policy.

examples of the cost
● Mr White, approaching the age of 25 and newly married, wants to be insured for £10,000 if he should die within the next 20 years: annual premium £11.40.

● A bank advance of £5,000 made to Mr Green, aged nearly 35, is to be repaid in 8 years. To ensure repayment in the event of his premature death, he takes out an 8-year term policy: annual premium £8.

● The sudden death of Mr Black, approaching the age of 42, technical director of an electronics firm, would be a calamity for the business. As a financial cushion in the event of his death, the company takes out a 'key man' insurance for £30,000, for a 23-year term, timed to finish just before Mr Black reaches the age of 65: annual premium £144.60.

● Another baby has been born to Mrs Grey. Mr Grey is aged just under 40 and in good health. To the insurance he already has, he wants to add £15,000 of cover for the next 18 years: the premium would be £4.10 per month (£49.20 per annum).

Increasing term insurance

There are policies where the amount payable if death is within the stated number of years gets higher as time goes by.

A common formula is for the sum assured to increase every 5 years. So, for example, if you take a 20-year policy, the position would be as follows:

death during	sum payable
years 1 to 5	£20,000
6 to 10	£25,000
11 to 15	£30,000
16 to 20	£35,000

Usually, the premium stays the same throughout the 20 years.

increasable term insurance
This is a type of term insurance in which you have the option to increase the sum assured if you wish. This has the advantage of greater flexibility but it is more expensive (except in the early stages). The premium will be increased for the extra cover at a rate for the age you are at the time you exercise your option.

Convertible term insurance

This is a term insurance policy with an option for you to convert to a permanent insurance at a later stage without any 'evidence of insurability' at that time. Evidence of insurability includes state of health, and your occupation.

The intention of such a policy is that you take out a relatively cheap policy (level term) to begin with, at a premium you can afford at the time. The terms of the policy enable you to change all or part of the policy to a more profitable type at a later stage within the original policy term (perhaps to a whole-life or endowment policy). Although you will not have to submit evidence of your state of health at the time of changing, the premium you pay for the next policy will be according to your age then.

Some convertible type policies also have an 'increasability' option, whereby you can at specified intervals (every 3 years, say, or every 5 years) increase the sum assured on the policy (for instance, upping it by 30%). Others allow you to extend the policy for a longer period, without checking on your health at the time.

Part of the March 1984 budget proposals mean that the exercise of any option constitutes varying the policy, so thereafter you may not get tax relief on the premiums even if the original policy was taken out on or before 13 March 1984.

There are so many types of insurance with confusing terminology and claims, it is difficult to see which offers the best deal. I missed an opportunity to convert a policy and would have appreciated a 'reminder' in the final year of option explaining (in simple language) the options offered. After policy has run for 10 years, it is not easy to recall advice given when taking out the policy nor the date at which special offers expire.
Which? reader B 306

The figures shown are the best premiums quoted by life insurance companies for a hypothetical 'normal' man at different ages. Last place on the list is not the worst on the market but the 10th best.

The information is taken from tables in *The Savings Market* February 1984.

Term insurance
annual and monthly premiums for a sum assured of £25,000

15-YEAR TERM

man aged 30 next birthday	premium annual	monthly
	£	£
Economic	(N)25.75	(M)4.00
Equitable Life	26.00	2.42
Zurich Life	(N)29.13	(M)3.00
Friends' Provident	(N)29.50	(M)3.00
Commercial Union	(N)31.42	2.83
Phoenix Assurance	(N)31.50	(M)3.00
National Provident	(N)32.01	2.75
Gresham Life	32.83	3.25
Guardian R E	(N)33.09	2.87
Sun Life	(N)34.00	3.00

man aged 45 next birthday		
Zurich Life	(N)101.36	8.70
Friends' Provident	(N)109.00	9.58
Equitable Life	110.00	9.42
Commercial Union	(N)111.21	9.65
Scottish Mutual	(N)113.49	9.75
UK Provident	(N)116.50	10.25
Economic Insurance	(N)118.25	10.51
London Life	119.25	10.34
Phoenix Assurance	(N)121.00	10.49
National Provident	(N)121.06	10.40

man aged 55 next birthday		
Zurich Life	(N)310.77	26.68
Equitable Life	313.00	26.33
Crusader	(N)316.72	27.30
Friends' Provident	(N)319.50	28.08
National Provident	(N)322.14	27.68
London Life	323.14	28.01
Sun Life of Canada	(N,I)323.75	28.38
Yorkshire General	(N)325.38	28.05
Economic Insurance	(N)325.75	28.67
Manulife	(N,I)331.00	28.50

(M) minimum premium allowed
(N) rates for non-smokers
(I) quoted on age nearest birthday

Convertible term insurance
annual and monthly premiums for a sum assured of £25,000 for policies convertible at any time during the term

15-YEAR TERM

man aged 30 next birthday	premium annual	monthly
	£	£
Economic	(N)27.75	(M)4.00
Equitable Life	28.00	2.58
Friends' Provident	(N)32.50	(M)3.00
Commercial Union	(N)33.76	3.03
Zurich Life	(N)34.08	(M)3.00
Crusader	(N)34.21	4.80
Phoenix Assurance	(N)35.00	3.03
Guardian R E	(N)35.25	3.06
Gresham Life	35.74	3.50
London Life	(*,M)36.00	(M)3.00

man aged 45 next birthday		
Zurich Life	(N)117.67	10.10
Equitable Life	121.00	10.33
Friends' Provident	(N)127.00	11.14
Crusader	(N)130.32	11.30
London Life	(*)130.50	11.31
Economic	(N)133.75	11.87
National Provident	(N)135.61	11.65
UK Provident	(N)135.75	12.00
Commercial Union	(N)136.95	11.85
Phoenix Assurance	(N)137.50	11.92

man aged 55 next birthday		
London Life	(*)364.23	31.57
Sun Life of Canada	(N,I)367.50	32.25
Economic	(N)373.75	32.87
Sun Life	(N)387.00	33.45
Gresham Life	390.76	34.00
Yorkshire General	(N)395.21	34.07
Confederation Life	(N)395.21	34.07
RNPF Nurses	416.63	35.59
Commercial Union	(N)423.01	36.30
Med.Sick/Permanent	428.25	36.57

* can be converted to a similar policy
(M) minimum premium allowed
(N) rates for non-smokers
(I) quoted on age nearest birthday

With many insurers, the premiums for non-smokers are nowadays lower than for smokers (but the premiums of other companies without non-smoker rates may be as low – or lower).

Decreasing term insurance

As its name implies, this means an insurance policy where the sum assured goes down from year to year. With most policies, the decline in the sum assured is by the same amount each year: for example, £10,000 in the first year, £9,500 in the second, £9,000 in the third and so on.

The premium for such a policy is averaged out to be the same throughout, although the sum assured is decreasing steadily. A few companies adjust their calculations so that no premiums need to be paid in the last few years of the term.

Report

mortgage protection policy

This is a particular variety of decreasing temporary insurance (although rarely referred to as such), taken out in conjunction with a repayment mortgage loan.

The period of the policy is the same as the term for which the mortgage loan is arranged, typically 25 years. The amount that would be paid out if you were to die is designed to go down on the same curve as the capital outstanding on the mortgage loan goes down (on the assumption that interest rates do not change drastically in the meantime). A few insurance companies provide the option to increase the sum assured and/or to extend the term of the policy. The policy remains valid (and premiums must be paid) even if the mortgage is paid off before the end of the term (for example, if you sell the house). It can be used to cover the mortgage on the next house.

Family income benefit (f.i.b.)

This is a temporary insurance policy where, if you should die within the term, a fixed sum is paid out tax-free for the remaining years of the term. For example, you could take out a policy where, in the event of your death within 20 years, £500 a quarter would be paid for the balance of that period – which could work out at £40,000 in total or as little as £500. Some companies allow part or all of the income that would be due to be paid as one lump sum instead.

increasing family income benefit

You can opt for an income which increases year by year. The rate of increase is specified at the outset. Some insurers do it on a simple increase basis, some on a compound basis. It is worth checking that the increases apply from the outset of the policy, and not just from the date of death.

Index-linking stops when payment starts.

A variation on the theme is an index-linked family income benefit policy: the income to be paid out will have increased in line with the retail price index (or some other index the policy is linked to), and so will the premiums.

Decreasing term insurance
(mortgage protection policy)
annual and monthly premiums
for a sum assured of £25,000

Family income benefit policy
annual and monthly premiums
for annual benefit of £5,000

Decreasing term insurance

25-YEAR TERM

man aged 25 next birthday		premium annual	monthly	
yrs*		£	£	%†
25	Equitable Life	20.00	1.92	10.49
25	Economic	(N)21.25	(M)4.00	10
25	Zurich Life	(N)25.93	3.00	12
21	Swiss Life	31.00	(M)5.00	13
18	FS Assurance	37.83	3.25	10
22	Ecclesiastical	31.01	2.75	15
21	Black Horse Life	32.50	(M)5.00	10
25	UK Provident	(N)27.50	2.75	15
25	Windsor Life	27.50	2.75	15
25	National Provident	(N)28.23	2.42	15.5

man aged 40 next birthday		premium annual	monthly	
yrs*		£	£	%†
25	Zurich Life	(N)73.69	6.33	13
25	Clerical Medical	(N)76.81	6.58	10.99
25	Equitable Life	78.00	6.75	10.49
25	Guardian R E	(N)79.32	6.88	20
25	National Provident	(N)80.02	6.88	10.49
25	Yorkshire General	(N)81.78	7.05	10
25	Economic	(N)82.00	7.34	10
25	UK Provident	(N)83.25	7.50	10
21	Swiss Life	100.75	8.65	12
22	Ecclesiastical	97.94	8.50	15

(M) minimum premium allowed
(N) rates for non-smokers
* years payable
† maximum mortgage interest rate covered under the policy

Family income benefit policy

25-YEAR TERM

man aged 25 next birthday		premium annual	monthly
yrs*		£	£
25	Economic	(N)39.90	(M)4.00
25	Equitable Life	43.00	3.83
25	National Provident	(N)45.40	3.90
20	Sentinel	57.50	4.94
25	UK Provident	(N)46.60	4.15
25	Crusader	(N)47.03	4.15
21	Time Assurance	56.31	4.80
23	London Life	51.50	4.46
25	Zurich Life	(N)48.35	4.15
25	Clerical Medical	(N)48.53	4.15

15-YEAR TERM

man aged 40 next birthday		premium annual	monthly
yrs*		£	£
15	Equitable Life	67.00	5.83
15	Zurich Life	(N)67.57	5.80
13	London Life	79.00	6.85
10	Sentinel	105.50	9.00
15	Economic	(N)70.95	6.37
15	Yorkshire General	(N)72.50	6.25
15	Scottish Mutual	(N)72.75	6.25
15	National Provident	(N)76.24	6.55
15	UK Provident	(N)79.10	6.95
15	Clerical Medical	(N)79.95	6.85

* years payable
(M) minimum premiums allowed
(N) rates for non-smokers

The figures shown are the best
premiums quoted by life insurance
companies for a hypothetical 'normal'
man at different ages. Last place on the
list is not the worst on the market but
the 10th best.

The information is taken from tables in
The Savings Market February 1984.

Which? calls permanent insurance 'investment-type' life insurance.

Permanent insurance

Policies where the sum assured is definitely going to be paid are referred to, in general, as 'permanent' insurances. There are various different types within that broad heading, the main distinction being between whole-life policies and endowment policies.

With a whole-life insurance policy, the lump sum becomes payable only when you die. With an endowment insurance policy, the lump sum is payable after a specified number of years or on your death if you die before the end of that period.

A whole-life insurance policy provides a sum assured payable on your death whenever that occurs, but with many of the insurance companies you do not have to go on paying the premiums all the time. The age at which you can stop paying ranges from 65 to 90; with some policies, you pay premiums for a defined number of years (30, perhaps).

Nowadays, the investment aspect of many life insurance policies tends to be the dominant element rather than the life cover.

Both whole-life and endowment insurance may be on a non-profit or on a with-profits basis.

Non-profit policies

Almost every type of temporary (term) life insurance is on a non-profit basis.

You agree to pay so-much every so-often, and the life insurance company agrees to pay so-much on your death (with an endowment policy, at the end of the specified period or on your death within that period).

Basically, what you are getting for your money from a permanent insurance on a non-profit basis is a guaranteed sum when the policy comes to an end. Because the sum is guaranteed, the insurance company has to be quite sure that it can be paid. So they are conservative in working out what sum can be guaranteed. This means that, in terms of investment, the return on non-profit policies is usually low.

For a non-profit policy, comparisons between different life insurance companies are relatively straightforward: tables are published in a number of specialist money magazines, showing precisely what sums will be paid for what premiums, and then you can make your choice.

The figures shown are the best premiums quoted by life insurance companies for a hypothetical 'normal' man at different ages. Last place on the list is not the worst on the market but the 10th best.

The information is taken from tables in *The Savings Market* **February 1984.**

Whole-life non-profit insurance
annual and monthly premiums for a sum assured of £25,000

man aged 30 next birthday	premium annual	monthly
	£	£
Yorkshire General	(N)183.28	15.80
Gresham Life	187.06	16.50
Ecclesiastical	188.15	16.25
Economic	(N)189.75	16.77
Premium Life	(N)189.99	17.40
Colonial Mutual	192.81	16.63
Equitable Life	195.00	16.50
Economic	198.75	17.55
Sentinel	201.00	17.26
American Life	206.25	18.50

man aged 45 next birthday		
Yorkshire General	(N)377.58	32.55
Colonial Mutual	393.39	33.93
Premium Life	(N)396.01	35.73
Economic	(N)398.00	34.99
Scottish Mutual	(N)398.67	34.25
Gresham Life	402.40	35.00
Equitable Life	410.00	34.42
Ecclesiastical	415.13	35.75
City Westminster	421.00	37.11
Clerical Medical	423.33	36.35

man aged 55 next birthday		
Yorkshire General	(N)644.38	55.55
Scottish Mutual	(N)651.84	56.00
Economic	(N)671.50	58.92
Colonial Mutual	671.65	57.93
Gresham Life	681.41	58.97
Premium Life	(N)691.51	62.03
Equitable Life	697.00	58.33
Ecclesiastical	709.04	61.00
Economic	711.25	62.48
Clerical Medical	714.33	61.35

(N) rates for non-smokers

Non-profit endowment insurance
annual and monthly premiums for a sum assured of £10,000

15-YEAR TERM

man aged 30 next birthday	premium annual	monthly
	£	£
Sun Alliance	447.29	38.56
Scottish Widows	450.00	38.60
Ecclesiastical	450.05	38.75
Scottish Provident	452.60	39.40
Life Assn Scotland	453.77	39.70
Equity & Law	456.22	39.16
Yorkshire General	(N)461.68	39.80
London Life	462.00	40.04
Economic	(N)465.40	40.89
Scottish Life	465.50	39.90

man aged 45 next birthday		
Ecclesiastical	469.84	40.45
Sun Alliance	469.91	40.51
Scottish Widows	471.00	40.40
Scottish Provident	473.40	41.20
Life Assn Scotland	474.35	41.50
Yorkshire General	(N)475.60	41.00
Equity & Law	479.52	41.16
London Life	482.00	41.77
Economic	(N)482.70	42.40
Equitable Life	483.40	40.53

(N) rates for non-smokers

With-profits policies

With life insurance arranged on a with-profits basis, whenever the sum assured is payable, the appropriate bonuses are payable as well. That is to say, if you take out a with-profits endowment policy and you survive to the end of the term, you get the sum assured plus all the bonuses which have accrued for the full term. If you die during the term of the policy, your estate (or the trustees if you have placed the policy in trust), get the sum assured plus the bonuses to the date of death.

The size of the lump sum grows as bonuses (depending mainly on how well the insurance company's investments have performed) are added. There is generally no guarantee that there will be a bonus every year, or how much each will be, but once they are declared, bonuses cannot be cancelled or withdrawn: they will be added to your sum assured.

You will be sent a notice every time a bonus is declared, showing the accumulated amount of the lump sum.

As well as these so-called reversionary bonuses, it is common for a terminal bonus to be added at the end of the life of a policy. A terminal bonus is a final share-out of the surplus to which the policyholder whose policy is coming to an end is entitled (as worked out by the actuary of the insurers).

For a with-profits policy, no one can know at the time you take it out exactly what it will pay at the end. Reversionary bonuses and a terminal bonus, if any, depend on the future profits of the life insurance company – they cannot be predicted. But every life insurance company calculates projected figures for its future bonuses, usually based on its current bonus rates.

Obtain a reasonable range of quotations to show:
● premium
● sum insured
● term
● with-profits – at what level
● terminal bonus
● when and how frequently are bonuses credited
● special options
Which? reader B 224

past performance or future projections

You have to decide
● should you go for the life insurance company which has produced the best past performance?
or
● should you go for the company which is currently producing the best projections?

Both criteria have drawbacks. Past performance is just what it says, and there is no guarantee that it will be repeated in the future. But the same life insurance companies seem to appear top or near top of 'past performance' tables year after year, so consistency is another criterion.

Future projections are based on today's bonus rates but, quite apart from differences in the precise methods of calculation, projections are just exercises in arithmetic and may or may not come about.

Past performance

With-profits endowment policies: the top ten companies

The table shows the maturity values over a decade paid on 1 February 1975 to 1984 on a policy taken out by a man who was 30 years of age next birthday at the outset, for a monthly premium of £10.

FIRST COLUMN: total maturity value – including sum assured
SECOND COLUMN: percentage coming from terminal bonus

from *Money Management*
May 1984

10 year term			15 year term			25 year term		

1974

10 year term	£	%	15 year term	£	%	25 year term	£	%
Equitable Life	1,874	9.1	Ecclesiastical	3,338	—	Standard Life	7,572	25.3
NALGO	1,816	11.9	NALGO	3,297	15.3	Ecclesiastical	7,508	—
RNP Fund for Nurses	1,780	4.4	Equitable Life	3,263	9.1	Equitable Life	7,208	9.1
Post Office	1,738	—	Clerical Medical	3,188	1.9	Scottish Widows	7,077	7.8
Avon	1,726	8.0	RNP Fund for Nurses	3,105	7.2	Sun Alliance (London)	6,986	3.5
N Farmers Union	1,691	7.5	Standard Life	3,074	15.5	Equity & Law	6,923	5.4
UK Provident	1,690	6.8	Sun Alliance (London)	3,041	1.1	NALGO	6,767	20.6
Crusader	1,685	9.0	UK Provident	2,996	9.0	Friends' Provident	6,736	7.6
Teachers	1,680	9.6	Legal & General	2,988	7.5	Clerical Medical	6,677	4.6
Royal London	1,671	7.5	Avon	2,970	9.7	Scottish Provident	6,657	6.6

1975

10 year term	£	%	15 year term	£	%	25 year term	£	%
Equitable Life	1,890	9.1	Clerical Medical	3,357	5.6	Scottish Widows	7,819	14.5
RNP Fund for Nurses	1,797	4.4	Ecclesiastical	3,305	—	Ecclesiastical	7,525	—
NALGO	1,781	7.6	Equitable Life	3,275	9.1	Equitable Life	7,355	9.1
Post Office	1,760	—	NALGO	3,197	9.8	Sun Alliance (London)	7,265	6.0
Avon	1,733	8.0	RNP Fund for Nurses	3,080	5.0	Standard Life	7,138	19.9
Royal London	1,713	9.2	Sun Alliance (London)	3,032	1.6	Clerical Medical	7,083	7.2
Irish Life	1,704	5.6	UK Provident	3,032	9.1	Equity & Law	6,999	5.4
N Farmers Union	1,702	7.6	Scottish Widows	3,022	4.8	Scottish Provident	6,930	8.4
Clerical Medical	1,701	4.7	Post Office	3,021	—	Friends' Provident	6,845	7.7
Crusader	1,701	9.0	Prudential	3,008	—	UK Provident	6,701	11.8
UK Provident	1,701	7.0						

1976

10 year term	£	%	15 year term	£	%	25 year term	£	%
Equitable Life	1,909	9.1	Clerical Medical	3,359	5.6	Scottish Widows	7,727	12.7
RNP Fund for Nurses	1,814	4.4	Equitable Life	3,302	9.1	Ecclesiastical	7,678	—
Post Office	1,794	—	Ecclesiastical	3,273	—	Standard Life	7,612	23.0
NALGO	1,789	7.5	NALGO	3,230	9.7	Equitable Life	7,479	9.1
Royal London	1,719	9.0	RNP Fund for Nurses	3,124	5.0	Sun Alliance (London)	7,270	4.5
Crusader	1,716	9.0	Post Office	3,089	—	Clerical Medical	7,239	7.0
Irish Life	1,716	8.3	Friends' Provident	3,064	7.7	Friends' Provident	7,118	10.1
UK Provident	1,713	7.0	UK Provident	3,063	9.2	Equity & Law	7,072	5.5
Friends' Provident	1,699	6.0	Crusader	3,056	13.0	Scottish Provident	7,012	7.5
Provident Mutual	1,689	7.0	Legal & General	3,044	—	Norwich Union	6,860	19.1

1977

1977	£	%		£	%		£	%
Equitable Life	1,914	9.1	Clerical Medical	3,579	10.1	Clerical Medical	8,146	12.8
London Life	1,834	10.3	Equitable Life	3,338	9.1	Norwich Union	8,013	18.2
RNP Fund for Nurses	1,812	3.8	NALGO	3,262	9.6	Sun Alliance (London)	7,868	10.3
Post Office	1,810	—	London Life	3,245	12.8	Ecclesiastical	7,818	—
NALGO	1,797	7.5	Teachers	3,185	18.3	Scottish Widows	7,778	11.9
Teachers	1,788	4.1	Friends' Provident	3,168	9.6	Standard Life	7,736	23.0
Friends' Provident	1,745	7.5	RNP Fund for Nurses	3,150	9.9	Equitable Life	7,594	9.1
UK Provident	1,745	3.3	Ecclesiastical	3,144	—	London Life	7,476	—
Irish Life	1,739	7.4	Provident Mutual	3,143	—	Friends' Provident	7,422	12.5
Clerical Medical	1,728	8.9	Post Office	3,141	—	Scottish Provident	7,399	9.3
Provident Mutual	1,728	8.0						

1978

1978	£	%		£	%		£	%
Equitable Life	1,916	9.1	Clerical Medical	3,581	10.4	Norwich Union	8,521	23.0
London Life	1,869	10.6	Equitable Life	3,369	9.1	Clerical Medical	8,424	12.5
Post Office	1,826	—	London Life	3,323	13.1	Ecclesiastical	8,283	—
RNP Fund for Nurses	1,823	4.3	Ecclesiastical	3,317	—	Equity & Law	8,200	19.4
NALGO	1,783	7.4	NALGO	3,314	9.5	Scottish Widows	8,179	14.2
Teachers	1,783	12.9	Norwich Union	3,254	14.4	Standard Life	8,169	26.0
Irish Life	1,769	8.4	Teachers	3,207	17.3	Sun Alliance (London)	8,125	11.3
UK Provident	1,763	3.4	Friends' Provident	3,204	9.2	London Life	7,718	16.5
Friends' Provident	1,755	7.6	Post Office	3,194	—	Equitable Life	7,635	9.1
Crusader	1,742	9.0	Crusader	3,186	—	Friends' Provident	7,528	12.6

10 year term	£	%	15 year term	£	%	25 year term	£	%
1979								
Equitable Life	1,936	9.1	Equitable Life	3,526	11.1	Norwich Union	9,022	20.8
London Life	1,930	12.6	London Life	3,516	15.6	Clerical Medical	8,783	13.9
Post Office	1,841	—	Clerical Medical	3,512	12.0	Sun Alliance (London)	8,655	15.0
RNP Fund for Nurses	1,816	3.8	Norwich Union	3,464	13.6	Standard Life	8,618	28.5
Norwich Union	1,810	8.5	Scottish Amicable	3,372	14.4	Equity & Law	8,590	23.1
Friends' Provident	1,806	9.1	NALGO	3,334	9.4	Ecclesiastical	8,554	—
Provident Mutual	1,795	9.0	Friends' Provident	3,329	11.6	Scottish Widows	8,506	21.0
Irish Life	1,794	8.2	UK Provident	3,292	7.2	Scottish Amicable	8,435	23.0
NALGO	1,794	7.4	Provident Mutual	3,281	13.0	London Life	8,235	19.5
Scottish Widows	1,766	—	Standard Life	3,275	13.5	Equitable Life	8,141	11.1
1980								
Equitable Life	1,996	13.0	Equitable Life	3,725	14.9	Equity & Law	9,664	32.4
London Life	1,970	13.6	Norwich Union	3,641	17.2	Norwich Union	9,574	25.1
RNP Fund for Nurses	1,947	4.1	London Life	3,635	16.8	UK Provident	9,246	18.2
Post Office	1,917	—	UK Provident	3,597	12.5	Sun Alliance (London)	9,160	18.7
Friends' Provident	1,877	12.0	Scottish Life	3,582	12.0	Clerical Medical	9,061	13.9
UK Provident	1,867	8.2	Clerical Medical	3,530	12.3	Scottish Amicable	9,007	25.6
Scottish Widows	1,851	9.9	Friends' Provident	3,525	15.2	Scottish Widows	8,978	19.7
Norwich Union	1,850	10.6	Scottish Amicable	3,507	16.3	Standard Life	8,936	29.8
Medical Sickness	1,845	8.3	RNP Fund for Nurses	3,477	6.4	London Life	8,749	21.0
Scottish Life	1,843	9.0	Equity & Law	3,453	—	Ecclesiastical	8,661	—
						Equitable Life	8,661	14.9
1981								
Equitable Life	2,004	13.0	UK Provident	3,836	17.7	UK Provident	10,171	24.3
London Life	1,997	13.9	Equitable Life	3,777	14.9	Ecclesiastical	9,997	12.3
UK Provident	1,976	12.8	Ecclesiastical	3,755	12.3	Equity & Law	9,940	33.8
Tunbridge Wells	1,966	17.0	Tunbridge Wells	3,753	26.75	Sun Alliance (London)	9,824	23.4
RNP Fund for Nurses	1,950	4.1	Norwich Union	3,751	19.1	Norwich Union	9,818	26.9
Ecclesiastical	1,948	12.3	Scottish Life	3,733	14.1	Clerical Medical	9,736	18.2
Post Office	1,924	—	London Life	3,720	17.2	Standard Life	9,730	35.5
Scottish Widows	1,922	13.0	Scottish Amicable	3,713	20.0	Tunbridge Wells	9,548	42.75
Royal London	1,914	11.9	Clerical Medical	3,708	15.8	Scottish Amicable	9,540	28.0
Sun Alliance	1,910	—	Royal London	3,642	19.6	Scottish Widows	9,434	22.2
1982								
Equitable Life	2,078	14.9	UK Provident	4,000	18.7	UK Provident	10,872	31.9
Ecclesiastical	2,072	17.4	Ecclesiastical	3,997	17.4	Ecclesiastical	10,753	17.4
Scottish Widows	2,060	18.0	Equitable Life	3,962	16.7	Equity & Law	10.741	36.3
London Life	2,053	15.4	Norwich Union	3,961	18.7	Norwich Union	10,508	25.1
UK Provident	2,053	15.5	London Life	3,893	19.1	Sun Alliance (London)	10,452	27.3
Friends' Provident	2,029	16.4	Scottish Widows	3,873	19.7	Clerical Medical	10,285	21.1
Sun Alliance	2,012	17.8	Friends' Provident	3,871	20.5	Scottish Amicable	10,193	31.0
Tunbridge Wells	2,009	17.4	Tunbridge Wells	3,854	27.3	Scottish Widows	10,157	26.5
N Farmers Union	2,005	12.9	Scottish Amicable	3,849	23.1	Sun Alliance (Alliance)	10,133	29.6
Avon	1,992	13.6	Standard Life	3,840	21.6	Standard	10,116	36.5
1983								
Ecclesiastical	2,263	23.1	Standard Life	4,511	31.0	Standard Life	12,422	45.9
Equitable Life	2,258	21.6	Norwich Union	4,458	26.0	Clerical Medical	12,135	31.7
Standard Life	2,255	27.3	Equitable Life	4,391	24.5	Scottish Amicable	11,763	38.8
Norwich Union	2,249	24.1	Scottish Amicable	4,317	30.8	Ecclesiastical	11,673	23.1
Scottish Widows	2,235	23.7	Ecclesiastical	4,291	23.1	Equity & Law	11,557	39.4
RNP Fund for Nurses	2,223	13.0	Scottish Widows	4,245	25.1	Norwich Union	11,516	31.6
Scottish Amicable	2,197	25.9	UK Provident	4,176	23.3	UK Provident	11,376	30.0
Scottish Mutual	2,155	23.1	RNP Fund for Nurses	4,170	18.4	Scottish Widows	11,136	31.0
UK Provident	2,137	18.2	Clerical Medical	4,136	25.7	Sun Alliance (London)	10,961	29.9
Clerical Medical	2,136	20.8	Friends' Provident	4,081	23.5	Equitable Life	10,922	27.3

Future projections

Estimated benefits obtainable from a policy effected on 1 April 1983 by a man age 30 next birthday at entry, paying an annual premium of £250.

	WHOLE-LIFE Payable on death on 1 April 2023 Total premiums paid: £10,000			ENDOWMENT – 15 YEARS Payable on maturity on 1 April 1998 Total premiums paid: £3,750		
	Guaranteed sum assured £	Sum payable excl. terminal bonus £	Sum payable incl. terminal bonus £	Guaranteed sum asssured £	Sum payable excl. terminal bonus £	Sum payable incl. terminal bonus £
American Life	11,558	55,490	81,849	3,313	5,967	6,763
Australian Mutual Provident	13,227	65,031	79,858	3,805	6,656	7,454
Avon Insurance	10,490	61,012	81,220	3,214	6,219	7,421
Black Horse Life	11,598	67,454	78,625	3,340	6,463	7,088
Canada Life	14,741	63,165	79,321	3,647	6,276	7,216
City of Glasgow	9,804	60,784	65,882	3,195	7,029	7,412
Clerical, Medical	10,477	68,341	87,828	3,645	7,362	8,947
Colonial Mutual Life	10,745	53,778	64,523	3,480	6,316	7,986
Commercial Union	10,358	101,312	101,312	3,373	7,451	7,451
Confederation Life	22,945	48,853	69,579	3,558	6,374	7,782
Cornhill Insurance	12,949	60,652	60,652	3,673	6,377	6,377
Crusader Insurance	9,486	73,450	110,170	3,372	7,213	8,565
Eagle Star Insurance	11,267	98,451	133,324	3,305	7,148	8,685
Ecclesiastical Insurance	12,241	68,738	83,173	3,587	6,871	8,314
Economic Insurance	9,840	49,093	49,093	3,660	6,497	6,497
Equitable Life	11,944	76,042	95,115	3,491	7,027	8,432
Equity & Law Life	9,442	57,138	94,440	3,426	6,629	9,214
Federation Mutual	10,313	49,513	55,391	3,524	6,346	6,769
Friends' Provident Life Office	11,965	84,233	123,981	3,557	7,395	9,506
FS Assurance	10,312	68,080	85,404	3,432	6,531	7,461
Gresham Life	12,748	61,203	78,158	3,617	6,514	7,527
Guardian Royal Exchange	13,800	51,060	60,375	3,306	6,529	7,335
Hearts of Oak	10,930	31,918	44,507	3,516	6,047	6,617
Hill Samuel Life	11,958	61,996	61,996	3,534	6,550	6,550
Irish Life	11,047	55,235	68,491	3,372	7,165	8,303
Legal & General	11,500	84,283	124,315	3,381	6,711	8,209
Life Association of Scotland	10,015	71,580	90,050	3,523	7,076	8,142
Lloyds Life	—	—	—	3,337	6,010	6,010
London & Manchester	11,921	38,147	47,493	3,408	6,220	7,252
London Life Association	12,323	95,411	136,955	3,614	7,786	9,872
Manufacturers Life[N]	12,742	69,227	83,072	3,833	6,558	7,214
Medical Sickness	12,079	93,522	117,955	3,437	7,405	8,595
MGM Assurance	11,400	41,042	52,440	3,456	6,566	7,862

from *Planned Savings* June 1983

	WHOLE-LIFE Payable on death on 1 April 2023 Total premiums paid: £10,000			ENDOWMENT – 15 YEARS Payable on maturity on 1 April 1998 Total premiums paid: £3,750		
	Guaranteed sum assured £	Sum payable excl. terminal bonus £	Sum payable incl. terminal bonus £	Guaranteed sum asssured £	Sum payable excl. terminal bonus £	Sum payable incl. terminal bonus £
NALGO Insurance	11,644	41,918	47,740	3,175	6,270	6,865
National Employers Life	12,081	35,034	47,115	3,278	5,613	6,842
National Farmers Union	10,786	62,734	83,513	3,234	6,258	7,467
National Mutual Life, Australasia	14,346	75,764	126,905	3,811	6,979	8,549
National Mutual Life	9,651	67,933	97,074	3,410	7,086	8,924
National Provident Institution	10,543	64,943	80,493	3,417	6,757	7,953
Norwich Union Life	12,572	80,461	101,205	3,537	7,095	8,704
Pearl Assurance	9,756	61,254	76,567	3,336	6,643	7,639
Phoenix Life	11,415	37,669	37,669	3,328	6,198	6,198
Pioneer Mutual	12,632	45,475	52,044	3,128	6,178	6,788
Post Office Insurance	12,400	42,160	42,160	3,723	6,792	6,792
Provident Life Assn of London	10,076	68,282	68,282	3,319	6,802	6,802
Provident Mutual	12,121	59,065	82,688	3,609	6,532	7,510
Provincial Life	10,655	51,932	56,056	3,408	6,168	6,445
Prudential Assurance[N]	13,547	42,266	74,507	3,336	5,988	7,922
Refuge Assurance	11,468	36,698	52,753	3,521	6,426	8,275
Reliance Mutual	8,581	45,350	45,350	3,447	6,436	6,436
Royal Life	7,421	102,699	110,369	3,357	7,707	8,285
Royal London Mutual	11,394	35,094	56,742	3,465	6,168	7,034
RN Pension Fund for Nurses	—	—	—	3,700	7,585	9,291
Save & Prosper	20,940	20,940	50,287	4,344	4,344	6,121
Scottish Amicable	10,084	72,072	114,375	3,511	7,051	9,166
Scottish Equitable	9,154	57,477	74,390	3,342	6,657	7,817
Scottish Life Assurance	10,040	76,272	100,115	3,484	7,453	8,881
Scottish Mutual[N]	11,440	86,280	129,420	3,459	7,015	8,769
Scottish Provident Institution	10,503	73,940	102,776	3,420	7,109	8,104
Scottish Widows Fund	10,083	77,247	119,870	3,366	7,098	8,834
Sentinel Insurance	12,137	37,625	37,625	3,621	6,473	7,055
Standard Life Assurance	9,416	78,663	110,515	3,425	7,213	9,418
Sun Alliance	9,453	67,967	84,888	3,550	6,855	8,453
Sun Life Assurance	10,942	70,018	87,740	3,466	6,949	7,994
Sun Life of Canada	10,868	79,521	79,521	3,463	16,929	6,929
Swiss Life & Pensions	20,504	49,931	58,759	4,315	6,025	6,538
Teachers Assurance	13,052	32,630	41,375	3,658	5,716	6,996
Tunbridge Wells Equitable	11,013	39,646	82,596	3,602	7,112	10,272
Time Assurance	11,628	55,826	55,826	3,351	6,722	6,722
UK Provident	10,751	72,848	110,106	3,460	7,089	9,084
Wesleyan & General	11,248	35,094	73,248	3,573	6,414	8,119
Yorkshire-General[N]	11,858	92,852	129,298	3,363	7,131	8,827
Zurich Life	9,518	53,447	53,447	3,560	3,768	8,827

[N] rates for non-smokers
from *Planned Savings* June 1983

Low-cost with-profits policies

It is possible to have an arrangement, part of which is on a with-profits basis and the other part non-profit.

Low-cost with-profits endowment policies have seen a great boost in recent years as collateral security for mortgage loans.

What is paid on death is a high sum assured on a non-profit basis, or a much smaller sum assured with bonuses if this produces a larger sum (as it may do towards the end of the term of the policy). What is paid at the end of the term if you survive is on a with-profits basis – that is to say, the smaller sum assured plus bonuses.

If you decide to use the endowment system for paying off a mortgage loan, you take out a low-cost endowment policy for the term of the mortgage and a sum assured equal to the amount of the loan. This would be paid if you died during the term of the mortgage. If you survive to the end of the specified term of years, the amount payable will be the smaller guaranteed amount but plus bonuses.

Why is there such a large difference in premiums between insurance companies that are offering the same amount and type of cover?
Which? reader A 84

Low-cost endowment policy
monthly premiums
for sum assured on death £10,000

25-YEAR TERM

man aged 30 next birthday	monthly premium
	£
Equitable Life	13.83
London Life	13.93
Commercial Union	14.20
Medical Sickness	14.36
Friends' Provident	14.50
Norwich Union	14.60
Yorkshire General	(N)14.60
Eagle Star	14.70
Crusader	14.80
Scottish Life	14.88

(N) rates for non-smokers

The figures shown are the best premiums quoted by life insurance companies for a hypothetical 'normal' man at different ages. Last place on the list is not the worst on the market but the 10th best.

The information is taken from tables in *The Savings Market* February 1984.

Unit-linked

With a unit-linked policy, the lump sum payable is expressed as being equal in value to so-many units in the particular investment fund (property, shares, equity).

The value of the investments to which the units are linked fluctuates with the market, and there is not the relatively steady with-profits basis where the results of a broader spread of investments average out, so you could do much better or much worse.

In spite of its name, unit-linked life insurance is intended mainly for saving and investing rather than to provide life insurance. You pay a lump sum (single-premium bond) to the insurance company who, after deducting their expenses, use a little of it to provide you with some life insurance and invest the rest.

Alternatively, instead of investing the single premium, you can pay regular smaller sums over a 10-year period. Technically, the payments into such a savings plan count as premiums and therefore used to get the 15% tax relief. Since the abolition of tax relief for premiums on new life insurance policies in March 1984, for regular savings you should consider going direct into units instead.

What you get at the end depends on the units' price at the time (it goes up and down according to the value of the investment funds to which the units were linked). Therefore, if you are going to need some money at a precise time which cannot be put off – for example, to repay a loan, to pay school fees or university expenses, to take retirement – you should not choose a unit-linked plan, because the time when you need the money might be a time when the unit price is low.

The type of policy commonly called 'unit-linked whole (of) life' is different and provides a relatively high level of life insurance cover plus an element of savings. However, you are likely to be better off, especially if you are young, if you arrange the life cover you need by means of temporary insurance policies and then save as a separate exercise.

What is called 'building society linked endowment' (also referred to as deposit administration, particularly in the context of pension schemes) is a variation on the unit-linked approach; with this, your premiums are invested as money rather than being used to buy units. What happens is that you pay a premium, and after the insurance company has taken an allowance for expenses and for the minimal life cover, the balance is invested in a building society (at a special rate of interest). If you die, the policy pays either the sum insured or whatever is in the account with the building society, whichever is the higher.

The *Which?* report in January 1983 on life insurance selling methods commented that 'It's important to buy the right sort of insurance. Too often, life insurance salesmen are offering plans which are extremely expensive for the insurance cover they give. They're really long-term savings plans. Unless this is what you want, don't buy them'.

Personal pension plans

Someone who is self-employed or an employee not in an employer's pension scheme can have life insurance and savings by what, technically, is a retirement annuity, approved under section 226 of the Income and Corporation Taxes Act 1970 and by a section 226A policy.

The tax advantages

The tax advantages of an approved retirement policy are that
● the premiums you pay are deductible in full from your earnings before tax assessment so you get tax relief on the premiums at the highest rate of income tax you are paying (excluding investment income surcharge in any year for which that applies)
● the retirement pension you get is regarded as earned income rather than investment income; if you take part of it as a cash sum, it is tax free.

The premiums

20% for people born between 1916 and 1933 inclusive; higher percentages for people born 1915 or before.

The premiums paid to an approved retirement policy on which you can get tax relief are limited to $17\frac{1}{2}\%$ of your so-called 'net relevant earnings' for each tax year: broadly, your earnings from self-employment and/or non-pensionable employment after business expenses but before tax.

There are complex 'carry forward' and 'carry back' rules if in any tax year you do not pay the full amount of premiums eligible for tax relief.

When you are taking out a retirement annuity policy, check what you would get from the premiums actually paid if you had to cease paying premiums at any time.

If you are ill, your earnings may reduce or cease so that you are not then eligible to pay premiums of the size you would wish to go into your retirement provision. Some retirement policies provide a 'waiver of premium' facility: the premiums which would have been paid are waived while you are ill and you will get the benefits at the end as though those premiums had all been paid. For this, you have to pay a higher rate of premium throughout.

Benefits from retirement policies

All or most of the benefit from a retirement policy has to be in the form of a pension. A lump sum can be paid but only at the precise point at which you start to draw the pension and the lump sum is not allowed to exceed 3 times the annual gross pension which will afterwards be paid.

The pension itself can have increases built in and, if you wish, part of it can be used to buy instead an annuity payable in the event of your death to your widow or widower, but the amount to be paid to your widow or widower cannot be greater than the amount of the pension to yourself would have been.

The pension can only commence (and correspondingly the cash sum can only be taken) between your 60th birthday and your 75th birthday, unless your occupation has an official earlier retirement age. (The Inland Revenue say, for example, that footballers can retire at 35.)

You can start to get your pension before the age of 60 if you take 'early ill health retirement'.

Section 226A policies

Anyone who can take out a personal pension scheme can also take out term insurance under section 226A of the Income and Corporation Taxes Act 1970 which provides full income tax relief (30% or more). As with retirement annuities, the tax relief is not by deduction from the premiums: it comes through your PAYE code or tax assessment and you pay the premiums gross.

The limit that you can spend on the premiums for 226A policies is 5% of your net earnings – and this counts as part of the 17½% (or 20%) limit for tax-deductible premiums for a retirement policy.

Policies under section 226A were given a boost by the Finance Act 1980, which removed the wording in the original legislation preventing such policies from being written under trust. This means that nowadays a section 226A policy can be used to provide not only for a spouse but somebody else: for example, your partner, your son or daughter, or your fellow-shareholding director.

Not all life insurance companies offer section 226A policies to any great extent. However, you should be able to find all the following policies available in special section 226A form, enabling you to obtain full income tax relief on the premiums you pay:

- temporary or term insurance
- increasing temporary or term insurance
- increasable temporary or term insurance
- decreasing temporary or term insurance (including mortgage protection policies)
- income for dependants (f.i.b.) policies (including increasing benefit).

Examples of section 226A policies

temporary insurance
Mr Brown, age 46 next birthday, leaves employment with a large company and sets up in business on his own account. As an employee, his salary was £12,000 a year and he was a member of a pension scheme which carried death-in-service benefits of 4 times salary as a lump sum plus a widow's pension of 4/9ths of salary. Now that he is self-employed and no longer has those death-in-service benefits, he decides to take out a 19-year policy which would provide £60,000 on death before his retirement pension starts.

His gross monthly premium is £28.22. Mr Brown is paying income tax at 30%, so the net monthly outlay is £19.75 (annual £237).

Should he die within the 19 years, his widow, if benefiting under the terms of his will or if the policy had been in trust for her benefit, would receive, free of all taxes, a lump sum of £60,000.

increasing temporary insurance

Mrs Morlais, age 40 next birthday, dressmaker, wishes to provide a sum on her death if she dies within 20 years, as follows

	sum assured
on death in years 1 to 5	£20,000
on death in years 6 to 10	£30,000
on death in years 11 to 15	£40,000
on death in years 16 to 20	£50,000

Her gross monthly premium is £6.80 throughout; so if her rate of tax is 30%, her net monthly outlay will be £4.76 (£57.12 a year).

mortgage protection policy

Mr Singh, self-employed illustrator and approaching the age of 30, has arranged a building society repayment mortgage loan of £15,000, repayable over 25 years at 10% interest. He takes out a mortgage protection policy with an initial sum assured of £15,000, running off over the 25-year term. His gross annual premium amounts to £18.77. He is paying income tax at 30%, so his net annual outlay is £13.14.

If he were to die just over 6 years later, £13,304 would be paid out on the policy. His widow could then use it to pay off the outstanding mortgage loan. (The outstanding mortgage loan would be within a few £s of £13,300 unless the interest rate had changed greatly during those six years or the basic rate of tax altered.)

Decreasing term policies are often quoted within an interest band, but there is no guarantee that there will be enough to pay off the mortgage if interest rates are considerably increased.

income for dependants

Mr Timeric is a self-employed builder. He is approaching age 30, married, with a small child.

He has already made substantial life insurance provision for his wife and made a will making her his beneficiary, and now wants to be sure that should he die while his child – and possibly children in the future – are still dependent, his widow would have regular income-like payments. He, therefore, takes out a family income benefit policy that would provide, in the event of his death within 25 years, payments of £3,000 a year (tax free) for the balance of that period.

His gross annual premium is £30.20. Mr Timeric is paying income tax at 30% so the net annual outlay is £21.14.

Should he die just over 8 years after taking out the policy, his widow would receive, free of all taxes, payments of £3,000 a year for 17 years.

Policies under trust and capital transfer tax

Married Women's Policies of Assurance (Scotland) Act 1880: a policy effected by a married man on his own life and expressed to be for the benefit of his wife or children or both shall be deemed a trust for them.

If you want the proceeds of a policy of life insurance to belong to someone other than yourself or your estate, the policy has to be under trust. It is a legal necessity to get the words just right. For instance, the form of trust for a life insurance policy under the Married Women's Property Act of 1882 has to be expressed to be 'for the benefit of a man's wife and/or his children'; similarly, a woman can effect a policy for the benefit of her husband and/or children.

The beneficiary, or each beneficiary if there are to be more than one, must be clearly specified by name or some other way of identification. This gives the beneficiary outright ownership or what is known as an interest in possession: he or she is regarded as the owner of the policy for capital transfer tax purposes, right from the outset. For example, if you decide to effect your policy for another adult by saying

'for the benefit of and in trust for John Smith if he shall be living at the date of the event upon which the sum assured is expressed in the policy to become payable'

the wording creates a trust and gives John Smith the interest in possession: John Smith is the owner of that policy and you are not. That means that each payment of premium represents a transfer of value, which is chargeable to capital transfer tax (to the extent, if any, that it is not exempt). The various capital transfer tax exemptions, such as the exemption between husband and wife, the £3,000 a year exemption, and the normal expenditure out-of-income exemption, mean that in the vast majority of cases such transfers are wholly exempt. When the beneficiary comes to take the proceeds of the policy, since he or she has been the owner of the policy right from the start, there is no transfer of value – and therefore no capital transfer tax liability.

If the specified beneficiary is someone under the age of eighteen, he or she does not have an interest in possession. But the capital transfer tax consequences are similar, provided the trust is such that the beneficiary will acquire an interest in possession (or will become entitled outright) at a specified age, which must not exceed twenty-five.

In cases of retirement policy death benefits, or policies written under section 226A, if the benefits are in trust even if the destination is not closely specified, the trustees can pay out those benefits without any liability to capital transfer tax when that happens.

For example, if you are self-employed and you are taking out life insurance for the benefit of your wife and children, you may wish to leave to the discretion of your trustees – perhaps your solicitor and your wife – the proportions in which you would like those various people to benefit. With a section 226A policy, this can be done without any capital transfer tax disadvantage.

If you are considering effecting a policy under trust, discuss what it is that you are trying to do with someone at the life insurance company (who cannot, however, be held responsible for any errors or omissions in a trust wording) or with a solicitor (who must take responsibility for any advice which he gives on trust wordings).

If you are arranging life insurance with the intention of benefiting your spouse, you could, instead of creating a trust, say in your will that the proceeds of the policy are to go to your spouse. Provided that your spouse has a permanent home in one of the countries of the United Kingdom (UK domicile), there is no advantage in terms of capital transfer tax in having a life insurance arrangement under trust, because there is no capital transfer tax on any transfers between husband and wife.

There are, however, other advantages (and possible disadvantages), which may follow from having the arrangements in trust.

■ *advantage 1*
On death of the life insured, the proceeds can be paid by the life insurance company without waiting for a grant of probate or letters of administration, provided there is a surviving trustee. The surviving trustee can collect the proceeds simply by producing a death certificate and the policy.

■ *advantage 2*
In the event of the bankruptcy of the individual who took out the policy, there is a degree of protection against creditors if it is under trust, particularly if the trust is within the Married Women's Property Act of 1882.

Married Women's Policies of Assurance (Scotland) Act 1880

The scottish legislation on bankruptcy is not the same but the effect is more or less similar.

■ *disadvantage 1*
It may be more difficult, or impossible, to use a policy that has been placed in trust as collateral security for a loan.

■ *disadvantage 2*
Problems could arise if the person for whom the policy is held in trust dies before the policyholder, or where a policy is in trust for husband or wife and the marriage breaks up.

Capital transfer tax planning

A person without a spouse, who wants to avoid assets having to be sold in order to meet capital transfer tax liabilities on his death, could arrange to take out a whole-life policy of approximately the prospective amounts of that tax.

For a married couple, depending on how the wills of the individuals are arranged, the answer may be a whole-life policy on each life, or where the first death will result in the surviving

spouse inheriting a large proportion of the estate, the married couple together taking out what is called a 'last survivor' policy. This is essentially a whole-life policy with the sum assured payable on the death of the second of the two people to die. The policies are effected under trust, and provided that suitable trusts are used, and that they have been written correctly, the payment of proceeds from such policies will be free of capital transfer tax.

Last survivor whole-life non-profit insurance
annual premium of £1000, payable to date of second death

The figures shown are the best premiums quoted by life insurance companies for a hypothetical 'normal' man and woman at different ages. Last place on the list is not the worst on the market but the 10th best.

The information is taken from tables in *The Savings Market* February 1984.

man aged 60 next birthday and woman aged 55 next birthday	sum assured £	man aged 70 next birthday and woman aged 70 next birthday	sum assured £
Yorkshire General	(N)61,889	Economic	(N)28,699
Economic	(N)59,903	Yorkshire General	(N)28,660
Scottish Mutual	(N)57,762	Scottish Mutual	(N)27,302
Scottish Provident	57,407	Provident Life	26,995
Clerical Medical	57,241	Clerical Medical	26,820
Gresham Life	56,896	Ecclesiastical	26,666
Ecclesiastical	55,699	Gresham Life	26,422
City Westminster	55,284	Scottish Widows	25,840
Sun Life	55,222	Life Assn Scotland	25,539
Equitable Life	55,144	Equity & Law	25,531

(N) rates for non-smokers

joint life policies

A policy can be on a joint life basis, with the sum assured payable on the death of the first of the two lives to die. This is sometimes suggested for mortgage protection. A possible better alternative, particularly where the mortgage loan repayments depend on both incomes, is that each of the couple should have a policy on his or her own life will to or in trust for the other. The two single life policies would cost very little more than the one joint life policy (possibly less if one or both individuals can qualify for a section 226A policy, with the tax relief on the premiums for such a policy).

It is not necessary to take two endowment policies because you do not need two lots of money at the end. One person could take out a low-cost endowment policy and the other a term insurance for the same period and the same sum assured.

Suitable types of insurance for different circumstances

Life insurance has to be reviewed regularly as one's circumstances change and as the economic climate changes. What may appear a very large sum assured initially is quickly reduced in value by inflation. Too few companies mention this in their sales literature.

My first insurance policy had a sum assured of £2500, then twice my salary. Now, 9 years later, the sum assured is ¼ of my salary. By the time it matures in 26 years' time, it will be practically worthless in purchasing power even allowing for attaching bonuses.
Which? reader B 80

I am single and don't intend having a family or getting married, so I see little benefit in taking out a policy.
Which? reader A 114

I see no reason, as a widow, to pay a life insurance for the benefit of others. It's a good thing for a family.
Which? reader A 115

When I was young and poorly paid, I could not afford it. Now I am too old to afford it. Anyway, I and my wife have superannuated posts.
Which? reader A 98

This outline suggests the various types of life insurance which may perhaps be suitable in the circumstances.

■ *young single man without dependants*
Unless you want to benefit somebody or some institution at your death or have a debt that will have to be paid off, there is no need for life insurance as such.

You may wish to buy a house later: concentrate on accumulating money in a building society or, as an alternative, take out a building society linked endowment policy (that may be better than starting the type of endowment policy whichg later may or may not be accepted as collateral: there is no guarantee that yours would be accepted by the building society you go to).

You may acquire dependants later on in life. While you are young and healthy, premiums will be low, so now may be the time to take out convertible term insurance, so as to give yourself the option to take out in the future whatever life insurance may then be suitable for your requirements without having to provide evidence of health.

■ *single woman without dependants*
There is no significant difference in your requirements, nor in the course of action you should consider, compared to the single man without dependants. There are a few policies aimed at women, but these may be no more than a marketing gimmick as far as straight life insurance is concerned. But all life insurance is cheaper for women anyway, and most of these policies seem only to take advantage of that. A policy may, for example, offer a discount of up to 25% on a 25-year term policy taken out by a woman at the age of 40. What is sold as if it were a discount is no more than an actuarial fact: to arrive at the rate for a woman, most insurers use the rate for a man less 4 years so that a woman of 40 is rated as a man of 36.

■ *single person with dependants*
You need life cover similar to a married couple's.

■ *married couple*
Your priority is likely to be adequate life cover so that in the event of your death, the proceeds payable are adequate for the needs of your widower or widow and other dependants; consider the various types of temporary insurance. If you are eligible, remember 226A policies.

If you are buying your home with a mortgage, you may decide to have an endowment policy to cover the loan or, with a repayment mortgage, may have to take out a decreasing term (mortgage protection) policy.

■ *for a child*

■ *for a child*
You can take out what is known as a child's option policy: an endowment policy taken out by you which, when it reaches initial maturity date (usually when the child is 18), provides the option for the 'child' then to transmute it into another kind of life insurance – for example, an endowment policy to the age of 65.

■ *unmarried couple*
If you are living with somebody to whom you are not married, no doubt your real life commitments and moral responsibilities are similar to those you would feel if you were married, but from a taxation point of view, you are either married or you are not. (Expressions such as 'common-law husband' or 'common-law wife' have no meaning in the context of UK taxation.) You do not get any tax relief on the premiums for a life insurance policy on the life of your partner nor if together you have a joint life policy, irrespective of when the policy was taken out.

If you want life insurance for the benefit of your partner, you can take out a policy on your own life in trust for your partner.

Capital transfer tax is an important aspect of being unmarried. For a married couple, there is total exemption from capital transfer tax on any transfers between them during lifetime or at death. There is no such exemption for an unmarried couple. Any transfer (apart from exemptions such as the annual £3,000) you make to your partner, during lifetime or at death, will be chargeable to capital transfer tax, and once your cumulative total of transfers reaches the point at which the zero-rated band runs out, tax will start to be payable. Therefore, any policies you take out with the intention of benefiting your partner should be under trust for his or her benefit.

Before taking out a policy, consider:
● possible additions to family – marriage, children – and make relevant allowances
● taking inflation into account, is sum assured likely to be adequate in a few years' time?
● when will policy expire and how old will you be then?
● if policy also a form of investment in addition to life cover, is the maturity date sensible?
● if regarding policy as form of investment, are there better alternatives, giving a better return?
● does your employer give insurance cover and is it adequate? consider effect if you changed jobs
● 'shop around' insurance companies – get details on different types of policies.

Which? reader B 200

How to insure yourself

Life insurance can be bought through
* insurance brokers
* full-time insurance company representatives
* bank insurance services
* solicitors, accountants
* other intermediaries: insurance agents, consultants; building societies
* directly from an insurance company.

Where to go for advice

There are numerous sources of advice, but whoever you decide to rely on, you should be as clear as possible first in your mind what you want – for instance, high insurance cover or good savings prospects.

Insurance broker

Get full details of alternatives. Be advised by non-interested party.
Be sure of your requirements.
Which? reader B 105

The expertise available differs enormously from one broker to another. Some brokers who specialise in perhaps car insurance or household and general insurance, may not be knowledgeable about life insurance.

Have a good broker – I think I have!
Which? reader B 112

Some insurance brokers are able to undertake a really comprehensive review of your requirements and come up with the right ideas for you, and be able to advise you on the choice of insurance company and policies, and get you competitive quotations. A good broker will have *Planned Savings* and *Money Management* and *Which?* information at his fingertips (and may be aware of mooted changes in the insurance companies' investment strategy which may affect future with-profits projections). The broker should advise not only on the most suitable insurance for you but also on the most tax-efficient way of arranging it.

The *Life & Pensions Brokers Directory* is available free from BIBA, 14 Bevis Marks, London EC3A 7NT, who can be asked for the names of other member brokers who have become eligible to be included in the directory since its publication in 1983.

The British Insurance Brokers' Association has compiled a directory of life and pensions brokers. This lists the individuals in firms, arranged in 22 regions of the UK, who have relevant experience and qualifications in life and pension business. The directory includes a summary of the code of conduct with which all registered brokers must comply.

Bank

A bank manager is often a source of financial advice, and some may be knowledgeable in the field of life insurance.

Most of the big banks have insurance departments acting as registered brokers, with specialists in life insurance.

Professional advisers

Your solicitor or accountant may be able to advise you on life insurance and pensions as part of the professional service for which he charges you. In particular, if you are in business as a self-employed person, he might prod you into doing something about your pension arrangements and some associated life insurance provision. Life insurance companies which do not pay commission get a substantial volume of business through accountants and solicitors.

Agents

A self-employed agent tied to one particular life insurance company may do a perfectly good job for you. But he is restricted to placing business with only the one company, which may not be the best one for the type of policy you require.

Other freelance agents will be able to offer policies for a number of insurance companies with which they have a tie-up, and their recommendations will be limited to these.

Building societies offering endowment-type mortgages to house buyers generally act as agents for the insurance company whose policy will be acceptable as collateral for the mortgage.

Company representatives

If you receive a call at your office or home from an insurance salesman wanting to sell you a life insurance policy, he may be a member of a direct-selling team employed (and trained) by one of the life insurance companies or firms of registered brokers or insurance consultants.

For salesmen who in insurance jargon are called 'introducers', the life assurance selling code of practice provides that they should
– *deal only in matters in which they are competent and seek assistance from the life office whenever necessary*
– *bring in a qualified representative of the life office to explain the contract to the 'prospect'*
– *not solicit business outside the terms of their appointment*
– *not attempt to influence the 'prospect' with regard to the completion of a proposal form.*

On the other hand, the person who calls may have received only a summary training from a less reputable insurance company, or from some unofficial body, and be able only to repeat salesman's jargon which may hide total ignorance of what the insurance is about.

First, ask your caller to identify himself: he should be able to produce an identity card issued by the insurance company which employs him or by a firm of registered brokers, or a salesman's practising certificate, such as the insurance intermediaries' card issued to their members by the Institute of Insurance Consultants.

Connection between broker and firm not always clear. Often, under pressure, firms will reduce premium by making the uninsured person an 'agent' and remitting some (2$\frac{1}{2}$% or more) of the yearly premium in order to ensure business.

Which? reader A 87

The Life Insurance Association and the Chartered Insurance Institute issue practising certificates for salesmen who have passed certain qualifying examinations.

Non-professional advisers

Find out as much detail as you can before meeting the insurance person so that you don't get dragged in by his patter. Always think about the policy before signing – preferably for 24 hours. Only if you are absolutely sure sign straightaway.
Which? reader B 39

Only registered brokers are allowed to call themselves 'brokers'. However, anybody can call himself something like 'life insurance specialist' or 'financial consultant' or 'investment adviser' or 'school fees planner'. He may be an expert, or a failed secondhand car salesman who has decided to try something else.

Do not sign a proposal form of any kind at the first contact but ask for the literature to be left with you to study carefully at your leisure. This will give you time to compare what others have to offer.

When dealing with a direct salesman, do not pay cash for the first premium, but make your cheque out to the insurance company or firm of brokers, not the salesman.

Insurance companies

Advertisements by off-shore (not authorised) insurance companies must include a warning statement that they do not come under DTI supervision and that their policyholders are not protected by the Policyholders Protection Act.

The specialist companies dealing with life insurance are referred to in the trade as life offices.

You can write (or go in person) for their literature or complete a coupon in a newspaper advertisement or direct mail shot.

A large number of life offices belong to

The Life Offices' Association or   Associated Scottish Life Offices
Aldermary House   23 St Andrew Square
Queen Street   Edinburgh EH2 1AQ
London EC4N 1TP

whose aim is to promote the interests of life insurance. The LOA and ASLO have issued a 'statement of long-term insurance practice' and each has a complaints procedure.

'industrial' insurance collectors

Money Which? June 1982 said that 'most of the policies are investment-type (endowment or whole-life) and provide only small amounts of insurance cover. In general, the policies are poor value because of the high expenses involved in collecting the premiums'.

Much life insurance, although not as much as some years ago, is done via life office employees who call on people at home, and collect premiums every month or two months. What this 'home service', as it is called, achieves is life insurance for many people who otherwise would not have any.

Most companies who transact home service business belong to
The Industrial Life Offices Association
Aldermary House
Queen Street
London EC4N 1TL

which has issued a statement of industrial insurance practice and has its own complaints procedure.

Commission

The majority of life insurance companies pay commission to brokers and other agents for each policy they bring to the office. There is at present no general scale of commission.

Different commission is paid depending on not only the company and the type of policy but also to whom it is paid – ranging from specialist registered insurance broker to non-specialist non-registered independent intermediary.

The commission is on the premium you pay, and the rate varies considerably according to the type of policy. For example, the commission rate on a whole-life policy can be 90% to 120% of the first year's premium; the commission rate is lower on many other policies. So, an agent or broker may be swayed to recommend a policy paying him a high commission rather than one that is best for your circumstances.

Be sure you really need whole-life insurance before taking it out: often convertible term insurance (lower commission) will do the job quite adequately and cost a lot less.

Commission is also paid on renewal premiums, but at a lower rate than on the first year's premium.

ask!
A registered insurance broker must, under his code of conduct, disclose the amount of his commission if asked, as must a chartered accountant.

Because of the inherent conflict of interest, you should always ask the broker, bank manager, building society manager, consultant, company representative or agent what the commission is on the policies he is suggesting. If he declines to give this information, draw your own conclusion.

No commission

I would like to see direct sale from company to individual, so cutting cost by removing commission. *Which?* reader B 130

A very few life insurance companies do not pay commission to brokers or other intermediaries – who are therefore unlikely to recommend their policies. You approach these companies direct, or through one of their full-time salesmen.

The non-commission-paying companies are mainly specialist ones (for nurses, for example) and the Ecclesiastical Insurance Office, the Equitable Life Assurance Society and the London Life Association.

Proposed self-regulation

The setting-up of a registry of life assurance commissions (ROLAC) has been initiated, on lines to be agreed by the life insurance industry. A registrar has been appointed. It is hoped that the ROLAC scheme will be operational in 1985.

The object of ROLAC is 'to ensure that the commission payable on the sale of long-term insurance policies shall not be capable of giving rise to any charge of bias in the advice given by the Intermediary relating to the selection of a Life Office.'

The proposal form

To most people, a life insurance proposal form may look long and complicated.

Some of the questions are very searching and may seem impertinent. Basically, what they are designed to find out from you is

* what sort of arrangements you wish to make (type of policy)
* how much you wish to pay (premium)
* what benefits you want to get (sum assured)
* your state of health (and that of parents and siblings)
* how old you are (next birthday)
* your height and weight (and recent change in weight)
* any factor which makes you other than a normal risk (smoking, drinking, 'hazardous' occupation).

On most proposal forms you have to do no more than put a tick against the type of policy you have chosen, and any optional extra arrangements.

In some cases, you are asked to complete a much shorter form: for instance, where the arrangements involve a substantial savings element and very little life cover.

Medical details

Be prepared to have to give detailed information about illnesses and treatment you have had. Forms vary in the manner in which you are asked.

Your age and the amount of insurance you want will have a bearing on what happens next. Most life insurance companies operate what they call non-medical age limits. If, at that age, the life insurance asked for does not exceed a certain figure, no medical examination may be required: for example, no medical examination up to age 40 for sum assured up to £125,000; to age 45 for sum assured up to £100,000.

If the amount you want to insure for exceeds the non-medical limits, or there appears from the form to be something in your medical or personal history on which the life insurance company would like more information to assess the correct premium, the insurance company may require a medical examination. Do not arrange that yourself, wait to be told what to do. Sometimes insurance companies will share one medical examination, so if you are getting quotations from three different companies, you may need to have just one medical.

For each quotation required, a questionnaire has to be completed.

The life insurance company may seek a private medical attendant's report, known as a 'PMAR'. With your authority, given by your signing the proposal form, the life insurance company will write to your doctor or any doctor whom you have consulted, and ask for information which could be relevant to a proposal for life insurance.

E   PERSONAL STATEMENT

TO BE ANSWERED BY LIVES TO BE INSURED

1   Have you made a previous proposal for life or accident or sickness insurance to the Society?

2   Has any proposal on your life ever been postponed, declined or accepted at special terms? (Details of companies and dates to be given)

3   Do you engage in any hazardous pursuits or occupation? e.g. aviation, working at heights, climbing, diving, motor sports, etc.

4   Do you intend to journey abroad or live outside the U.K.? (excluding holidays)

5   Have you had any X-rays, medical tests, investigations or operations, or attended any hospital, consultant, or clinic?

6   Are you now or have you recently been on a diet, treatment, or taking any pills or drugs?

7   HAVE YOU EVER HAD—

   (i)   asthma, bronchitis, chest pain, high blood pressure, rheumatic fever, disease of the lungs or heart?

   (ii) indigestion, ulcer, colitis, bladder, thyroid, kidney or prostate trouble, rheumatism, gout or diabetes?

   (iii) depresssion, anxiety, breakdown, blackouts, faints, fits or any mental or nervous trouble, or pains in joints or muscles?

   (iv) any other illness or injury, disability or need for medical attention?

8   (a) What is your Height without shoes?   (b) Weight?

9   (a) How much do you Smoke?   (b) Drink?

   (c) If you do not smoke or drink, state for how long, reason for discontinuing and previous consumption

10 Reason for last medical consultation with date and details of treatment

11 Name and address of your present doctor

12 Have either parents, brothers or sisters died?

   If 'YES' state cause and age at death

4. Health & Activities

1 (a) Please state the name and address of your doctor

   (b) If you have been registered for less than six months, please state the name and address of your previous doctor

2 (a) Please state your height

   (b) Please state your weight

3 (a) Please provide details of consultations you have had with your doctor in the last five years

   (b) Please state the names of any drugs or medicines you are currently taking

4 Please provide details of any hospital admissions or examinations

5 (a) Please state the exact nature of your occupation

   (b) Please provide details if you intend to reside outside the UK

6 (a) Please provide details of any hazardous sports or activities in which you intend to, or participate in

   (b) Please provide details of any anticipated aviation other than as a fare-paying passenger

Above from Norwich Union Life Insurance Society *proposal*

Right from Hill Samuel Life Assurance Ltd *application*

Additional information

If you are taking out life insurance where yours is not the life which is being insured, it is likely there will be two forms: one for you to complete and the other to be completed by the person whose life is going to be insured. His or her personal details and medical history will have to be given. Yours is likely to be a simple form, calling for a brief statement of your insurable interest in the life to be insured.

Similarly, if you and another person (typically, your spouse) are going to take out an arrangement together, it is likely that each of you will have to fill up an individual form and then the two of you will have to complete together a third form which acts as a link document, tying together the others, to form the basis on which the contract is entered into. This arises mainly with last survivor policies, and joint life/first death policies.

If the arrangement you are entering into is a retirement annuity under section 226 or a section 226A life insurance policy with full tax relief on the premiums, part of the documentation you must complete is a declaration to the effect that you are eligible: either self-employed or an employee in non-pensionable employment, as laid down by the Inland Revenue.

Payment of premiums

Some professional associations are linked with insurance companies and discounts on premiums are allowable. Worth looking for on large policies.

Which? reader B 293

Generally speaking, you have a choice of ways in which to pay premiums.

You can usually pay annually, half yearly, quarterly or monthly. Some insurers charge more for monthly payments than for annual – partly because they are not getting the money so soon, and partly because they are having to collect 12 times instead of once. If you are going to pay on a periodic basis, you may have to use some kind of standing order and may be asked to complete a direct debiting mandate rather than the old-style banker's order. Under the direct debiting system, it is the payee (the insurance company) who initiates the payment.

If it is a variable direct debit order you are asked to sign, it may be for 'an unspecified amount' or 'not exceeding the amount of . . .' (the premium). This enables the insurance company to change the amount without further authority from you.

Direct debiting is ultimately safe, because bond insurance has to be taken out by all operators of direct debiting systems, so that any money wrongfully taken will be re-paid immediately. But watch the payments, especially at the beginning and at any change of policy. The bank's computer is linked to the insurance company's computer and the whole thing untouched by human brain. Strange things can happen: a debit every day – or week – no debits at all (but you have to pay in the end).

Suicide

Most life insurance policies contain a provision that the sum assured will not be paid in the event of death by suicide within a specified time. The specified time varies from policy to policy; 12 or 13 months is the most common.

The suicide clause often contains an exception to protect the bona fide interest of a third party, such as a building society or bank which has made a loan with the policy as collateral security.

What happens next

Normally, you will get an illustration form or an acceptance letter which tells you the terms of the insurance and the premium. If these details differ in any way from what you have been led to believe, you should enquire why.

The acceptance letter will invite you to complete the business by paying the first premium. This may be more or less than the amount originally quoted because standard age-and-sex based quotations do not take into account an individual's health, habits and occupation.

The acceptance letter stage may be missed out if the first premium has been paid at the time the proposal form was completed.

The cooling-off period

Read the small print. Make sure you can get out without costing too much. *Which?* reader B 117

In a very complicated business, with a lot of small print, changing your mind can cause you a loss on what you have actually paid in. *Which?* reader A 16

You have a legal right to a so-called cooling-off period. After you complete a proposal form for life insurance, you have the right to change your mind and get back any money without penalty. The life insurance company is obliged to send you a notice, in statutory form, to inform you of your rights within the 10-day cooling-off period.

However, the cooling-off period does not apply to all types.

There is no cooling-off period with a single-premium policy: once you have paid your money, that is it. Anything you get back thereafter, even if the next day, is in accordance with the terms of the contract you have entered into and could, for instance, be considerably less than the amount you had paid. Such a policy is excluded presumably because before parting with so large a sum, you are likely to have given considerable thought to the transaction. But these are the very policies sold by high-pressure techniques.

This gives rise to the absurd position that somebody who parts with his first £5 monthly premium gets it back if he changes his mind, but somebody who is persuaded to part with his £20,000 life savings as a single premium has no such protection.

Also there is no cooling-off period for retirement policies under section 226 nor life insurance policies under section 226A.

Discontinuing the policy

One of the reasons for discontinuing the premiums for a section 226A policy may be that you become ineligible – for example, by moving to employment where there is a pension scheme.

What happens if you find you have to, or want to, discontinue paying premiums depends on the type of insurance.

If you discontinue the premiums for a term (or temporary) insurance policy of whatever sort, the policy comes to an end, and that is that. You do not get any return from it. That is because, under a term policy, you buy life insurance cover and nothing else, premium by premium, as you pay each month or year.

If you have to discontinue premiums for a permanent life insurance policy, there are broadly two alternatives: the policy can be changed to a paid-up policy or it can be surrendered (cashed-in).

■ *making the policy paid-up*
You stop paying the premiums, and ask the insurance company to reduce the guaranteed sum in relation to the premiums you have already paid. This new guaranteed sum (the paid-up value) is paid out at the end of the period you insured for (or when you die, if this is earlier). Most companies continue to add bonuses to the paid-up value of a with-profits policy – check whether yours will do so.

■ *surrendering the policy*
If you take out an endowment policy, make sure you understand the implication of cashing in the policy.
Which? reader B 10

You stop paying the premiums and give the policy back to the insurance company. In return, the company pays out a sum (the surrender value) then and there. The amount you get is at the discretion of the insurance company. With most companies, you get nothing back if you cash in a policy within the first two years; for a few years after that, what you get back would probably be less than the premiums you have paid out, even with a with-profits policy.

The reduction is by an amount dependent on, but not in proportion to, the unexpired term of the policy and the number of premiums paid. For whole life policies, the unexpired term is usually taken as a figure equivalent to the expectation of life 'for the age of the life assured concerned'.

Tax
Does not apply to section 226 retirement annuities or section 226A life policies nor to any life insurance policy taken out after 13 March 1984.

If within the first four years of its life you stop paying premiums for a qualifying policy taken out before 14 March 1984 and make a profit by cashing it in – that is, what you get for the policy is more than the net outlay for the premiums you paid – there is clawback of all or part of the tax relief you had on the premiums. That amount is deducted from the payment you get for the policy (the life insurance company pays this deducted amount over to the Inland Revenue). There is similar clawback if you make the policy paid-up within that time and you would have made a profit if you had cashed it in then.

There is an exception to the rule that the proceeds of a qualifying policy are tax-free: where you cash in the policy or subject to tax at your highest rates less basic rate. For example, if your highest rate of tax is 55%, you will have to pay tax at 25% on your gain from the policy (while the basic rate of tax is 30%).

Any gain you make at any time from a non-qualifying policy (for example, single-premium policy or bond) will be subject to tax, at your highest rate less the basic rate.

Different, and generally more favourable, rules apply in respect of any life insurance policy taken out on or before 19 March 1968 and for any life annuity contract effected on or before 26 March 1974.

If the gain from the policy which is to be charged to tax straddles more than one tax band when it is added to your income, you may be able to benefit from what is called 'top-slicing relief'. What this means is that if, for example, you are cashing-in a policy which you have held for just over six years, the gain is divided by six and only the resulting fraction is treated as part of your income for the tax year in which the policy is cashed, for the purpose of calculating the rate of tax to apply. You then have to apply the rate so calculated, minus basic rate, to the whole of the gain and not just the fraction.

If you are going to cash-in a non-qualifying policy, the great thing is to try to do so in a tax year where your income is low. However, a point to watch is that if you are over 65 and entitled to the age allowance (which is higher than the ordinary personal tax allowance), as soon as your total income exceeds a certain figure (different each tax year), the special age allowance is reduced by £2 for every £3 of excess income, until it is down to the level of the ordinary personal allowance. A consequence is that a gain from a life insurance policy, which is subject to tax at higher rates but less basic rate, may be taxed in your hands at 20% instead of at nil.

Cover preservation

Life insurance policies other than term insurance often contain a clause relating to the preservation of cover in the event of non-payment of premium. Not all companies operate on this 'automatic loan' principle for preventing the policy from ceasing.

An insurance company cannot grant a loan on the surrender value of a term policy – because there isn't any.

With policies such as whole-life or endowment policies, if premiums are discontinued but no notice is given of an intention to cash-in the policy or make it paid-up, the insurance company takes out a loan on the surrender value of the policy – on behalf of the policyholder but without asking his permission – in order to pay the next premium. (Interest is charged on the loan and is added to the amount borrowed.)

This continues as each premium becomes due until the size of the loan has reached the surrender value of the policy. At that time, the life insurance company surrenders the policy and uses the proceeds to repay the loan.

By this practice, the policy continues in force for the full sum assured for a length of time which depends on the size of the surrender value at the moment when premiums stopped being paid, and on the type of policy. For example, after a given number of years' premiums have been paid, an endowment with-profits with a term of 10 years has a much larger surrender value than, say, a whole-life policy without profits.

Advantages
• The life cover under the policy is kept in force for as long as possible and in the event of death while this system is operating, the sum paid would be the full sum assured (less the total of premiums advanced under the loan).

• When the policyholder's financial position improves, he can resume the payment of premiums on the original terms and could arrange to make gradual repayments of the loan and interest as his circumstances permit.

• Policy remains in force, so eligibility for tax relief retained when you resume paying premiums.

Disadvantages
• If you are getting tax relief, this will not be available on premiums advanced in this way, so they will cost more.

• Normally you would only stop paying premiums because you were hard up. If you let your policy continue under the cover preservation system, eventually the surrender value will be completely used up and you will be left with nothing.

warning
Once the insurance company has informed you that the cover preservation system is in operation, they will not normally contact you again until they have surrendered your policy to repay that loan. No further reminders of outstanding premiums would be sent.

Substitution

Some policies lack flexibility to meet changing family circumstances and the cost penalties of cashing in one policy and starting an alternative are too high. Therefore careful planning and consultation with more than one agent/broker is recommended as advice varies.
Which? reader B 255

Before you surrender a policy, find out if the insurance company will let you take out a new policy in substitution for the one you are surrendering.

It is important if you decide on a swap that you take out the new policy at exactly the same time as you surrender the original policy. If the new policy is of a different type or for a longer term or greater sum assured than the original, you will need to give evidence of continuing good health.

The rates of premium for policies issued in substitution are usually slightly cheaper than the equivalent policy if taken out not using substitution.

No commission is paid to intermediaries or salesmen for substitution policies, so you have to go direct to the head office of the company with your request. This also ensures that the timing of the surrender and the issue of the new policy are coincidental.

Remember, however, that you will not get tax relief on the premiums for the new life insurance policy. So, try to keep the old one going if you can.

Passing on the policy

Although there is no capital gains tax payable on the lump sum that you receive when a policy matures, if the beneficial ownership of the policy changes hands during its currency for a consideration in money or in money's worth, CGT becomes payable. So, if you buy a policy and then sell it at a gain, it is in principle subject to capital gains tax. Similarly, if there is a change in beneficial ownership of a policy – for example, if you are in partnership with somebody else, and the two of you decide that each should take out a policy of life insurance on his own life and then assign the beneficial ownership to the other, each assignment will rank as money's worth for the other assignment – the ultimate gain under each policy will, in principle, be subject to capital gains tax.

If you give away a life insurance policy, there should be no capital gains tax problem because the person who ultimately takes the proceeds did not acquire the interest in the policy for any 'consideration'. Make sure, however, that the deed or document you use to make the gift makes clear that it is not any part of a more complex transaction under the terms of which consideration is being given and that it includes somewhere words such as 'in consideration of my natural love and affection for so-and-so . . .'.

We asked a number of *Which?* readers, some of whom ('B') already had a life insurance policy and some ('A') who did not, to tell us what they knew or wanted to know about life insurance and to let us have their comments generally. We are quoting from some of their responses.

❛ . . . Now that you've got me to get out my policy, I realise how underinsured we are and shall go to my brokers forthwith.
Which? reader B 323

Salesmen seem to presume that everyone understands insurance procedures. There should be better explanations.
Which? reader B 103

I now have a close friend who is an insurance salesman. I wish I had known him four years ago!
I recently had occasion to fill in a form for insurance of household contents. It was an all-embracing form which also had a section for life insurance. I was disturbed at the lack of guidance on the completion of the form. It appeared that one could quite easily sign for far more cover than was really required.
Which? reader B 310

I feel that written matter from insurance companies contains far too much technical jargon and not enough plain English to make it readily and easily understandable without having to consult the agent or salesman.
Which? reader B 236

I work for a bank who have a very good insurance dept. However, to approach them you have to have an idea about what type of policy you want and how much you want to pay – which is fine if someone has told you about the different kinds of policies.
Which? reader B 34

Know what you want before approaching a broker or agent. Use a big broker who handles a large range of companies – that way he is less likely to try to sell only his line.
Ask as many relevant questions as possible concerning tax situation, payments etc.
Which? reader B 31

1 Learn different insurance terms
2 Compare policies offered by different companies
3 Beware of the friend-of-a-friend who has an 'interesting proposition' to put to you
4 Be sure you know what you are buying and why you want it.
Which? reader B 321

When I first bought life insurance, a whole life with-profits policy, it was not what I needed. However, I was talked into it by a persuasive salesman who came armed with an impressive array of statistics and 'facts' to show me that it was the perfect policy for me. The lesson I learned, which has been reinforced by reading *Money Which?*, is that salesmen sell not for the customer but for the commission.
Which? reader B 15

Obtain fullest information in writing. Discuss benefits with rep of competing company. No snap decisions. Sleep on information received until more relaxed. The final decision is yours so treat the responsibility accordingly.
Which? reader A 9

Once considered taking life insurance, put off by pushy broker!
Which? reader A 85

I would warn anybody taking out life insurance to beware of dishonest salesmen only out to make their commissions – also to always obtain advice from several different insurers, and compare the policies as they vary greatly. A broker can shop around and find the best deals for you.
Which? reader B 139

I don't understand all the terms so clearer explanations in the prospectus would help.
Which? reader A 108   ❜

❛Life insurance is a long time commitment and should not be entered into if the policy is to be cancelled in the early years because of low surrender value. Perhaps the insurance companies ought to spell out exactly what a policy can do, apart from death and maturity, i.e. fund school fees by way of policy loans, good security at bank, etc.
Which? reader B 13

I think that there is a danger of being over-insured. Also, one does tend to be contacted rather more often than one needs by salesmen from different companies, and this can result in confusion.
Over the years one can forget what insurance one has!
Which? reader B 126

Various salesmen have called from time to time selling 'insurance'. Normally they are selling investment schemes with some life cover. I consider life insurance as being something which pays my dependants if I should die. Therefore, it follows that any policy which pays the proposer money if he survives a term is a glorified savings scheme. With such policies, the amount paid out if the proposer does die is normally so small it wouldn't protect any dependants.
Which? reader B 101

Insurance brokers don't give you information on different types of cover that is available but try and sell the one they think is good.
Which? reader A 51

I feel one has to shop around to find a policy which fits one's needs properly. Insurance salesmen seem to want to sell people the most expensive policy, supposedly because they get more commission, and no doubt many people are persuaded to buy such policies. The policies could be written in a language ordinary people could understand.
Which? reader B 202

Originally we got the insurance really through heredity almost. The man from the Pru had always called to my mother's house ever since her days in Lancashire and it was either them or the Co-op insurance. Now that was continued fortunately through my uncle-in-law who had connections with the Pru.
I now know more about the business and would use my friend the insurance broker to arrange things.
Which? reader A 47

None of the hard-sell tactics of my car insurance company have yet convinced me that I need take out life insurance.
Which? reader A 114

I disapprove of insurance in general terms as I would prefer to look after my own money. However, I do realise the need for life insurance to safeguard the welfare of wife and children if I had any.
Which? reader A 38

What to do if things go wrong

We have been increasingly disturbed by instances of insurance intermediaries misleading their clients or failing to advise them adequately. They are a minority, but their inadequacies can have serious consequences for policyholders. It is manifestly necessary for the public to have reliable sources of advice on a subject so important to them, yet so complex. The Ombudsman's terms of reference do not permit him to deal with intermediaries. Complaints about registered brokers can be – and ought to be – referred to the British Insurance Brokers' Association if they are members. Lawyers who give incorrect advice can be – and ought to be – reported to the Law Society. But there are unregistered intermediaries, whose activities are unsupervised.
INSURANCE OMBUDSMAN BUREAU
annual report for 1982

BIBA
BIBA House
14 Bevis Marks
London EC3A 7NT

IBRC
15 St Helen's Place
London EC3A 6DS

Even with the utmost good faith operating on both sides, things occasionally go wrong (sometimes drastically).

When you are dissatisfied with your insurers or any of their agents, first have it out with whoever you think is at fault. This applies to complaints of all descriptions. Most complaints are about claim settlements, because insurance is not 'used', so to speak, unless it is called upon to pay out.

If your complaint is about an agent's or other intermediary's services and he refuses to take appropriate action or puts you off too many times, contact the insurance company with whom he has insured you. The insurance company should be concerned enough to treat your complaint seriously – although the agent may well have been acting on their instructions.

Also – and in a way more worrying to you – there are rogue intermediaries who may not have passed on clients' premium payments, or the policy they purport to have sold is not operative. If you are at all uneasy, get in touch with the insurance company direct.

An insurance company is not responsible for the ways of a broker, but if in difficulty with a broker, you can go direct to the company.

Most brokers are members of the British Insurance Brokers' Association – their trade association – which has a consumer relations department to which complaints against members may be made. The Insurance Brokers Registration Council also will deal with complaints against registered brokers involving breaches of the Insurance Brokers Registration Act or the code of conduct.

Insurance company

If you are dissatisfied with the way an insurance company has been dealing with you, your first complaint should be to the branch manager. If you want to see him in person, make an appointment and say what your complaint is about, so that they will get out the right papers. Take with you all the documentary evidence that you have got.

If you remain unsatisfied, your next step is to write to the general manager of the company. You can get the name of the top man in any company from *The Insurance Directory and Year Book*, available at reference libraries; the information given about each insurance company includes the names of managerial staff, even at the branches. (Make sure that you are looking at an up-to-date edition of the Directory; it is reissued every year.)

In your letter, set out the details of what has been happening and say why you think the company's action is wrong and what you are asking to be done. Keep a copy of your letter, to save having to write out all the facts again if the matter is not resolved and you have to take it still further.

insurance company a member of the BIA

The British Insurance Association was set up to protect the interests of its members (currently, some 340 companies) and it is financed by these members. (Membership is not open to brokers or other intermediaries, private individuals, Lloyd's syndicates or underwriters.)

In addition to its work for its members, the BIA can be approached by individual policyholders who have been unable to resolve their differences directly with a member company.

If you are unsatisfied with the treatment of your complaint by your insurance company and they are members of the BIA, write with the details to the British Insurance Association, Aldermary House, Queen Street, London EC4N 1TU.

The BIA can only advise: they have no statutory rights, and an insurance company is not bound to do what the BIA recommend (although it is difficult to visualise a situation where a company would not).

If you feel that a trade association is bound to favour its members and you would like a more impartial assessment, you can turn to either the Insurance Ombudsman Bureau or the Personal Insurance Arbitration Service – provided the insurance company is a member of either of these organisations. To find out, you can ask the insurance company (who should tell you even if you are in dispute) or ask the BIA (telephone 01-248 4477).

The insurance ombudsman

The Insurance Ombudsman Bureau was set up in March 1981 to deal with complaints relating to personal insurances issued in the UK by members of the ombudsman scheme. (At present, there are 50 insurance groups comprising some 120 companies belonging to the scheme.) Although the Bureau is paid for by insurance companies, the ombudsman is an independently appointed lawyer and his work is supervised by an independent council. Together, the ombudsman and the council are called The Insurance Ombudsman Bureau.

The Insurance Ombudsman
Bureau
31 Southampton Row
London WC1B 5HJ

Insurance advertising has a tendency to tell the public what is covered by a policy but not what is omitted; so the prospective policyholder is likely to be dazzled by the variety of different advantages offered and to fail to observe the flat spaces between. The Bureau can often explain to enquirers in what areas an ordinary household, car or personal accident policy will never offer cover.
INSURANCE OMBUDSMAN BUREAU
annual report for 1982

A free leaflet *How the insurance ombudsman could help you* is available from the IOB and also from the BIA and member insurance companies, and brokers and agents.

PERSONAL INSURANCE ARBITRATION SERVICE

If you have failed to reach agreement with your insurance company at senior management level, you can write to ask the ombudsman to help you. There is no fee for appealing to the ombudsman. You must do so within six months of the date when the company told you of their final decision on your dispute. You have to give the company's name and, if possible, the policy number, and explain the problem as briefly as you can.

The ombudsman will let you know if he can deal with your dispute. If it is just a matter of a misunderstanding over policy wording, he may give you what he calls 'summary advice' – basically, a letter saying 'The facts are not in dispute (*listing the policy wording*). The policy does not cover you because (*listing the reasons*). However, you are entitled to a full investigation if you think it would serve a useful purpose.'

If he decides to make a full investigation, he will send for the insurance company's files. He sometimes investigates further into the facts, and often calls in expert advice. You could be asked to attend a hearing.

The ombudsman decides whether your claim should succeed or fail and gives his reasons for this. He may be able to bring about an improvement in the company's offer. He has power to tell the company to make you a cash payment of up to £100,000 (or £10,000 per annum in a permanent health insurance case).

The insurance company is bound to abide by his decision once you have accepted it. You, however, have the right to reject the decision and are then free to do as you wish: if you want to take legal action, your legal rights will not have been affected by the ombudsman's decision.

Arbitration

As an alternative to the Insurance Ombudsman Bureau, a Personal Insurance Arbitration Service was set up also in 1981 by some insurance companies. The service can be invoked when a policyholder alleges financial loss caused by an insurance company failing to fulfil its obligations under a personal insurance policy issued in the UK. About 30 insurance groups participate in the PIAS scheme.

Under the PIAS, an independent arbitrator is appointed by the Chartered Institute of Arbitrators to resolve a dispute in cases where the insurance company's normal procedure, at the most senior level, has failed to achieve 'an amicable settlement'. The insurance company pays the costs of arbitration.

A PIAS claim has to be initiated by the aggrieved policyholder but the agreement of the insurance company to the application is necessary. The normal procedure under the PIAS rules requires both sides to submit documentary evidence within set time limits and the arbitrator then decides the case on the basis of the documents submitted. He can ask for an informal hearing (and so can the policyholder) which both parties would be required to attend. The arbitrator's decision is final and binding on both you and the insurance company.

The PIAS cannot usually be used for disputes involving claims of more than £25,000 (the limit varies with different insurance companies) or those arising from third party claims or those involving complicated issues.

Disputes not admissible under the PIAS may be referred to arbitration under the standard rules of the Institute. Arbitration is available as an alternative to litigation in any case where both sides to a dispute agree to arbitration.

The Chartered Institute of Arbitrators will provide information on the Personal Insurance Arbitration Service and on arbitration generally.

Arbitration in England and Wales is subject to the Arbitration Acts 1950–1979 (in Scotland and Northern Ireland, different Acts apply).

The Chartered Institute of Arbitrators
75 Cannon Street
London EC4N 5BH

Other ways of redress

Should your insurance company not be a member of the BIA, the IOB or the PIAS and all your representations to the company have failed, you may be able to sue the company for breach of contract, or possibly for misrepresentation, or for debt. But first get advice from a citizens advice bureau or a consumer advice centre, or perhaps the local trading standards officer – or a solicitor.

The only certainty if you get in touch with a solicitor is that you will get a solicitor's bill.
Which? reader Q 58

When insured at Lloyd's

A Lloyd's policyholder cannot get in direct contact with either the underwriter who issued his insurance or the claims manager who is handling his claim. All problems must be directed through the broker.

In the event of a dispute concerning a Lloyd's policy, the matter should first be raised with the broker through whom the insurance was placed.

If it is not resolved by him, write with full details to the manager of the advisory department, Lloyd's, Lime Street, London EC3M 7HA. Lloyd's is outside the Insurance Ombudsman Bureau and the Personal Insurance Arbitration Service, but it has a complaints department to take up disputes about insurances at Lloyd's.

In the (unlikely) event that a member of Lloyd's is unable to meet his obligations, the Corporation of Lloyd's has a central fund from which the policyholder would be reimbursed for any unexpired premium and the settlement of any impending claim.

Company defaults

There have always been some members of the public who fall for the offer of cheaper than cheap premiums and always some brokers or agents lured by high commissions to recommend companies of whom they know little financially. But there is now some legislation to cushion the effects.

If an authorised insurance company were to fail, the Policyholders Protection Act 1975 would live up to its name. This Act provides a scheme for the continuity of life insurance and the meeting of claims in the event of an insurance company being unable to meet its liabilities to individual policyholders.

The scheme is administered by a statutory body called the Policyholders Protection Board, Aldermary House, Queen Street, London EC4N 1TP

Where there is a claim in the pipeline, the board secures the payment of 90% of any valid claim (100% of any compulsory insurance, such as motor insurance).

The Act does not apply to insurance companies who are not authorised to do business in the UK. Nor do they come under the Department of Trade and Industry's supervision. Most of these 'off-shore' insurance companies sell mainly life insurance. In their advertisements, these companies have to state that they are not supervised by the DTI nor come under the Policyholders Protection Act.

Also – and in a way more worrying to you – there are rogue intermediaries who may not have passed on clients' premium payments, or the policy they purport to have sold is not operative. If you are at all uneasy, get in touch with the insurance company direct.

What the ombudsman said

The first annual report from the Insurance Ombudsman Bureau makes the following points.

• Every word of an insurance policy is put there for a purpose; if that purpose is not clear, get sound advice – preferably before the policy is bought.

• Insurance protects against the unexpected; not against the inevitable effects of time, wear and use.

• Don't choose your policy from the advertisement alone.

• When insurance policies come up for renewal, both parties are free to make a new bargain.

• When contemplating available policy options, the choice is between paying for the insurer to take the risk of loss, or saving the money and taking the chance that it will never happen.

Some relevant *Which?* reports

H = *Holiday Which?*
M = *Money Which?*
W = *Which?*
* not a full comparative report

Index

C

SO.

OGY,

EX.